THE NELSON-ATKINS MUSEUM OF ART

CULINARY MASTERPIECES

RIZZOLI
NEW YORK

First published in the
United States of America in 1993 by
Rizzoli International Publications, Inc.
300 Park Avenue South
New York, New York 10010
in association with the
Nelson-Atkins Museum of Art
4425 Oak Street
Kansas City, Missouri 64111

Library of Congress
Cataloging-in Publication Data

Culinary masterpieces /
The Nelson-Atkins Museum of Art.
      p. cm.
    "A tasteful collection from the
    Nelson-Atkins Museum of
    Art"—half t.p.
    Includes index
    ISBN 0-8478-1765-2
    I. Cookery. 2. Menus.
  3. Nelson-Atkins Museum of Art.
  TX714.C833   1993
  641.5—dc20   93-857
              CIP

A Tasteful Collection from the Nelson-Atkins Museum of Art

TABLE OF CONTENTS

FOREWORD

THIS COOKBOOK IS A TANGIBLE CELEBRATION OF THE SIXTIETH BIRTHDAY OF THE NELSON-ATKINS MUSEUM OF ART AND OF THE ENERGY AND DEDICATION OF THE VOLUNTEERS WHO ENVISIONED AND CARRIED OUT ITS PRODUCTION.

THE INSTITUTION WHICH THESE VOLUNTEERS SUPPORT IS WORTHY OF THEIR EFFORTS. The Nelson-Atkins Museum has especially fine collections of Asian art, with a particularly distinguished collection of Chinese art. There are small but choice collections of antiquities and the arts of Africa; European paintings and sculpture of international renown by artists such as Petrus Christus, Caravaggio, Monet, and Cézanne; one of the world's best collections of seventeenth- and eighteenth-century British ceramics; and nearly 7,000 prints and drawings. Additionally, there are superb American paintings by Sargent, Eakins, Benton, and Church, and the twentieth-century collection includes masterpieces by Hartley, de Kooning, Kelly, Kline, and Rauschenberg.

Thus, the intention of this book has been to create culinary equivalents to the Nelson's outstanding works of art. The Museum is fortunate to be the beneficiary of the time, skill, and talent of these and all volunteers who make the Museum richer and more enjoyable. Volunteers infuse the Museum with their enthusiasm, dedication and genuine love for this institution, and they are allies and ambassadors who extend the Museum's reach into the community. Their devotion to its welfare is a source of sustained encouragement to the trustees, to me and to the staff. Without them, this would be an impoverished place.

The cookbook has been an undertaking of exceptional teamwork and organization. A few staff members and volunteers must be singled out for special recognition: Ellen Goheen, the Museum's advisor to the project, and Helen Windsor, Volunteer Coordinator for the Museum, gave untold hours of personal time to organize, advise, and support. Maureen Gamble, Volunteer Council chairman, had the vision, enthusiasm, perseverance, and leadership to oversee the project from idea to completion. Candy Linn assumed the daunting task of Recipe Chairman, and, with her legions of testers and tasters, refined and brought order to the final selection of recipes. Jo Ann Krekel, computer wizard, transferred all manuscripts, from draft to final copy, to disks that greatly facilitated the production of the book. And, finally, Editor Crennan Ray made whole and consistent a mass of disparate materials from numerous committees and writers.

My heartfelt thanks and appreciation go to each one who has worked to bring this beautiful book to fruition. Bon appétit!

MARC F. WILSON

Director

INTRODUCTION

TO BE HAPPY, YOU MUST HAVE TAKEN THE MEASURE OF YOUR OWN POWERS, TASTED THE FRUITS OF YOUR PASSION, AND LEARNED YOUR PLACE IN THE WORLD—A HEADY ADMONISHMENT FROM GEORGE SANTAYANA, THE AMERICAN POET AND PHILOSOPHER. AN ART MUSEUM IS A FINE PLACE TO BEGIN AT LEAST TWO OF THESE TASKS. It may not allow you to take the measure of your own powers, but it can indeed enable you to taste the fruits of your passion and to learn your place in relation to the rest of the world.

The Nelson-Atkins Museum of Art celebrates its sixtieth anniversary this year. Before the Museum opened in December, 1933, the first trustees had directed that it should display the fine and decorative arts of all civilizations, cultures and periods, thereby ensuring that the collections represent the finest works of art from ancient Mesopotamia to the present. Through the contemplation and comparison of these treasures, we may learn about our place in the world.

The Nelson-Atkins Museum can fulfill Santayana's other requirement for happiness, that of tasting the fruits of passion, both literally and figuratively. Exquisite food and memorable art are two of the greatest products of creative passion. With this book, we offer you the opportunity to sample the fruits of the artist's passion. As you progress through its pages, you will be introduced to the Museum and, we hope, be enticed to visit if you have not already done so. The masterpieces of art may be seen only in the Museum, but the culinary masterpieces can be found in the pages that follow.

In splendid photographs, the galleries and public spaces of the Museum have been dressed in creative finery to serve as backdrops for masterpieces of both art and food. The great south lawn, home to a baker's dozen of Henry Moore's large sculptures, is the venue for a leisurely picnic. Majestic Kirkwood Hall is set for a fanciful fall dinner party, its signature columns an inspiration for the columns of type throughout this book. You will encounter the arts of China, which comprise the best known part of the Museum's collections. The beautiful French cloister has metamorphosed into a *millefleurs* garden, and the marble columns at the head of Atkins Staircase have been transformed into the site of a gala celebration. Imagination reigns in the lively, vibrant Creative Arts Center, which has nurtured the creativity of generations of Museum-goers. Finally, Rozzelle Court, once open to the sky, now houses Henry Moore maquettes and small sculptures on its balcony and plays host to diners around its fountain in the Rozzelle Court Restaurant. We offer you a feast for the eye as well as for the palate.

ELLEN R. GOHEEN

Administrator, Special Exhibitions and Collections

THE BASICS

OF MATCHING WINES

WITH FOOD

SOME GENERAL RECOMMENDATIONS FOR COMBINING WINES WITH FOOD ARE GIVEN AT THE BEGINNING OF EACH SECTION OF THIS BOOK; WHERE APPROPRIATE, A SPECIFIC WINE RECOMMENDATION WILL FOLLOW A RECIPE. NO MATTER HOW CLOSELY YOU READ A RECIPE, ANY WINE SUGGESTION IS AN EDUCATED GUESS UNTIL YOU TASTE THE DISH. The recommendations have been made based upon the recipe ingredients, but the best way to find the perfect match is to test food and wine together. If the wine seems too tart, add some acid (wine, vinegar or lemon juice, for example) to the dish. If the wine tastes too sweet, add some richness to the dish (cream, butter, fruit).

Bear in mind also that wines change—that is why we enjoy collecting them! Shop at a reliable retailer and insist on properly stored wines. And if you are reading this cookbook in 1995 or beyond, remember that these recommendations date from 1993, and you will want to buy a younger version of the recommended wine, or a worthy substitute. These suggestions are intended to encourage you to pair certain foods with specific wines. However, choosing a wine should not be an unbearably complicated affair. Wine is specifically matched with a particular food because it can be. A good match is symbiotic, and a dinner will take on a strength and interest that celebrate the joy of dining and the mystery of flavors.

Wine is composed in varying intensities of fruit and tannin or fruit and acid. When combining a wine with food, first consider the primary character of the wine—tannin (an acid with a dusty effect) or fruit. Does it have the flavor of cherries or blackberries, oranges or honey, gardenias or peaches, leather or coffee, chocolate or wood? Some characteristic will be foremost. Making this judgment requires some familiarity with all wines—not an unpleasant task! Begin by drinking good wines from every area and from every type of grape.

After determining a wine's chief characteristic, look for a food that exhibits some of the same characteristics, and that matches the wine's body—light, medium or heavy. In America, people often begin with the food and then, at the last moment, try to select a wine from whatever is at hand. Abandon that practice! Take the recipe to a reliable wine merchant and put the best wine clerk to work. Let your wine merchant know the results of the selection; this is a learning process that never ends.

Matching weights of dishes with weights in wines is simplistic, but a very good starting point. A pâté de foie gras is quite rich, but at most medium in weight, so choose a wine of similar weight and richness, perhaps a Sauternes. Shrimp is light and barely sweet; it would not go well with anything heavier than medium-weight white wine, such as a crisp Chardonnay. Roast beef should be paired with a wine as heavy as itself, perhaps a Châteauneuf-du-Pape. Spicy foods are more difficult. Generally speaking, massive fruit will overcome the heat and blend well, but spicy foods usually require non-tannic wines. Consider rich, slightly sweet wines, such as Spätlese or Vouvray.

Salt and acidity cancel each other. The acidity of a dish can be adjusted to bring it up to the level of the salt. When shellfish, which are often naturally salty, are served with an acid wine, there is usually a friendly match of contraries. However, if a dish tastes briny, try a slightly sweet wine with very high acidity, such as German Kabinett or Alsatian Pinot Gris.

Oil or fat and tannins also cancel each other out, which is why red meat usually goes well with red wine. Marbled cuts of red meat taste cleaner when combined with a tannic wine. Conversely, a tannic wine tastes less tannic when drunk with a marbled cut of meat.

Experiment on your own or ask your wine merchant for advice. A good wine can turn an everyday meal into a special one, and it can transform a very special meal into a memorable experience.

DOUG FROST
Master Sommelier

MENUS

LUNCHEON ON THE SOUTH LAWN
A Picnic
Henry Moore Sculpture Garden

GOAT CHEESE TART
Paul Figeat Pouilly Fumé 1 9 9 0 (Loire)
SAUTÉED SUNFLOWER LAMB CHOPS
ASPARAGUS IN LEMON VINAIGRETTE
VEGETABLE PASTA SALAD
Ridge Howell Mountain Zinfandel 1 9 8 8
BLUEBERRY RICOTTA TART

...

BARONIAL SPLENDOR
A Formal Fall Dinner Party
Kirkwood Hall

ROQUEFORT NAPOLEON
Château Rabaud Promis 1 9 8 3 (Sauternes)
CHICKEN DELLA ROBBIA
GOLDEN VEGETABLE PURÉE
ENGLISH PEAS WITH SHERRY
RICH CREAM BISCUITS
Robert Arnoux 1 9 8 8 Bourgogne Rouge
MIXED SALAD OF FRESH GREENS
FRESH COCONUT MOUSSE
WITH HOT CARAMEL SAUCE

...

FESTIVAL OF LANTERNS
A Cocktail Buffet
Main Chinese Gallery

CHINESE CRÊPES WITH MANY FLAVORS
ORIENTAL STUFFED MUSSELS
ROOT VEGETABLE CHIPS
KOREAN SHORT RIBS
CURRIED ALMOND CHICKEN
WITH HOMEMADE TOAST POINTS
von Hovel Oberemmeler Hutte Kabinett 1 9 9 0
(Mosel - Saar - Ruwer)
Rosemount Show Reserve Chardonnay 1 9 9 0
(Hunter Valley - Australia)

...

FOUR AND TWENTY BLACKBIRDS
Medieval Garden Party
The Cloisters

BLACKBERRY TARTS
GINGERBREAD HEART COOKIES
SPRINGERLE BIRD COOKIES
CITRUS TORTA
RED, WHITE AND BLUEBERRY
HERBED APPLE CIDER
Bonny Doon's Blackberry Infusion

...

A CELEBRATION OF SURPRISES
Desserts, Champagne & Coffee
Atkins Staircase

LEMON RASPBERRY TART
Schramsberg Demi-Sec 1 9 8 8 (Napa)
GREEK ORANGES
WHITE CHOCOLATE CHEESECAKE WITH LIME CURD
Domaine Durban Muscat Beaumes de Venise (Southern Rhône)
ICED LEMON SOUFFLÉ
ORANGE PECANS
ROASTED WALNUTS
Roederer Estate Brut nv (Anderson Valley)
Taittinger Blanc de Blanc nv (Champagne)

...

THE MEXICAN MAD HATTER
Brunch
Creative Arts Center

RED PEPPER CORN CHOWDER
SPICY CHILI CHEESE BREAD
FLOUR TORTILLAS WITH CHICKEN AND SPINACH FILLING
ZUCCHINI FLAN
SPICY POTATO SALAD
CLASSIC MARGARITAS
CORN THINS
ALMOND TORTE
COFFEE AND TEA

...

CARNEVALE
A Gala
Rozzelle Court

COLD POTATO SOUP WITH SPINACH AND WATERCRESS
SALTY CARAWAY CRESCENTS
Morton Estate Sauvignon Blanc 1 9 9 0
SALMON FILLET WITH GREEN PEPPERCORN CRUST
POTATOES GRUYÈRE
SNOW PEAS WITH CARROTS AND RED PEPPER
BAKED APPLES IN PHYLLO
Adelsheim Pinot Noir 1 9 8 9 (Oregon)

...

PRECEDING PHOTOGRAPHS:

Pages 17-19:

Henry Moore Sculpture Garden

The Museum building, completed in 1933, is neoclassic in inspiration. Built of Indiana limestone selected for its warm buff color, its south facade overlooks a superbly landscaped greensward that is now the setting for the Henry Moore Sculpture Garden.

Pages 20-24:

Kirkwood Hall

The Museum's interior is marked by its simplicity and perfection of proportions, with the great central Kirkwood Hall an impressive introduction to the treasures within. The space is punctuated by twelve colossal columns of Pyrenées Black and White marble; the walls and floors are covered in Travertine.

Pages 22-23:

Main Chinese Gallery

The dramatic setting of the great wood and polychrome Kuan-yin sculpture makes the main Chinese gallery a place of pilgrimage for many Museum visitors.

Pages 24-25:

The Cloisters

The French cloister once belonged to an Augustinian complex said to have been built near the northern town of Beauvais. In its center stands a large capital encircled by dancing figures and stylized foliage.

Pages 26-27:

Atkins Staircase

The grand sweep of the Atkins Staircase, built of Hauteville marble from France and Siena grey and yellow marble from Tuscany, spills out into the east corridor, leading to the European painting galleries.

Pages 28-29:

Creative Arts Center

For Museum-goers of all ages, the Creative Arts Center offers a challenge to the imagination and an opportunity to explore all of the visual arts.

Pages 30-32:

Rozzelle Court

Once open to the sky, Rozzelle Court is built of pink and yellow Mankato stone from Minnesota. In the center is a classical fountain of Cipolino Marine marble, surrounded by twelve bronze zodiac medallions set into the marble floor. Now enclosed, the court is home to the Museum's popular restaurant and the site of many Museum functions.

APPETIZERS

&

FIRST COURSES

WINE WITH APPETIZERS

In a restaurant setting, the function of an aperitif wine is simple—it should be sufficiently dry to cause the drinker to begin ordering more food and wine. In theory, a great deal of Muscadet should be available by the glass in America's restaurants; but in practice, this is not so. An aperitif wine should be dry, and therefore something that stimulates the appetite, but most Americans are a little uneasy with utterly dry wines. Often, America's aperitif wines have some fruitiness to them. Most Sauvignon Blanc is a tiny bit sweet, as is most sparkling wine or champagne.

A good choice is something light and fairly dry. A big oaky Chardonnay is so rich that it satisfies the appetite instead of stimulating it. When selecting an aperitif, find a wine that is suitably refreshing for the season. In summer, light German and Alsatian wines are perfect; in the cold of winter, a rich but light Pinot Noir from Burgundy or America gets the juices flowing.

Sometimes the aperitif wine is an accompaniment to the appetizer. Received wisdom dictates that one should begin with the lightest wines and proceed smoothly to the heaviest, which accompanies the entrée or the cheese course. Received wisdom is often wrong, but it is hard to argue the relative merits of the concept. Try drinking a light Riesling after drinking grand cru classe Bordeaux—the intensity of the Bordeaux destroys one's appreciation of the subtlety of the Riesling. But, as with most rules about wine, this one need not be taken to an extreme. It is possible to enjoy Burgundy (Pinot Noir) after Bordeaux (heavier wines such as Cabernet Sauvignon, Cabernet Franc, and Merlot), and the order in which they are served will not disrupt the flow of a perfect dinner. As well, one may go from lighter red to heavier white, especially if a sorbet or salad is served in between.

 Preceding page: Oriental Stuffed Mussels, page 51

SALMON-WRAPPED ASPARAGUS WITH SWEET MUSTARD SAUCE

3	TABLESPOONS DIJON-STYLE MUSTARD
3	TABLESPOONS SUGAR
1	TABLESPOON WHITE-WINE VINEGAR
3	TABLESPOONS VEGETABLE OIL
1/4	TEASPOON SALT
TWENTY	3-INCH TIPS CRISPLY COOKED FRESH ASPARAGUS
TWENTY	3-INCH STRIPS THINLY SLICED SMOKED SALMON

In a small bowl, whisk together mustard, sugar, vinegar, oil and salt. (The sauce may be prepared several hours ahead, covered and refrigerated. Bring to room temperature before assembling.) Just before serving (or up to 1 hour ahead), wrap each asparagus tip in a salmon strip. Place on a serving dish with the rolled edge down. Do not use toothpicks; the salmon will adhere to asparagus.

When ready to serve, pour mustard sauce into a small serving dish and arrange asparagus rolls around the sauce.

5 SERVINGS

GOAT CHEESE TART

1/2	CUP FRESH HERBS, LOOSELY PACKED (ANY COMBINATION OF BASIL, PARSLEY, MARJORAM, TARRAGON, ROSEMARY OR THYME)
1	SMALL CLOVE GARLIC, MASHED OR PRESSED
12	OUNCES GOAT CHEESE (CHÈVRE), SOFTENED
1/2	CUP RICOTTA CHEESE, AT ROOM TEMPERATURE
2	TABLESPOONS UNSALTED BUTTER, SOFTENED
1/3	CUP CRÈME FRAÎCHE (PAGE 198), AT ROOM TEMPERATURE
2	TABLESPOONS ALL-PURPOSE FLOUR
2	EGGS, AT ROOM TEMPERATURE
	SALT, TO TASTE
	FRESHLY GROUND BLACK PEPPER, TO TASTE
1	PREBAKED 9-INCH PIE CRUST

In the bowl of a food processor, mince herbs and garlic. Then add goat cheese, ricotta cheese, butter, crème fraîche, flour, eggs, salt and pepper. Process until mixture is smooth and thoroughly blended. Pour mixture into prebaked pie crust. Bake in a preheated 375 degree oven until puffed and golden, about 30 minutes.

Serve tart warm or at room temperature, as an appetizer, first course, or luncheon entree.

MAKES 24 APPETIZERS,
8 FIRST COURSE SERVINGS,
OR 6 LUNCHEON SERVINGS.

Paul Figeat Pouilly Fumé 1 9 9 0 (Loire)

SHERRIED SHRIMP COCKTAIL

ROASTED WALNUTS

Begin several hours to 1 day before serving.

- 1/2 CUP MAYONNAISE
- 1/2 TABLESPOON WHITE-WINE VINEGAR
- 1/2 TABLESPOON RED-WINE VINEGAR
- 1 TEASPOON ANCHOVY PASTE
- 1/2 TEASPOON DRY MUSTARD
- 1 TABLESPOON DRY SHERRY
- 2 TABLESPOONS MINCED FRESH PARSLEY
- 1/2 TEASPOON GRATED ONION
- 2 TABLESPOONS CAPERS, DRAINED
- 1/8 TEASPOON GARLIC POWDER
- 1/4 TEASPOON SALT
- 1 POUND SHRIMP, SHELLED, DEVEINED AND COOKED

Combine mayonnaise, vinegars, anchovy paste, dry mustard, sherry, parsley, onion, capers, garlic powder and salt in the bowl of a food processor. Process until smooth. Refrigerate, tightly covered, for several hours or overnight. May be made one day in advance. Serve as sauce for shrimp cocktail.

4 SERVINGS

- 2 1/2 CUPS WALNUT HALVES
- 3 TABLESPOONS VEGETABLE OIL
- 2 TABLESPOONS SUGAR
- 3/4 TEASPOON SALT
- 1/2 TEASPOON GROUND CUMIN
- 1/4 TEASPOON DRIED RED PEPPER FLAKES

Place walnuts in a small bowl, add oil and stir to coat. Add sugar, salt, cumin and red pepper flakes and toss gently. Place nuts in a small baking pan in a preheated 350 degree oven, and roast until golden brown, stirring occasionally, about 15 minutes. Serve warm or at room temperature.

MAKES ABOUT 2 1/2 CUPS.

Valentini Trebbiano d'Abruzzo 1 9 8 7 (Abruzzi)

TRIPLE BOURSIN CHEESE

Begin 1 day before serving.
BOURSIN BASE
3/4   POUND UNSALTED BUTTER, SOFTENED
24   OUNCES CREAM CHEESE, SOFTENED

With an electric mixer, cream butter and cheese in a large bowl, and divide into three equal portions.

GARLIC-HERB CHEESE
1   CLOVE GARLIC, CRUSHED
3/4   TEASPOON DRIED OREGANO
1/2   TEASPOON DRIED MARJORAM
1/2   TEASPOON DRIED THYME
1/2   TEASPOON DRIED BASIL
1/2   TEASPOON FRESHLY GROUND WHITE PEPPER
1/2   TEASPOON DRIED DILLWEED
2   CUPS WHOLE BLANCHED ALMONDS, LIGHTLY SALTED AND TOASTED

Combine garlic, oregano, marjoram, thyme, basil, white pepper and dillweed, and blend into one portion of cheese mixture. Heap into an oval mound on a square of foil. Stud the cheese with the almonds, pointed end down and at an angle. Insert toothpicks to stand higher than the nuts, cover with plastic wrap and refrigerate overnight so flavors will blend.

OLIVE-NUT CHEESE
6   OUNCES SALAD OLIVES, DRAINED AND COARSELY CHOPPED
2   CUPS LIGHTLY SALTED AND TOASTED PECAN HALVES

Add olives to second portion of cheese mixture, stirring to blend. Heap the cheese into an oval mound on a square of foil. Stud cheese with pecans, wide ends down. Insert toothpicks to stand higher than the nuts, cover with plastic wrap and refrigerate overnight.

RAISIN-WALNUT CHEESE
1/2   CUP GOLDEN RAISINS, DIVIDED
1/2   CUP CHOPPED ENGLISH WALNUTS, DIVIDED
3   TABLESPOONS HONEY

Set aside two tablespoons of raisins and chopped walnuts for garnish. Combine third portion of cheese mixture with remaining raisins, nuts and honey. Heap the cheese into an oval mound on a square of foil. Press remaining nuts and raisins onto the cheese mound. Cover with plastic wrap and refrigerate overnight.

To serve, slide cheeses off foil onto a serving plate and arrange water biscuits or whole wheat crackers between the cheeses. Pass with three spreading knives.

Abbazia di Rosazzo Ronco della Acacie 1 9 9 0
(Friuli - Venezia)

AVOCADO MOUSSE
WITH SHRIMP AND CAVIAR

Begin at least 4 hours before serving.

1	TABLESPOON UNFLAVORED GELATIN
1/4	CUP COLD WATER
1	CUP MASHED AVOCADO
1	TABLESPOON FRESHLY SQUEEZED LEMON JUICE
6	OUNCES DRY ITALIAN SALAD DRESSING
2	CUPS SOUR CREAM
3	TABLESPOONS CHOPPED PARSLEY A DASH OF HOT PEPPER SAUCE
2 TO 3	DROPS GREEN FOOD COLORING, IF DESIRED

miniature shrimp, red or black caviar, chopped cucumber, chopped green onions and chopped tomatoes, for garnish

In a small saucepan, sprinkle gelatin over water and stir. Let stand for 5 minutes, then cook over medium heat until dissolved. Place avocado, lemon juice, Italian dressing, sour cream, parsley and hot sauce in food processor and blend until smooth. Mix in gelatin and add green food coloring, if used. Oil a 9 1/2-inch flan pan or mold. Pour mixture into the mold and refrigerate for 3 to 4 hours.

Invert mold onto a large platter. Arrange the garnishes around mousse, and spoon caviar in the center. The mousse can be prepared up to 2 days ahead and refrigerated. Serve with crackers or lavosh.

MAKES 3 CUPS.

Roederer Estate Brut nv (Anderson Valley)

CURRIED ALMOND CHICKEN

1/3	CUP CHOPPED BLANCHED ALMONDS
2	LARGE SHALLOTS
1/4	CUP FRESH PARSLEY LEAVES
4	OUNCES CHOPPED COOKED CHICKEN BREAST
1	CUP MAYONNAISE
1 1/2	TEASPOONS CURRY POWDER
2	TEASPOONS FRESHLY SQUEEZED LEMON JUICE
2	DROPS HOT PEPPER SAUCE
1/2	TEASPOON SALT FRESHLY GROUND BLACK PEPPER, TO TASTE
3	OUNCES MONTEREY JACK CHEESE, SHREDDED

Homemade Toast Points (see recipe below), as an accompaniment

Place almonds, shallots and parsley leaves in a food processor and pulse for 5 seconds. Add chicken and pulse. Add mayonnaise, curry powder, lemon juice, hot pepper sauce, salt and pepper and blend. Add shredded cheese and pulse to blend until thoroughly mixed. Transfer mixture to a bowl, cover and refrigerate.

Serve cold with Homemade Toast Points. For a warm appetizer, spread on toast points and heat under a broiler for 5 minutes.

MAKES 2 CUPS.

Rosemount Show Reserve Chardonnay 1 9 9 0 (Hunter Valley - Australia)

HOMEMADE TOAST POINTS

1	LOAF THINLY SLICED WHITE BREAD, CRUSTS REMOVED
12	TABLESPOONS BUTTER, MELTED

Cut bread slices diagonally and arrange in a single thickness on a baking sheet. Brush liberally with melted butter and crisp in a preheated 300 degree oven until golden brown, about 20 minutes. Cool on wire rack to room temperature. If not used immediately, store in an airtight container.

48 SERVINGS

GRILLED BACKYARD SHRIMP

3 TO 4	LARGE SHRIMP OR 6 SMALL SHRIMP PER PERSON
1	CUP OLIVE OIL
	FRESHLY SQUEEZED JUICE OF 3 LEMONS
1/4	CUP SOY SAUCE
1/4	CUP FINELY CHOPPED FRESH PARSLEY
2	TABLESPOONS CHOPPED FRESH TARRAGON OR 2 TEASPOONS DRIED

With a sharp scissors cut the back of each shrimp shell and remove black vein, but do not remove shell. Wash shrimp, pat dry and place in a large bowl. Combine olive oil, lemon juice, soy sauce, parsley and tarragon and pour over shrimp. Marinate shrimp for 2 hours in refrigerator, tossing occasionally. Bring to room temperature before grilling.

Arrange shrimp in a basket grill and cook over hot coals 5 to 6 minutes. The shrimp should be tender and moist with slightly charred shells. The recipe makes enough marinade for 3 pounds of shrimp.

This makes good picnic or tailgate party fare—provide finger bowls and plenty of paper napkins.

Shafer Chardonnay 1 9 9 0 (Napa)

KOREAN SHORT RIBS

	Begin 1 day before serving.
6	POUNDS BEEF SHORT RIBS, BONED AND CUT IN 2-INCH CUBES
1	CUP SOY SAUCE
1/2	CUP VEGETABLE OIL
1/2	CUP LIGHT BROWN SUGAR
4	CLOVES GARLIC, CRUSHED
1	BUNCH GREEN ONIONS, SLICED

Combine soy sauce, vegetable oil, brown sugar, garlic and green onions. Score ribs and place in a large glass or plastic container. Pour marinade over the ribs and refrigerate overnight. Grill over hot coals, turning frequently until browned, 6 to 8 minutes for rare; 10 to 12 minutes for well-done.

MAKES 16 SERVINGS AS AN APPETIZER;
6 TO 8 SERVINGS AS A MAIN COURSE.

Storybook Mountain Zinfandel 1 9 8 9 (Napa)

COGNAC ALMOND MOLD

Begin 1 day before serving.

1	TABLESPOON UNFLAVORED GELATIN
1/4	CUP COLD WATER
1/2	CUP SUGAR
12	OUNCES CREAM CHEESE, SOFTENED
8	TABLESPOONS BUTTER, SOFTENED
1/4	CUP SOUR CREAM
1	CUP WHITE SEEDLESS GRAPES, SOAKED OVERNIGHT IN COGNAC OR BRANDY TO COVER ZEST OF 2 LEMONS
1	CUP SLIVERED ALMONDS

Dissolve gelatin in water and set aside. In a food processor, blend sugar, cream cheese, butter and sour cream. Add softened gelatin and blend again. Drain grapes and cut in half lengthwise. Fold into gelatin mixture. Add lemon zest and almonds. Pour into a 1-quart mold and refrigerate at least 4 hours, or overnight.

To serve, invert mold onto a serving platter. Serve with salty crackers for an appetizer or with wheat crackers and fruit as a dessert.

24 SERVINGS

*Château St. Jean Pinot Blanc
Robert Young 1 9 8 8 (Sonoma)*

MELTED BRIE WITH WINTER FRUITS

Begin 3 hours before serving.

3/4	CUP CHOPPED, PITTED DATES
1	SMALL APPLE, PEELED AND DICED
1	FIRM RIPE PEAR, PEELED AND DICED
1/2	CUP CURRANTS
1/2	CUP CHOPPED PECANS
1/3	CUP ROSÉ WINE OR APPLEJACK
2-POUND	WHEEL RIPE BRIE, WELL CHILLED
	thin baguette slices, toasted, as an accompaniment

In a bowl, mix dates, apple, pear, currants, pecans and wine. Set aside to let fruit soften, about 2 hours. Cut brie in half horizontally to make two round layers. Place one layer, cut side up, in a 10-inch shallow-rimmed baking dish or quiche pan. Spread cut side with 2 1/4 cups fruit. Place remaining cheese layer, cut side down, on fruit. Spoon remaining fruit onto center of cheese. The recipe may be prepared to this point up to 2 days ahead, covered and refrigerated.

When ready to serve, bake brie, uncovered, in a preheated 300 degree oven until cheese melts at the edges and the center is warm, about 15 to 20 minutes. Serve hot brie from baking dish, spread on thin toasted baguette slices.

16 SERVINGS

*Henschke Shiraz "Mount Edelstone" 1 9 8 8
(Barossa Valley - Australia)*

ROQUEFORT NAPOLEON

1/2 POUND FROZEN PREPARED PUFF
PASTRY
3/4 POUND ROQUEFORT CHEESE
8 OUNCES CREAM CHEESE
4 OUNCES MASCARPONE CHEESE
1 OUNCE PORT WINE
2 VERY RIPE PEARS
1/4 CUP CRÈME FRAÎCHE (PAGE 198)
1 TABLESPOON HEAVY CREAM
1 TABLESPOON PAPRIKA
1/3 CUP FINELY CHOPPED WALNUTS
sliced pears, mint leaves and red grapes, for garnish

Use parchment paper to line a 12- by 18-inch
baking pan. On a lightly floured surface, roll out
the pastry to a thickness of 1/8 inch, close to the
size of the baking sheet. Lightly sprinkle
parchment with water and place the pastry on
the sheet. Pierce the dough with the tines of a
fork and bake in a preheated 375 degree oven
for 12 minutes, or until golden. Remove pastry
and parchment to a wire rack and cool.

Blend Roquefort and cream cheese until smooth,
then fold in the mascarpone and port. Set aside.
Use a sharp serrated knife to cut the pastry
crosswise into six equal strips (each will be about
2 inches by 10 inches). Core and peel the pears
and cut into 1/4-inch slices. With a long metal
spatula, coat one strip of pastry with a thin layer
of the cheese mixture. Place a layer of pears
over the cheese, coat the pears with cheese
mixture, and cover with a strip of pastry. Repeat
for the second layer and cover with a final strip
of pastry. Make the second Napoleon in the
same way. Any remaining cheese mixture may
be used as a spread on crackers.

In a small bowl, whisk crème fraîche with heavy
cream and set aside. Lightly dust tops of
Napoleons with paprika through a fine-meshed
sieve. Dip the tines of a fork into cream mixture
and rapidly drizzle the cream over the tops.
Sprinkle with chopped walnuts.

Cut Napoleons into 6 triangles to serve as a first
course or cheese course. Garnish with sliced
pears, mint leaves and red grapes.

*Napoleons should be made and served the same day at
room temperature. Do not refrigerate. The cheese mixture
may be made in advance, refrigerated, then brought to room
temperature before assembling.*

6 SERVINGS

Château Rabaud Promis 1 9 8 3 (Sauternes)

ROASTED CORN AND AVOCADO SPREAD

1   CUP FROZEN YELLOW CORN
     KERNELS, THAWED
2   TEASPOONS OLIVE OIL
2   LARGE AVOCADOS, PITTED AND
     PEELED
1   RIPE MEDIUM TOMATO, CHOPPED
3   TABLESPOONS FRESHLY SQUEEZED
     LIME JUICE
2   TABLESPOONS MINCED GREEN
     ONION
2   CLOVES GARLIC, PRESSED
4   OUNCES CHOPPED JALAPEÑO
     PEPPERS
1/4   TEASPOON GROUND CUMIN
chopped ripe tomatoes, for garnish
yellow, red and blue corn chips, as accompaniments

Combine corn and olive oil in a shallow pan. Bake in a preheated 400 degree oven for 8 minutes or until lightly browned, stirring occasionally. Remove from oven and cool.

Mash one avocado and set aside. Coarsely chop the second avocado. In a mixing bowl, combine roasted corn with mashed and chopped avocado, tomato and lime juice. Add green onion, garlic, jalapeño peppers and cumin and stir until well blended. Cover and refrigerate up to 24 hours.

Place spread in serving dish and garnish with chopped tomato. Serve with yellow, red and blue corn chips.

MAKES ABOUT 3 CUPS.

Rothbury Chardonnay 1 9 9 1
(Hunter Valley - Australia)

BARBECUED PORK TENDERLOIN

Begin 1 day before serving.
2   WHOLE PORK TENDERLOINS (ABOUT
     12 OUNCES EACH)
1/4   CUP SOY SAUCE
2   TABLESPOONS BEER
1   TABLESPOON BROWN SUGAR
1   TABLESPOON HONEY
1/3   TEASPOON GROUND CINNAMON
1   CLOVE GARLIC, MINCED
party rye slices, horseradish and Dijon-style mustard,
as accompaniments

Remove membrane from tenderloins and place the meat in a heavy-duty plastic bag. Combine soy sauce, beer, brown sugar, honey, cinnamon, and garlic. Pour mixture over tenderloins in bag and seal. Refrigerate overnight, turning once.

Preheat oven to 350 degrees. Remove pork from marinade, reserving liquid. Place tenderloins on a wire rack over a baking pan containing a small amount of water. Bake about 45 to 50 minutes, turning occasionally and basting frequently with marinade until done. Allow tenderloins to cool 10 minutes before slicing.

Thinly slice at a slight angle. Serve on slices of party rye with horseradish and Dijon-style mustard.

16 SERVINGS

Bert Simon Serriger Würtzberg Auslese 1 9 9 0
(Mosel - Saar - Ruwer)

MUSHROOM FILLED CROUSTADES

CROUSTADES

24   SLICES THINLY SLICED FRESH WHITE
BREAD
BUTTER OR NONSTICK VEGETABLE
SPRAY

Butter 2-inch muffin tins or spray with a nonstick vegetable spray. Using a 3-inch biscuit cutter, cut one round from each slice of bread. Carefully fit each bread round into a muffin tin, molding bread into the center and sides of the tin with fingertips. Bake croustades in a preheated 400 degree oven for about 10 minutes, or until lightly browned. Remove, cool and set aside.

DUXELLES FILLING

2   TABLESPOONS BUTTER
3   TABLESPOONS FINELY CHOPPED
GREEN ONION
1/2   POUND FRESH MUSHROOMS, FINELY
CHOPPED
2   TABLESPOONS ALL-PURPOSE FLOUR
1   CUP HEAVY CREAM
1/2   TEASPOON SALT
1/8   TEASPOON CAYENNE PEPPER
1   TABLESPOON FINELY CHOPPED
FRESH PARSLEY
1/2   TABLESPOON FINELY CHOPPED
FRESH CHIVES
1/2   TEASPOON FRESHLY SQUEEZED
LEMON JUICE
2   TABLESPOONS FRESHLY GRATED
PARMESAN CHEESE

In a heavy, 10-inch frying pan, melt butter and sauté green onion, stirring constantly over medium heat, about 4 minutes. Do not brown. Add mushrooms, stirring frequently until all moisture has evaporated, about 10 to 15 minutes. Remove from heat.

Sprinkle flour over mushrooms and stir until thoroughly mixed. Immediately pour on cream and return to heat. Bring the mixture to a boil, stirring constantly. Reduce heat, simmer briefly and remove from heat. Add salt, cayenne pepper, parsley, chives and lemon juice. Cool, then cover and refrigerate until ready to use.

To assemble, use a small spoon to mound filling into the croustades. Sprinkle each croustade with Parmesan cheese and a small dot of butter, if desired. Arrange on a baking sheet and place in a preheated 350 degree oven for 10 minutes. Brown quickly under broiler, taking care that croustades do not burn. Serve hot.

The croustades freeze very well. They may be filled while frozen and heated as described above. Other fillings may be used as long as they do not contain too much liquid.

24 SERVINGS

Aubert de Villaine Bourgogne Rouge "le Digoines" 1 9 8 9 (Red Burgundy)

SMOKED SALMON CHEESECAKE

Begin at least 5 hours before serving.

1 TABLESPOON BUTTER
2 TABLESPOONS FRESHLY GRATED
   PARMESAN CHEESE
3 TABLESPOONS BREADCRUMBS
3 TABLESPOONS HEAVY CREAM
2 EGGS
14 OUNCES CREAM CHEESE, SOFTENED
1/2 CUP CHOPPED LEEKS (WHITE PART
   ONLY)
3 TABLESPOONS UNSALTED BUTTER
1/4 POUND DICED SMOKED SALMON
1/3 CUP GRATED GRUYÈRE CHEESE
1/2 TEASPOON FRESHLY GROUND BLACK
   PEPPER
3/4 TEASPOON SALT, OR TO TASTE

Butter an 8- or 9-inch springform pan. Coat sides and bottom of pan with a mixture of the Parmesan cheese and breadcrumbs. Combine cream, eggs and cream cheese in bowl of a food processor and process until smooth. Sauté leeks in butter until soft and translucent, but not browned. Add leeks to cheese mixture, then add smoked salmon, Gruyère and pepper and salt. Pulse to blend. Turn mixture into pan and place the pan in a larger baking pan. Pour hot water into the larger pan, halfway up the sides of springform pan. Bake in a preheated 300 degree oven for 1 hour and 40 minutes. Turn off oven and leave cheesecake in oven 1 hour longer. Remove and let stand at room temperature for at least 2 hours.

Invert cheesecake onto serving tray and slice. Serve at room temperature. If cheesecake has been refrigerated, reheat in 300 degree oven until warm but not hot.

6 FIRST COURSE SERVINGS

Nautilus Sauvignon Blanc 1 9 9 0 (New Zealand)

PISSALADIÈRE

4 TABLESPOONS OLIVE OIL
4 POUNDS YELLOW ONIONS, THINLY
   SLICED
1 TABLESPOON ALL-PURPOSE FLOUR
   SALT, TO TASTE
   FRESHLY GROUND BLACK PEPPER,
   TO TASTE
12 OUNCES BREAD DOUGH
16 ANCHOVY FILLETS IN OLIVE OIL,
   SLICED LENGTHWISE IF FLAT
4 OUNCES PITTED NIÇOISE OLIVES,
   SPRINKLED WITH OIL FROM
   ANCHOVIES

Heat oil in a large skillet. Add onions and cook, stirring, over low heat until onions are golden but not brown, about 45 minutes to 1 hour. Stir in flour, salt and pepper and remove from heat. Lightly oil a 9- by 14-inch baking sheet (with sides) or a 12-inch round tart pan. Roll out bread dough to fit, and place in pan. Spread cooked onion mixture over dough. Arrange anchovy fillets in a decorative lattice or diamond pattern on top, with an olive in the center of each diamond. Bake in a preheated 425 degree oven for 30 minutes, or until golden brown.

For a richer crust, use pâte brisée in place of the bread dough.

12 SERVINGS

Château de Beaucastel Blanc 1 9 9 0
(Châteauneuf-du-Pape Blanc)

POLENTA PIZZA

POLENTA

4 1/2	CUPS WATER
1 1/2	CUPS COARSELY GROUND YELLOW CORNMEAL
2	TABLESPOONS BUTTER
1/2	CUP FRESHLY GRATED PARMESAN CHEESE

Bring water to a boil in a deep saucepan. Whisk cornmeal into boiling water and simmer, stirring constantly, for 15 to 20 minutes or until mixture is very thick and pulls away from sides of pan. Remove from heat and add butter and Parmesan cheese.

Pour polenta into an oiled 12-inch round quiche pan and flatten into a circle. Cool at room temperature for at least one hour or until top feels dry. Bake for 20 minutes in a preheated 350 degree oven. If the polenta puffs up, prick bubbles with a fork.

PIZZA TOPPING

1	MEDIUM ONION, CHOPPED
1	CLOVE GARLIC, CRUSHED
2	TABLESPOONS OLIVE OIL
1	POUND FRESH MUSHROOMS, SUCH AS SHIITAKE, BOLETES OR CHANTERELLE, SLICED; OR 4 TO 5 OUNCES DRIED MUSHROOMS, SOAKED IN WARM WATER FOR 15 MINUTES AND SLICED
1	CUP CRUSHED TOMATOES
1/4	TEASPOON DRIED OREGANO
1/4	TEASPOON DRIED BASIL
1/4	TEASPOON SALT
	FRESHLY GROUND BLACK PEPPER, TO TASTE
2	TABLESPOONS CHOPPED FRESH PARSLEY
6	OUNCES GRATED GRUYÈRE CHEESE, IF DESIRED

In a large skillet, sauté onion and garlic in oil until the onion is translucent. Add mushrooms, increase heat to medium-high and cook, stirring constantly, until the liquid evaporates and mushrooms begin to brown. Add tomatoes, oregano, basil, salt and pepper. Reduce heat and cook for 7 to 10 minutes, stirring occasionally. Remove from heat and add parsley. Spoon pizza topping over polenta and sprinkle grated cheese on top. Bake for 5 to 7 minutes until the cheese melts. Cut in wedges and serve immediately.

The pizza tastes even better on the second day. It may be served as a first course or as an accompaniment to grilled meats. Try it with Splendid Beef Tenderloin (page 120).

10 TO 12 SERVINGS

Girard Chardonnay 1 9 8 8 (Napa)

ROQUEFORT ROUNDS

ROUNDS

7   TABLESPOONS BUTTER
7   TABLESPOONS ROQUEFORT CHEESE
1   CUP FLOUR
4   TEASPOONS HEAVY CREAM
    SALT, TO TASTE
1   EGG YOLK
    CAYENNE PEPPER, TO TASTE

Cut butter and cheese into flour with a pastry cutter. Mix in cream, salt, egg yolk and cayenne pepper and blend well. Let stand in refrigerator 20 minutes. Shape dough into a long roll and wrap in plastic wrap; refrigerate 20 minutes longer. Thinly slice dough into rounds and place on a baking sheet. Bake in a preheated 400 degree oven for 8 to 10 minutes, or until lightly browned. Carefully remove rounds from baking sheet and cool.

TOPPING

3   EGG YOLKS
2/3 CUP HEAVY CREAM
    SALT, TO TASTE
    CAYENNE PEPPER, TO TASTE
5   TABLESPOONS ROQUEFORT CHEESE
3   TABLESPOONS BUTTER
1   TEASPOON KIRSCH
1 finely chopped green onion, for garnish

In a saucepan, mix egg yolks, cream, salt and cayenne pepper. Cook, stirring, over low heat. Whisk in Roquefort and butter and cook until thickened; add Kirsch.

Spread cooled topping on rounds and garnish with green onion.

10 TO 12 SERVINGS

Château Roumieu-Lacoste 1 9 8 6 (Sauternes)

SUN-DRIED TOMATO AND ROASTED RED PEPPER DIP

1   14-OUNCE JAR ROASTED RED PEPPERS, DRAINED AND PATTED DRY
1/2 CUP SLICED SUN-DRIED TOMATO HALVES, SOAKED IN HOT WATER 5 MINUTES, DRAINED AND PATTED DRY
1   CLOVE GARLIC, MINCED OR PRESSED
1   TABLESPOON FRESHLY SQUEEZED LEMON JUICE
2   TABLESPOONS FRESH FLAT-LEAF PARSLEY
4   OUNCES CREAM CHEESE, SOFTENED
1/2 CUP SOUR CREAM
    SALT, TO TASTE
    FRESHLY GROUND BLACK PEPPER, TO TASTE
toasted pita triangles and assorted raw vegetables, as accompaniments

Purée peppers, tomatoes, garlic, lemon juice and parsley in a food processor. Add cream cheese, sour cream, salt and pepper and continue to blend until mixture is smooth.

Transfer dip to a serving bowl and serve with toasted pita triangles and assorted raw vegetables.

MAKES 2 1/4 CUPS.

St. Supéry Sauvignon Blanc 1 9 9 0 (Napa)

MARINATED GOAT CHEESE

Prepare at least 1 week before serving.

12   OUNCES GOAT CHEESE, SUCH AS
      MONTRACHET
TWO 4-INCH SPRIGS THYME
ONE 2-INCH SPRIG ROSEMARY
 2   BAY LEAVES
12   PEPPERCORNS, LIGHTLY CRUSHED.
      EXTRA-VIRGIN OLIVE OIL TO COVER,
      ABOUT 1 CUP

Slice goat cheese into 1/2-inch discs (dip knife in hot water if cheese crumbles). Place in a jar just large enough to hold cheese. Add thyme, rosemary, bay leaves and peppercorns. Pour oil over cheese to cover. Close lid tightly and store at least one week in a cool place. The cheese will keep one month, refrigerated. Drain cheese before using.

To marinate quickly, combine seasonings and oil in a small saucepan. Cook over medium heat until oil is very hot. Pour over cheese in a heat-proof container. Cool to room temperature and store tightly covered in a cool place for at least four hours.

First course serving suggestions:
Toast French bread rounds on both sides. Place a slice of marinated cheese on each round, entirely covering the bread. Broil until cheese is melted. Serve immediately on greens tossed in a vinaigrette dressing.

Coat slices of cheese with breadcrumbs which have been sautéed in olive oil. Place slices on a baking sheet and heat in a preheated 350 degree oven for 6 to 8 minutes, or until softened. Serve with a green or fruit salad.

Babcock Sauvignon Blanc Eleven Oaks 1 9 9 0
(Santa Barbara)

FRESH BASIL TAPENADE

1/4   CUP PITTED GREEN OLIVES
1/2   CUP PITTED NIÇOISE OR OTHER
       BRINE-CURED BLACK OLIVES
 2   SMALL CLOVES GARLIC
 4   ANCHOVY FILLETS, DRAINED AND
       RINSED IN WATER
 2   TABLESPOONS CANNED TUNA,
       DRAINED
2 1/2 TABLESPOONS CAPERS, DRAINED
1 1/4 CUPS FRESH BASIL LEAVES
 1   TABLESPOON FRESHLY SQUEEZED
       LEMON JUICE
1/4   CUP OLIVE OIL
1/2   CUP MAYONNAISE, IF DESIRED
1 artichoke, cooked and cooled, as an accompaniment
cold cooked shrimp, as an accompaniment

Combine green and black olives, garlic, anchovy fillets, tuna, capers, basil and lemon juice in a food processor. Purée, then add the oil slowly while processor is still running. For a milder sauce, thin with mayonnaise.

To serve, scoop out the center of the artichoke, and fill with tapenade. Surround artichoke with cold shrimp for a first course.

Makes 1 1/2 cups.

B.R. Cohn Cabernet Sauvignon 1 9 8 8 Olive Hill
(Sonoma)

CHINESE CRÊPES
WITH MANY FLAVORS

1 1/2   CUPS ALL-PURPOSE FLOUR
1/4   TEASPOON SALT
2   EGGS
1 1/2   CUPS MILK
1   CUP WATER

In a small bowl, combine flour and salt. In a separate bowl, whisk together eggs, milk and water. Add flour mixture and beat until smooth. Cover lightly and let stand at room temperature. Lightly oil a 10-inch non-stick skillet and place over medium-high heat. Pour just enough batter in skillet to make a thin, even coating. Cook until set, then turn crêpe and brown a few seconds on the other side. Continue until all crêpes are cooked, brushing skillet with oil after every third or fourth crêpe.

Roll each crêpe, cover with plastic wrap and refrigerate. Bring to room temperature before serving.

MAKES 12 TO 14 CRÊPES.

FILLINGS

- SHREDDED ROAST DUCK, CARROT FLOWERETS, GREEN ONION CURLS AND HOISIN SAUCE
- SHREDDED CHINESE BARBECUED DUCK
- SHREDDED ROASTED CHICKEN OR PORK
- FRESH SHIITAKE MUSHROOMS, CUT INTO JULIENNE AND SAUTÉED IN VEGETABLE OIL WITH A DASH OF SOY SAUCE AND A PINCH OF SUGAR
- ASSORTED VEGETABLES, SUCH AS CARROTS, ONIONS, ZUCCHINI AND DAIKON, CUT INTO JULIENNE AND STIR-FRIED UNTIL CRISP-TENDER
- BAMBOO SHOOTS
- WATER CHESTNUTS
- BEAN SPROUTS
- CILANTRO LEAVES
- PRESERVED PICKLED GINGER, CUT INTO JULIENNE

To serve, surround pancakes with fillings. Allow guests to serve themselves.

6 TO 8 SERVINGS

*von Hovel Oberemmeler Hutte Kabinett 1 9 9 0
(Mosel - Saar - Ruwer)*

ORIENTAL STUFFED MUSSELS

1 1/2   CUPS RICE
3/4   CUP SAKE (JAPANESE RICE WINE)
3/4   CUP WATER
3   DOZEN FRESH MUSSELS, CLEANED
   AND RINSED
1 OR 2   LINKS DICED CHINESE SAUSAGE
2 TO 4   OUNCES FRESH SHIITAKE
   MUSHROOMS, OR 1 OUNCE DRIED
   MUSHROOMS, SOAKED, STEMS
   REMOVED, AND CHOPPED
2   TABLESPOONS THINLY SLICED GREEN
   ONION
2   TABLESPOON COARSELY CHOPPED
   FRESH CILANTRO LEAVES
1/4   CUP PINE NUTS, IF DESIRED
2   TABLESPOONS DARK SESAME OIL
   SALT, TO TASTE
   FRESHLY GROUND BLACK PEPPER,
   TO TASTE
raw white rice, for garnish if desired

Steam rice until tender; reserve. Bring sake and water to a boil in a large skillet or Dutch oven; add mussels, cover and steam until shells open, about 5 to 10 minutes. Remove and reserve mussels in their shells, discarding any unopened ones. Combine cooked rice, Chinese sausage, mushrooms, green onions, cilantro, pine nuts, sesame oil, salt and pepper.

Gently pull apart mussel shells. Fill the empty half with the rice mixture. Tie the two halves together with raffia or string. Mussels can be removed from shells, placed on a rice-filled shell half, and served open-faced, omitting the tie, if desired. Serve mussels at room temperature, arranged on a bed of raw rice. Or arrange mussels on top of raw rice or the remaining cooked rice mixture and bake in a preheated 300 degree oven for 15 minutes. Serve hot.

8 TO 12 SERVINGS

Babcock Gewurztraminer 1 9 9 0 (Santa Barbara)

ROOT VEGETABLE CHIPS

- WHITE POTATOES, SWEET POTATOES, PARSNIPS, TARO, YUCA, LOTUS ROOT, BEETS, OR OTHER ROOT VEGETABLES, THINLY SLICED
- SALT
- VEGETABLE OIL

Heat oil in a deep fat fryer to 375 degrees. Separating slices, drop vegetables into hot oil and fry until golden brown. Chips should turn a deeper color as they crisp. Watch carefully to prevent burning. Remove from oil and drain. Sprinkle with salt.

Adelsheim Pinot Blanc 1 9 9 0 (Oregon)

ROLLED SALMON SOUFFLÉ
WITH ARTICHOKE FILLING

SOUFFLÉ

3	TABLESPOONS BUTTER
2	CLOVES GARLIC, MINCED
2	FINELY CHOPPED SHALLOTS
3	TABLESPOONS ALL-PURPOSE FLOUR
2 1/4	CUPS MILK
1/8	TEASPOON NUTMEG
1	TEASPOON SALT
1/4	TEASPOON FRESHLY GROUND WHITE PEPPER
5	EGG YOLKS
7	OUNCES COOKED SALMON, FLAKED, BONES REMOVED
6	EGG WHITES, BEATEN UNTIL STIFF BUT NOT DRY

lemon slices and sprigs of fresh dill, for garnish

Oil a jelly-roll pan (10 1/2- by 15- by 1-inch) and line with a piece of waxed paper long enough to extend over the short edges by about 1 inch. Oil the paper lightly. Melt butter in a medium saucepan and add garlic and shallots. Sauté over low heat until soft, then sprinkle with flour and cook one minute, stirring constantly. Gradually add milk and whisk steadily until the mixture nears boiling. Add nutmeg, salt, and pepper. Transfer one cup of sauce to a medium bowl and set the remainder aside to use with filling. Whisk egg yolks into the one cup of sauce and blend well. Add flaked salmon. Stir about 1/4 cup of beaten egg whites into the soufflé, then fold in the remainder. Spread mixture evenly into prepared jelly-roll pan. Bake in a preheated 400 degree oven for 14 to 16 minutes, or until cake tester comes out clean and top is browned.

Lay a clean dish towel on a flat surface and spray with nonstick cooking spray. Loosen sides of soufflé from pan with a knife and turn out onto prepared cloth. Remove wax paper carefully. Beginning at a short end, roll the soufflé in the towel, jelly-roll fashion, and cool thoroughly.

FILLING

ONE	14-OUNCE CAN ARTICHOKE BOTTOMS, DRAINED
3	TABLESPOONS BUTTER
1/2	POUND COARSELY CHOPPED FRESH MUSHROOMS
4	OUNCES GRATED MONTEREY JACK CHEESE (ABOUT 1 CUP)
1 1/2	TABLESPOONS CHOPPED FRESH DILL OR 1 1/4 TEASPOONS DRIED
2	TABLESPOONS FRESHLY SQUEEZED LEMON JUICE

Chop 5 artichoke bottoms coarsely. Melt butter in a medium skillet and add mushrooms and chopped artichokes. Sauté until liquid has evaporated, stirring occasionally. Stir in reserved sauce, cheese, dill and lemon juice and simmer until cheese melts. Unroll the soufflé and spread about three fourths of the filling evenly over soufflé to within 2 inches of one shorter end. Beginning at the filling-covered end, reroll soufflé gently, using the towel as an aid. It is normal for cracks to appear. Place on a lightly oiled baking sheet, cover loosely with foil, and heat in a preheated 400 degree oven for 15 minutes.

Slice soufflé into 1-inch rounds. Heat remaining sauce, thinning with a little milk if desired, and spoon over individual slices. Garnish with lemon slices and fresh dill.

The soufflé may be refrigerated overnight or frozen. Bring to room temperature before reheating as directed.

8 TO 10 SERVINGS

Kuentz Bas Pinot Blanc 1 9 9 0 (Alsace)

LAYERED OMELET TERRINE

TOMATO LAYER

1	TABLESPOON OLIVE OIL
6	FINELY CHOPPED SHALLOTS
6	LARGE TOMATOES (ABOUT 3 POUNDS), COARSELY CHOPPED
FOUR	4- OR 5-INCH SPRIGS OF FRESH OREGANO, LEAVES REMOVED FROM STEMS AND MINCED
	SALT, TO TASTE
	FRESHLY GROUND WHITE PEPPER, TO TASTE

Heat oil over medium heat and sauté shallots until soft. Add tomatoes, oregano, salt and pepper and cook uncovered about 30 minutes until almost all liquid has evaporated. Correct seasoning. Drain in a strainer and set aside.

ZUCCHINI LAYER

1/2	TEASPOON OLIVE OIL
2	SMALL CLOVES GARLIC, MINCED
2	SMALL ZUCCHINI (ABOUT 3/4 POUND), FINELY CHOPPED
	SALT, TO TASTE
	FRESHLY GROUND WHITE PEPPER, TO TASTE
10	EGGS

chopped hard-cooked egg and tiny cooked vegetables, such as peas and cubed carrots, for garnish

Heat oil over low heat and sauté garlic until soft. Add zucchini, salt, and pepper. Increase heat to medium-high and cook uncovered about 5 minutes. Correct seasoning. Drain and set aside.

Whisk 6 eggs together. Add tomato mixture and blend well. Pour into a medium saucepan and cook over low heat until just set, but not dry, stirring occasionally. Season with salt and pepper. Reserve one half of tomato mixture and spoon the other half evenly into a lightly oiled 8 1/2-inch loaf pan.

Whisk 4 eggs together. Add zucchini mixture. Cook, stirring occasionally, until set but not dry. Correct seasoning and spoon over tomato layer.

Spoon reserved portion of the tomato mixture over the zucchini layer and smooth the top. Cover pan with foil, and bake in a preheated 300 degree oven about 20 minutes, or until set. Cool to room temperature. The terrine may be served immediately or refrigerated overnight. If refrigerated, return to room temperature before serving.

To serve, turn terrine out of pan and slice. Garnish with hard-cooked egg and tiny cooked vegetables at room temperature or spoon Sweet Red Pepper Sauce (page 199) around sliced terrine on plate. The terrine may also be served with Tapenade Provence (page 198).

This makes an excellent first course, or luncheon or brunch entrée. Other vegetables may be substituted for tomatoes and zucchini. Increasing the number of layers results in an even prettier dish.

6 TO 8 SERVINGS

Domaine Tempier Bandol Rosé 1 9 9 0 (Provence)

CLASSIC MARGARITAS

2/3   CUP TEQUILA
2/3   CUP FRESHLY SQUEEZED LIME JUICE
1/3   CUP COLD WATER
1/3   CUP TRIPLE SEC LIQUEUR
1/4   CUP SUPERFINE SUGAR
4 TO 5   CUPS ICE
coarse salt, for garnish, if desired
lime wedges, for garnish

In a 6-cup blender, place tequila, lime juice, water, Triple Sec and sugar. Add ice—4 cups for a strong margarita or 5 cups for a milder drink. Blend at highest speed until ice is finely crushed. If desired, dip glass rim in coarse salt. Fill glass with frozen margarita and garnish with a lime wedge. Margaritas may be made ahead and placed in freezer, then whirled in blender before serving.

These margaritas are authentic and worth the extra effort.
The key ingredient is the freshly squeezed lime juice—
do not substitute.

6 SERVINGS

HOLLY COCKTAIL

12   OUNCES FROZEN LIMEADE
     CONCENTRATE, THAWED
32   OUNCES FROZEN SWEETENED
     STRAWBERRIES, THAWED
1 1/2   CUPS LIGHT RUM
1 1/2   CUPS FINELY CRUSHED ICE
1/4   CUP TRIPLE SEC LIQUEUR

Place limeade and strawberries in food processor and pulse to blend. Add rum, ice and Triple Sec; pulse until slushy. Serve in large, stemmed glasses.

This holiday beverage is just as good without the alcohol.
If rum is used, the recipe may be doubled and
stored in a large container in the freezer, ready to serve.
For extra zip, splash Triple Sec over the top
of each glass at serving time.

8 TO 10 SERVINGS

WATERMELON AND LIME DAIQUIRI

Begin at least 6 hours before serving.

4   CUPS SEEDED WATERMELON, CUT IN
      1-INCH CHUNKS
1/4   CUP FRESHLY SQUEEZED LIME JUICE
      (2 TO 3 LIMES)
3/4   CUP WHITE RUM
1   TABLESPOON PLUS 1 TEASPOON
      SUGAR
      lime slices, for garnish

Place watermelon chunks in a large plastic bag
and freeze 6 hours or more. Combine lime juice,
rum and sugar, stirring to dissolve sugar. Pour
mixture into blender; add frozen watermelon
chunks and blend until smooth, about 1 minute.
Pour into martini glasses and garnish with lime
slices.

4 SERVINGS

HERBED APPLE CIDER

8   CUPS FRESH APPLE CIDER OR PEAR
      JUICE
1/3   TEASPOON GROUND NUTMEG
1/4   TEASPOON GROUND THYME
1/2   TEASPOON GROUND GINGER
4   CINNAMON STICKS, BROKEN IN HALF
      sprigs of fresh thyme, for garnish

In a large, nonreactive pot, heat the apple cider
to simmering. Stir in the nutmeg, thyme and
ginger and simmer for 8 minutes, uncovered.
Cool slightly. To serve, place a piece of
cinnamon stick in a heavy glass or mug, pour in
the warm cider and garnish with a sprig of
thyme.

*The thyme gives this cider drink a fresh and unexpected
flavor. The recipe can be easily made in larger quantities
and stored in the refrigerator. Reheat before serving.*

6 TO 8 SERVINGS

SOUPS

&

BREADS

WINE WITH SOUPS

Soups are difficult to match with wines. Because they are often warm liquid, they may not seem right with another liquid, usually a cold glass of wine, although sometimes the contrast can be interesting. Too, there are times when it is not necessary to serve wine. Let the recipe be a guide. If sherry is an ingredient of the soup, it will probably make a good accompaniment. Serve a true sherry from the sherry region of Spain, not a fortified American wine misleadingly labeled as sherry.

True sherry is very often underpriced. There are two basic types—fino (dry), and oloroso (sweet). Many intermediate styles exist, but bear in mind these two parameters and a good wine merchant will find the right one. If the soup is light and crisp, including perhaps a touch of rich fish, then a very dry fino will work well. If the soup is exotic and rich, made with sweet vegetables (onions, carrots, parsnips, turnips), then try an oloroso. Cream sherries, as very sweet olorosos are often called, are appropriate only to dessert.

With soups made with fish or chicken, serve wines that would normally accompany a fish or chicken dish—Sauvignon Blanc or German wines. Stews, which are usually hearty, require hearty wines, such as Italian red wines, Rhône wines or Zinfandel.

Preceding page: Rozzelle Court Scones, page 91

TORTILLA CORN SOUP

3 1/2 TO 4 CUPS FRESH YELLOW CORN KERNELS
1 1/2 CUPS CHICKEN BROTH, PREFERABLY HOMEMADE
4 TABLESPOONS BUTTER
2 CUPS MILK
1 1/4 TEASPOONS GROUND CUMIN
1 LARGE CLOVE GARLIC, PRESSED
ONE 4-OUNCE CAN GREEN CHILIES
HOT PEPPER SAUCE, TO TASTE
1 TEASPOON FRESHLY GROUND BLACK PEPPER
8 CORN TORTILLAS, CUT INTO SMALL STRIPS
VEGETABLE OIL, FOR FRYING
SALT, TO TASTE
1 1/2 CUPS DICED TOMATOES
2 CUPS DICED COOKED CHICKEN BREAST
1 1/2 CUPS SHREDDED MONTEREY JACK CHEESE WITH JALEPEÑO PEPPERS

tomato salsa, sliced black olives, sour cream, sliced green onions and diced avocados, as accompaniments

Using a food processor, purée corn in chicken broth. Melt butter in a stockpot, add corn purée and simmer 5 minutes over low heat, stirring. Add milk, cumin and garlic and bring to a boil. Reduce heat and add green chilies, hot pepper sauce and pepper. (The soup may be prepared to this point, cooled and frozen.)

Fry tortilla strips in 1/2 inch oil in a heavy skillet. Drain on paper towels and sprinkle with salt to taste. Divide tomatoes and chicken among individual soup bowls. Add cheese to hot soup and stir until cheese is melted. Ladle soup into bowls and garnish with tortilla strips. Pass accompaniments.

This soup and its accompaniments make a colorful main course for a casual buffet dinner. Serve with Classic Margaritas (page 54) and Corn Thins (page 85).

8 TO 10 SERVINGS

MANDARIN SCALLOP SOUP WITH SNOW PEAS

Begin 4 hours to 1 day before serving.

2 TABLESPOONS FRESH GINGER, PEELED AND MINCED
2 MEDIUM CLOVES GARLIC, THINLY SLICED
3/4 TEASPOON WHOLE BLACK PEPPERCORNS
3/4 CUP THINLY SLICED GREEN ONIONS, DIVIDED
6 CUPS CHICKEN STOCK, PREFERABLY HOMEMADE
2 CUPS WATER
1 1/2 TEASPOONS SOY SAUCE
2 TABLESPOONS DRY SHERRY, OR TO TASTE
1 1/2 TEASPOONS SESAME OIL
FRESHLY GROUND BLACK PEPPER, TO TASTE
1/4 POUND SNOW PEAS, TRIMMED AND CUT INTO 1/2-INCH PIECES
1/2 TO 3/4 POUND SEA SCALLOPS, RINSED, DRAINED, AND HALVED HORIZONTALLY

In a stockpot, combine ginger, garlic, peppercorns, 1/2 cup green onions, chicken stock and water. Bring to a boil and simmer for 10 minutes, then remove stockpot from heat and cool. Strain the mixture into a large bowl. Stir in soy sauce, sherry, sesame oil and pepper. Cover and chill for at least 3 hours, or until cold. In a medium saucepan bring salted water to a boil, add snow peas and scallops, and cook for 1 minute. Drain the scallops and peas in a colander, then rinse with cold water. Stir snow peas and scallops into the chilled soup with the remaining 1/4 cup green onions.

Variations: 1/2 pound small shrimp, shelled, or 1/2 pound cooked chicken breast, shredded, may be substituted for the sea scallops.

6 TO 8 SERVINGS

Moriette Vouvray 1 9 8 9 (Loire)

RED PEPPER CORN CHOWDER

1/4 POUND BACON, CUT IN 1/2-INCH PIECES
1 LARGE ONION, DICED
2 POUNDS WHITE POTATOES, PEELED AND CUT INTO 1/2-INCH CUBES
1 LARGE RED BELL PEPPER, DICED
6 CUPS CHICKEN STOCK, PREFERABLY HOMEMADE
3 SPRIGS FRESH THYME
8 MEDIUM EARS OF FRESH YELLOW CORN, KERNELS REMOVED (ABOUT 4 CUPS CORN)
1/2 CUP HEAVY CREAM
1 TEASPOON SALT
1/4 TEASPOON FRESHLY GROUND BLACK PEPPER
cooked, crumbled bacon, for garnish
large red peppers, halved, as serving bowls

Brown bacon in a stockpot, remove and set aside. Add onion to drippings in pot and sauté 3 to 5 minutes. Add potatoes and sauté 3 minutes, then add red pepper and cook 1 minute longer. Blend in stock and thyme. Bring soup to a boil, then reduce heat and simmer, partially covered, until potatoes are tender, about 20 minutes. Discard thyme. In a food processor, purée potato mixture and return to stockpot. Add corn, cream, salt and pepper and heat gently for 5 minutes. The soup may be prepared up to 8 hours ahead and reheated before serving.

Serve soup in red pepper halves, garnished with crumbled bacon.

6 SERVINGS

Matrot Meursault 1 9 9 0 (White Burgundy)

THAI SOUP

1 CAN UNSWEETENED COCONUT MILK (DO NOT SHAKE)
3 TO 4 SLICES FRESH GINGER (THAI GINGER, IF AVAILABLE), SOAKED IN WARM WATER 10 MINUTES
2 CUPS CHICKEN BREAST, BONED, SKINNED AND CUT INTO THIN STRIPS
2 TO 3 TABLESPOONS FISH SAUCE
1/4 TO 1/2 CUP WATER
ONE 15-OUNCE CAN STRAW MUSHROOMS, DRAINED
2 TO 3 TABLESPOONS FRESHLY SQUEEZED LIME JUICE
1 STALK FRESH LEMON GRASS, CUT IN 1-INCH PIECES AND BRUISED WITH THE DULL EDGE OF A KNIFE
1 TEASPOON SUGAR
4 FRESH TINY GREEN CHILI PEPPERS, HALVED
1 TEASPOON THAI CHILI IN OIL
fresh cilantro, for garnish

Heat thickened half of coconut milk to boiling. Reduce heat and add ginger, chicken and fish sauce. Stir until chicken is cooked, about 3 minutes. Add remaining half of coconut milk, water and mushrooms and bring to boil. Stir in lime juice, lemon grass, sugar, chili peppers and chili in oil. Stir, taste and add more fish sauce, lime juice and sugar if desired. The chili peppers, ginger and lemon grass are for flavoring and are usually removed.

Garnish with cilantro and serve with sesame rice wafers.

4 SERVINGS

Schlossgut Diel Dorsheimer Goldloch Auslese 1 9 9 0 (Nahe)

JAPANESE GAZPACHO

Begin 4 hours to 1 day before serving.

1	CUP CHOPPED, SEEDED CUCUMBER
1	LARGE RED BELL PEPPER, CHOPPED
1/2	CUP SLICED GREEN ONION
1/2	CUP CHOPPED CELERY
1	CUP ZUCCHINI, CUT INTO JULIENNE
1/2	CUP DAIKON (JAPANESE RADISH), PEELED AND CHOPPED
1	TABLESPOON SOY SAUCE
1 1/2	TEASPOONS SESAME OIL
	HOT PEPPER SAUCE, TO TASTE
1/3	CUP RICE OR WHITE-WINE VINEGAR
4	CUPS CHICKEN BROTH, PREFERABLY HOMEMADE

1/4 cup chopped cilantro, for garnish
1/2 cup enoki mushrooms, for garnish

In a large mixing bowl, combine cucumber, red pepper, green onion, celery, zucchini and daikon. Stir in soy sauce, sesame oil, hot pepper sauce, vinegar and chicken broth. Cover and chill 4 hours or overnight. Garnish with cilantro and mushrooms.

6 TO 8 SERVINGS

Dr. Loosen Bernkasteler Lay Kabinett 1 9 9 0
(Mosel - Saar - Ruwer)

WINTER SQUASH SOUP

2	LARGE BUTTERNUT SQUASH (ABOUT 2 POUNDS EACH)
6	TABLESPOONS UNSALTED BUTTER
1	LARGE YELLOW ONION, SLICED
6	CUPS CHICKEN STOCK, PREFERABLY HOMEMADE
	SALT, TO TASTE
	FRESHLY GROUND WHITE PEPPER, TO TASTE
	FRESHLY GRATED NUTMEG, TO TASTE
	A PINCH OF GROUND CLOVES
1/2	CUP FRESHLY GRATED PARMESAN CHEESE

fresh croutons, for garnish

Place squash in a shallow baking pan in the center of a preheated 400 degree oven. Bake until the point of a knife pierces skin easily, about 1 hour. Remove squash from the oven, cut in half and cool to room temperature. Melt butter in a skillet and cook onions over low heat, partially covered, until soft, about 15 minutes. Remove seeds from squash and scoop out the pulp. In a food processor, purée the pulp and onions. Whisk the purée into the stock in a saucepan and simmer, covered, for 10 minutes. Season with white pepper, nutmeg and cloves.

Ladle into warmed soup bowls and garnish with Parmesan cheese and croutons. For an elegant buffet, serve the soup in a squash or small pumpkin shell.

10 TO 12 SERVINGS

Villa Sparina Gavi di Gavi 1 9 9 0 (Piedmont)

VEGETABLE CHICKEN NOODLE SOUP

10 CUPS HOMEMADE CHICKEN STOCK
(SEE RECIPE)

6 POUNDS CHICKEN BREASTS

3 CARROTS, SLICED

3 CELERY STALKS, SLICED

1 RED BELL PEPPER, CUBED

1 BUNCH BROCCOLI, FLOWERETS
ONLY

1 ZUCCHINI, CUBED

8 OUNCES COOKED THIN NOODLES

1 BUNCH GREEN ONIONS, THINLY
SLICED
SALT, TO TASTE
FRESHLY GROUND BLACK PEPPER,
TO TASTE

2 tablespoons chopped fresh parsley, for garnish

Place chicken breasts and homemade stock in a large pot and bring to a boil. Reduce heat and simmer, covered, for about one hour. Let chicken stand in broth until it is cool enough to handle. Remove skin and bones and discard. Cut the meat into chunks, return to broth and refrigerate. When fat solidifies on top, skim off. Bring the broth to a boil, then add carrots, celery and red pepper. Simmer for 10 minutes. Add broccoli and simmer 5 minutes. Add zucchini and simmer 2 minutes longer.

Just before serving, add noodles, green onions, salt and pepper and heat just to boiling. Serve garnished with chopped fresh parsley.

8 TO 10 SERVINGS

Alexander Valley Vineyards Chardonnay 1 9 9 0
(Alexander Valley)

HOMEMADE CHICKEN STOCK

6 POUNDS CHICKEN WINGS

1 CARROT, CHOPPED

2 STALKS CELERY, CHOPPED

1 ONION, PEELED AND QUARTERED

1 LEEK, WHITE PART ONLY, CHOPPED

3 SPRIGS FRESH PARSLEY

1 BAY LEAF

6 WHOLE BLACK PEPPERCORNS

1 TEASPOON SALT

Place chicken wings, carrot, celery, onion, leek, parsley, bay leaf, peppercorns and salt in a large stockpot with enough cold water to cover ingredients by 1 inch. Bring to a boil, and skim. Reduce heat to low and simmer for about 3 hours. Remove chicken wings and bones and discard. Cool, then strain the stock and refrigerate. When fat is solidified on top, skim off. This stock will keep in the refrigerator up to 1 week, or it may be frozen.

MAKES ABOUT 10 CUPS.

PIQUANT SHRIMP SOUP

Begin 4 hours before serving.

1   QUART BUTTERMILK
1   TABLESPOON ENGLISH-STYLE DRY
     MUSTARD
1/2   TEASPOON SALT
1   TEASPOON SUGAR
1/2   POUND COOKED SHRIMP, COOLED,
     SHELLED, DEVEINED AND CHOPPED
1   CUCUMBER, PEELED, SEEDED AND
     CHOPPED
2   TABLESPOONS SNIPPED FRESH
     CHIVES

2 to 3 whole shrimp, halved lengthwise, for garnish
cucumber slices, for garnish

In a large bowl, combine the buttermilk, mustard, salt, sugar, chopped shrimp, cucumber and chives. Whisk until soup is well blended. Chill, covered, for 3 hours, or until soup is very cold. Garnish each serving with a shrimp half and a slice of cucumber.

4 TO 6 SERVINGS

Morgan Chardonnay 1 9 9 0 (Monterey)

COLD POTATO SOUP
WITH SPINACH AND WATERCRESS

Prepare 1 day before serving.

3   TABLESPOONS VEGETABLE OIL
4   LEEKS, WHITE PART ONLY, RINSED
     WELL AND CHOPPED
1 1/2   POUNDS POTATOES, PEELED AND
     CUBED
1   LARGE BUNCH FRESH SPINACH,
     WASHED AND STEMMED (12 TO 14
     OUNCES)
1   BUNCH WATERCRESS, WASHED AND
     STEMMED
8   CUPS CHICKEN STOCK, PREFERABLY
     HOMEMADE
1/2   TEASPOON SALT, OR TO TASTE
1/2   TEASPOON FRESHLY GROUND
     WHITE PEPPER, OR TO TASTE
3   TABLESPOONS FRESHLY SQUEEZED
     LEMON JUICE, DIVIDED
1/2   CUP SOUR CREAM
1   TABLESPOON FINELY CHOPPED
     FRESH CHIVES

In a medium stockpot, heat oil over medium heat and sauté leeks until soft, stirring occasionally. Add potatoes and cook until tender. Stir in spinach and watercress and sauté until wilted, about 3 minutes longer. Blend in chicken stock and bring to a simmer. Cook, partially covered, about 15 minutes, then cool. Purée soup in a food processor, and season with salt, pepper and 1 tablespoon lemon juice. Chill overnight.

Whisk together sour cream, 2 tablespoons lemon juice and chives. Serve soup topped with a spoonful of lemon-chive cream.

8 SERVINGS

Creston Vineyards Chevrier Blanc 1 9 9 0 (Monterey)

BASIL CREAM MINESTRONE

2 TABLESPOONS OLIVE OIL
2 MEDIUM ONIONS, FINELY CHOPPED
4 MEDIUM CARROTS, CHOPPED
1/2 POUND WHITE POTATOES, PEELED AND CUBED
1 MEDIUM ZUCCHINI, CUBED
1 MEDIUM YELLOW ZUCCHINI, CUBED
1 1/2 CUPS FRESH GREEN BEANS, CUT IN 1-INCH PIECES
1/2 SMALL CABBAGE, SHREDDED
2 CUPS CANNED ITALIAN PLUM TOMATOES, DRAINED AND PURÉED
6 CUPS CHICKEN STOCK, PREFERABLY HOMEMADE
2 CLOVES GARLIC, MINCED
1 TABLESPOON FINELY CHOPPED FRESH BASIL
1 TEASPOON SALT
1/2 TEASPOON FRESHLY GROUND BLACK PEPPER
1/4 CUP ORZO
1 CUP CANNED WHITE BEANS, DRAINED

In a large stockpot, heat olive oil and sauté onion until translucent. Add carrots, potatoes, zucchini and beans. Sauté 3 minutes longer, stir in cabbage and sauté until softened. Add tomatoes, chicken stock, garlic, basil, salt and pepper. Bring to a boil, reduce heat and simmer, uncovered, until vegetables are tender and soup is slightly thickened, about 25 minutes. In the last 10 minutes of cooking add orzo and cook until done. Stir in the white beans and heat briefly.

BASIL CREAM

1/2 CUP BASIL PESTO, PREFERABLY HOMEMADE
1 TABLESPOON RED-WINE VINEGAR
1/2 CUP HEAVY CREAM
1/2 TEASPOON SALT
1/4 TEASPOON FRESHLY GROUND BLACK PEPPER

Combine basil pesto, vinegar, cream, salt and pepper in a small bowl and whisk until smooth. Refrigerate.

The soup can be served hot, cold or at room temperature. Add a spoonful of Basil Cream to each bowl. Serve with Tuscan Peasant Bread (page 90).

6 TO 8 SERVINGS

Regaleali Rosso del Conte 1 9 8 6 (Sicily)

RED PEPPER SOUP WITH FRESH DILL

4	LARGE RED BELL PEPPERS, CHOPPED
2	MEDIUM ONIONS, CHOPPED
6	TABLESPOONS BUTTER
1/2	LARGE POTATO, PEELED AND GRATED
2 1/2	CUPS CHICKEN STOCK, PREFERABLY HOMEMADE
1/2	CUP HEAVY CREAM
2	TABLESPOONS FRESHLY SQUEEZED LEMON JUICE
	SALT, TO TASTE
	FRESHLY GROUND BLACK PEPPER, TO TASTE
2	TABLESPOONS CHOPPED FRESH DILL

sour cream and fresh dill, for garnish

Melt butter in a large saucepan and add peppers and onions. Cover and cook 35 to 45 minutes over medium-low heat, stirring occasionally. Add grated potato and chicken stock and bring to a boil. Simmer, covered, over low heat for about 15 minutes. Purée the mixture in a food processor or blender. Return to pan and add cream, lemon juice, salt, pepper and dill.

Serve hot or cold, topped with a spoonful of sour cream and garnished with dill, accompanied by Garlic Popovers (page 236).

This soup may also be made with green or yellow peppers. To make a rainbow soup, prepare two batches, with two different color peppers, making slightly more of one soup than the other. When ready to serve, pouring from dry measuring cups, pour one soup slowly down one side of each soup bowl while simultaneously pouring the other soup down the opposite side.

6 TO 8 SERVINGS

Cullens Sauvignon Blanc 1 9 8 9 (Margaret River - Australia)

CREAM OF MUSHROOM SOUP WITH FRESH MINT

4	MEDIUM ONIONS, COARSELY CHOPPED
1	CLOVE GARLIC, CRUSHED
4	TABLESPOONS BUTTER
1	POUND FRESH MUSHROOMS
2	TEASPOONS FRESHLY SQUEEZED LEMON JUICE
2	TABLESPOONS ALL-PURPOSE FLOUR
8	CUPS CHICKEN STOCK, PREFERABLY HOMEMADE
2	CUPS LIGHT CREAM
1/4	CUP CHOPPED FRESH MINT
1/3	CUP DRY SHERRY
	SALT, TO TASTE
	FRESHLY GROUND BLACK PEPPER, TO TASTE

Sauté onions and garlic in butter until tender but not brown, about 3 to 4 minutes. Add the whole mushrooms and lemon juice and cook slowly for 10 minutes. Coarsely chop the mixture in a food processor. Return to the pan, stir in flour and stock and simmer until soup is slightly thickened. Add cream and mint, then season with sherry, salt and pepper. Do not boil during cooking or reheating. The soup may be refrigerated for up to 3 days.

12 SERVINGS

Lavantureaux Chablis 1 9 8 6 (Chablis)

OVEN VEGETABLE CHOWDER

1	LARGE ZUCCHINI, CUT IN 1/4-INCH SLICES, THEN QUARTERED
2	MEDIUM ONIONS, CUT IN 1/4-INCH SLICES, THEN QUARTERED
ONE	14 1/2-OUNCE CAN CHOPPED TOMATOES, WITH LIQUID
ONE	15-OUNCE CAN GARBANZO BEANS, WITH LIQUID
2	TABLESPOONS MELTED BUTTER
1 1/2	CUPS DRY WHITE WINE
2	LARGE CLOVES GARLIC, MINCED
2	TEASPOONS MINCED FRESH BASIL
1	BAY LEAF FRESHLY GROUND BLACK PEPPER, TO TASTE
1 1/2	CUPS SHREDDED MONTEREY JACK CHEESE
1	CUP FRESHLY GRATED PARMESAN CHEESE

Combine zucchini, onions, tomatoes and beans in a 3-quart baking dish. Pour melted butter over vegetables. Add wine, garlic, basil and bay leaf and stir gently. Cover and bake in a preheated 400 degree oven for 1 hour, stirring occasionally. Remove bay leaf. Season with pepper and stir. Sprinkle with Monterey Jack cheese, replace cover and bake for an additional 10 minutes.

When ready to serve, preheat broiler. Divide soup among 6 to 8 ovenproof bowls. Sprinkle with Parmesan cheese and place under broiler until cheese is golden and chowder is bubbling.

Serve this unusual chowder, baked in the oven, with Caesar Salad (page 181) and Bruschetta (page 92) for a warming meal.

6 TO 8 SERVINGS

Castallare Bianco 1 9 9 0 (Tuscany)

SENEGALESE SOUP

Begin 4 hours or 1 day ahead.

3	LARGE STALKS CELERY, FINELY CHOPPED
3	ONIONS, MINCED
3	GRANNY SMITH APPLES, PEELED AND FINELY CHOPPED
3	TABLESPOONS BUTTER
3	TABLESPOONS CURRY POWDER
1/2	CUP ALL-PURPOSE FLOUR
6	CUPS CHICKEN BROTH, PREFERABLY HOMEMADE SALT, TO TASTE CAYENNE PEPPER, TO TASTE
1 1/4	CUPS FINELY CHOPPED, COOKED CHICKEN BREAST
3	CUPS HALF-AND-HALF

fresh lime and avocado, thinly sliced, for garnish

In a stockpot, sauté celery, onions and apples in butter until soft, but not brown. Add curry powder and cook, stirring, for 2 minutes. Blend in flour, and cook 2 minutes longer. Add broth gradually, stirring with a whisk, and cook until soup is smooth and slightly thickened. Season with salt and cayenne pepper. Add chicken, cool, then stir in half-and-half.

Serve the soup chilled, garnished with thin slices of lime and avocado.

8 SERVINGS

Adelsheim Chardonnay 1 9 9 0 (Oregon)

PACIFIC CHOWDER

8   TABLESPOONS BUTTER
1   SMALL ONION, DICED
1/2   GREEN BELL PEPPER, DICED
1/4   RED BELL PEPPER, DICED
2   STALKS CELERY, DICED
1/3   CUP ALL-PURPOSE FLOUR
1   TABLESPOON OLD BAY SEASONING
   FRESHLY GROUND BLACK PEPPER,
   TO TASTE
8   CUPS MILK
ONE   14-OUNCE CAN SALMON, DRAINED
1/4   CUP DRY SHERRY, OR TO TASTE

Melt butter in a large stockpot. Sauté onion, green and red peppers and celery until onions are translucent. Add flour, Old Bay Seasoning, and pepper. Cover and cook over medium heat for 1 minute. Add half of the milk, stirring to blend until mixture begins to thicken. Add remaining milk and simmer 5 minutes. Add salmon and sherry and heat briefly.

6 TO 8 SERVINGS

Lustau Fino Amontillado (Sherry - Spain)

COLD DILLED TOMATO SOUP

Prepare at least 4 hours before serving.

3   TABLESPOONS BUTTER
2   ONIONS, COARSELY CHOPPED
4   SHALLOTS, COARSELY CHOPPED
6   CARROTS, COARSELY SHREDDED
2   MEDIUM POTATOES, PEELED AND
   COARSELY CHOPPED
4   CUPS CHICKEN STOCK, PREFERABLY
   HOMEMADE
3   POUNDS RIPE TOMATOES, PEELED
   AND COARSELY CHOPPED
3   TABLESPOONS FINELY CHOPPED
   FRESH DILL
   SALT, TO TASTE
   FRESHLY GROUND BLACK PEPPER,
   TO TASTE
sour cream and sprigs of fresh dill, for garnish

Melt butter in a large stockpot and add onions, shallots and carrots. Sauté 5 minutes, then stir in potatoes and chicken stock and simmer, covered, for 10 minutes. Add tomatoes and continue cooking for 15 minutes, stirring occasionally. Purée in a food processor and return to stockpot. Add dill, salt and pepper and simmer 5 minutes. Remove from heat and chill for 3 to 4 hours. Serve topped with a spoonful of sour cream and a sprig of dill.

6 SERVINGS

Sanford Sauvignon Blanc 1 9 9 0 (Santa Barbara)

RIO GRANDE CHILI

3 POUNDS LEAN GROUND SIRLOIN
1 POUND CUBED PORK TENDERLOIN
2 LINKS OF ITALIAN SAUSAGE
SALT, TO TASTE
2 LARGE YELLOW ONIONS, CHOPPED
3 CLOVES GARLIC, CHOPPED
2 TABLESPOONS CHILI POWDER
2 TABLESPOONS GROUND CUMIN
1 TABLESPOON DRIED OREGANO
2 TABLESPOONS ALL-PURPOSE FLOUR
1 CUP TOMATO SAUCE
6 OUNCES TOMATO PASTE
2 POUNDS TOMATOES, CHOPPED
2 STALKS CELERY, CHOPPED
1 MEDIUM GREEN BELL PEPPER,
CHOPPED
2 BAY LEAVES
1 TABLESPOON BROWN SUGAR
2 TABLESPOONS FRESHLY SQUEEZED
LEMON JUICE
THREE 15-OUNCE CANS PINTO BEANS,
DRAINED AND RINSED
ONE 16-OUNCE CAN RED KIDNEY BEANS,
DRAINED AND RINSED
ONE 4 1/2-OUNCE CAN MILD JALAPEÑO
PEPPERS, CHOPPED
1 CUP RED WINE
sour cream and lime wedges, for garnish
warmed flour tortillas, as an accompaniment

In a large skillet, brown ground sirloin, pork and sausage. Drain off all but 2 tablespoons of fat and transfer meat to a large stockpot. Salt to taste and keep warm over low heat. In the same skillet, sauté onions and garlic until tender. Add to meat and mix thoroughly. In a small bowl, combine chili powder, cumin, oregano and flour. Sprinkle over meat in the stockpot and stir to coat well. Stir in tomato sauce, tomato paste and tomatoes, and increase heat to medium. Add water if mixture seems too dry.

Then add celery, green pepper, bay leaves, brown sugar and lemon juice. Simmer, covered, for 2 hours or more, stirring occasionally. During the last 40 minutes, add pinto beans, red kidney beans, jalapeño peppers and wine.

Garnish bowls of chili with sour cream and lime wedges and serve warmed flour tortillas as an accompaniment.

8 SERVINGS

Samuel Adams Lager (Boston beer)

SAUSAGE LENTIL SOUP

2   TABLESPOONS OLIVE OIL
2   MEDIUM ONIONS, FINELY CHOPPED
4   CELERY STALKS, CHOPPED
1   POUND FRESH SEASONED SAUSAGE,
    SAUTÉED, DRAINED AND CRUMBLED
3 1/2 CUPS CHICKEN BROTH, PREFERABLY
    HOMEMADE
4   CUPS WATER
2   CUPS LENTILS
    ZEST OF 1 SMALL ORANGE, CUT IN
    1 OR 2 LARGE STRIPS
1/2 TEASPOON DRIED SAVORY
1/2 TEASPOON DRIED MARJORAM
6   CARROTS, CHOPPED
    SALT, TO TASTE
    FRESHLY GROUND BLACK PEPPER,
    TO TASTE

In a stockpot, heat oil and cook onion over low heat for about 5 minutes. Add celery and sausage and cook 10 minutes, stirring occasionally. Add broth, water, lentils, orange zest, savory and marjoram. Bring to a boil, then reduce heat and simmer, partially covered, for another 15 minutes. Add carrots and continue cooking, partially covered, until lentils are tender and can be mashed with a spoon, about 45 minutes. Remove orange zest and season with salt and pepper.

This substantial main course soup can be prepared up to 2 days ahead. Serve with a salad of fresh greens and Bundt Pan Cornbread (page 235).

4 SERVINGS

Domaine St. Charles Brouilly 1 9 9 0 (Beaujolais)

HEARTY POTATO CHOWDER

2   CUPS PEELED, DICED POTATOES
3/4 CUP DICED ONION
1/2 CUP FINELY DICED CELERY
2 1/2 CUPS WATER
2   TEASPOONS SALT, OR TO TASTE
4   TABLESPOONS BUTTER
4   TABLESPOONS ALL-PURPOSE FLOUR
3/4 TABLESPOON DIJON-STYLE
    MUSTARD
1/4 TEASPOON FRESHLY GROUND
    BLACK PEPPER
2   CUPS MILK, OR MORE FOR DESIRED
    CONSISTENCY
1   TEASPOON WORCESTERSHIRE SAUCE
1/4 POUND CHEDDAR CHEESE,
    SHREDDED
1   CUP CANNED TOMATOES, DRAINED
    AND DICED
    DICED COOKED HAM, IF DESIRED
    chopped fresh dill or chives, for garnish

In a large stockpot, combine potatoes, onion, celery, water and salt and cook until vegetables are tender. Do not drain. While the vegetables are cooking, melt butter in a large heavy saucepan. Whisk in flour, mustard and pepper. Add milk slowly, whisking until thick and smooth. Stir in Worcestershire sauce and cheese. Add potato mixture and tomatoes and heat thoroughly, but do not boil. For an even heartier soup, diced ham may be added while heating. Garnish with chopped dill or chives.

Served with a green salad and Salty Caraway Crescents (page 80), this chowder makes a substantial cold weather main course.

4 TO 6 SERVINGS

*Ronco del Gnemiz Chardonnay 1 9 8 8
(Friuli - Venezia)*

OLD-FASHIONED FISH CHOWDER

Prepare 1 day before serving.

1 1/2 POUNDS SKINLESS FILLETS OF HALIBUT, HADDOCK, OR WHITING FISH BONES (REQUEST FROM FISH MARKET)

6 CUPS WATER

2 OUNCES DICED SALT PORK

8 TABLESPOONS BUTTER

1/2 CUP CHOPPED ONION

1 SMALL LEEK, FINELY CHOPPED

1/2 CUP CHOPPED CELERY, INCLUDING LEAVES

1 TEASPOON SALT

1/4 TEASPOON CURRY POWDER

3 TABLESPOONS ALL-PURPOSE FLOUR

2 CUPS POTATOES, PEELED AND CUT IN LARGE CUBES

1 CUP LIGHT CREAM

1/2 CUP MILK

2 tablespoons chopped fresh parsley, for garnish

Cut fish into 1/2-inch chunks. In a large stockpot combine fish and water, including any large bones from the fish. Bring to a boil, reduce heat and simmer for 15 minutes. Drain fish, discard bones and set aside. Reserve one quart of stock.

Rinse and dry the cooking pot. Place diced salt pork in the pot and cook over medium heat until the pork is crisp and golden brown. Drain on paper towels and set aside. Add butter to pork drippings, along with onion, leek and celery. Sauté several minutes until vegetables are wilted, but not brown.

Add salt and curry powder and whisk in flour, beating until smooth. Blend in reserved fish stock and potatoes. Cook over medium heat until potatoes are tender, stirring occasionally, about 15 minutes. Remove from heat and add cream, milk, fish, and salt pork. Cover and refrigerate several hours or overnight to blend flavors.

To serve, reheat gently, but do not allow the chowder to boil. Add chopped parsley and dots of butter, if desired, to each bowl or tureen. Pass a peppermill at the table.

6 SERVINGS

Chereau Carré Muscadet Comte Leloup 1 9 9 0 (Loire)

SWEET GREEN PEA SOUP

Begin at least 4 hours before serving.

1	POUND SHELLED FRESH PEAS OR FROZEN PEAS, THAWED
1	LARGE ONION, SLICED
1	LARGE POTATO, PEELED AND SLICED
2	CARROTS, THINLY SLICED
2	STALKS CELERY WITH LEAVES, SLICED
2	CLOVES GARLIC, CRUSHED
1	TEASPOON SALT
1 1/2	TEASPOONS CURRY POWDER
3	CUPS CHICKEN STOCK, PREFERABLY HOMEMADE
1	CUP HEAVY CREAM

sprigs of fresh mint and whipped cream, for garnish

Place peas, onion, potato, carrots, celery, garlic, salt, curry powder and chicken stock in a medium saucepan. Bring to a boil, reduce heat and simmer 20 to 30 minutes. Purée in a food processor. Add cream and chill for 3 to 4 hours.

Serve topped with a spoonful of whipped cream and a sprig of mint.

The soup may be served warm, omitting mint. The taste of curry complements the flavor of delicate spring peas.

8 SERVINGS

Kumeu River Sauvignon Blanc 1 9 8 9 (New Zealand)

RUSSIAN VICHYSSOISE

Prepare at least 3 hours before serving.

4	CUPS CHICKEN BROTH, PREFERABLY HOMEMADE
1	POUND POTATOES, PEELED AND THINLY SLICED
1	LARGE ONION, CHOPPED
3	LEEKS, WHITE PART ONLY, RINSED WELL AND CHOPPED
2	STALKS CELERY, THINLY SLICED
3	TABLESPOONS CHOPPED FRESH MARJORAM, OR 1 TABLESPOON DRIED
3/4	CUP CRÈME FRAÎCHE (PAGE 198), DIVIDED
1/2	CUP HEAVY CREAM, DIVIDED
	SALT, TO TASTE
	FRESHLY GROUND BLACK PEPPER, TO TASTE

1 bunch of minced fresh chives, for garnish
2 ounces black caviar, for garnish

Combine broth, potatoes, onion, leeks, celery and marjoram in a stockpot. Bring to a boil and simmer for 1 hour or until vegetables are very soft. Purée the mixture in batches in a food processor, and strain into a large bowl. Stir in 1/2 cup of the crème fraîche and 1/4 cup of the cream. Season with salt and pepper. If soup is too thick, add the remaining 1/4 cup cream. Cover and chill soup for at least 2 hours or overnight.

To serve, ladle soup into bowls, sprinkle with chives, and garnish with caviar. Top each serving with a spoonful of the remaining crème fraîche.

4 TO 6 SERVINGS

Taittinger Blanc de Blanc nv (Champagne)

PASTA E FAGIOLI

Begin 1 day before serving.

- 1/4 CUP OLIVE OIL
- 2 CARROTS, CHOPPED
- 2 CUPS FINELY CHOPPED ONIONS
- 1/2 CUP CHOPPED CELERY
- 4 CLOVES GARLIC, MINCED
- 1/2 TEASPOON DRIED BASIL
- 1/2 TEASPOON DRIED OREGANO
- 2 BAY LEAVES
- 3/4 TEASPOON DRIED RED PEPPER FLAKES
- 1 CUP DRIED WHITE BEANS, SOAKED IN WATER OVERNIGHT AND DRAINED
- 8 CUPS CHICKEN STOCK, PREFERABLY HOMEMADE, DIVIDED
- 4 OUNCES SMALL SHELL PASTA OR ORZO
- 1/2 CUP FINELY CHOPPED OIL-PACKED SUN-DRIED TOMATOES
- 1/4 CUP FINELY CHOPPED PARSLEY SALT, TO TASTE FRESHLY GROUND BLACK PEPPER, TO TASTE FRESHLY GRATED PARMESAN CHEESE

In a stockpot, heat oil over medium heat. Add carrots, onions, celery, garlic, basil, oregano, bay leaves and red pepper flakes. Cover and cook about 15 minutes until onions are soft, stirring occasionally. Add beans and 7 cups stock and bring to a boil. Reduce heat, partially cover and simmer about 1 hour and 15 minutes, or until beans are tender. (The soup can be prepared to this point ahead of time. Refrigerate, covered. Bring to a simmer and proceed.)

Add shell pasta or orzo and tomatoes to hot soup and simmer about 15 minutes, partially covered, until pasta is cooked. If soup is too thick, add 1/2 to 1 cup additional stock. Remove bay leaves and stir in parsley, salt and pepper. Pass cheese separately.

6 SERVINGS

Gundlach Bundschu Cabernet Franc 1 9 8 9 (Sonoma)

CARIBBEAN BLACK BEAN SOUP

Begin 1 day or more before serving.

- 1 POUND BLACK TURTLE BEANS
- 3 TABLESPOONS BUTTER
- 2 CUPS CHOPPED ONION
- 1 CUP CHOPPED CELERY BOUQUET GARNI OF 6 SPRIGS PARSLEY, 2 SPRIGS THYME AND 1 BAY LEAF
- 1 HAM BONE (OR SMOKED HAM HOCK)
- 6 CUPS BEEF BROTH, PREFERABLY HOMEMADE
- 4 CUPS WATER
- 1 TEASPOON SALT
- 1/4 TEASPOON FRESHLY GROUND BLACK PEPPER
- 1/3 CUP DARK RUM FRESHLY SQUEEZED LEMON JUICE, TO TASTE

cooked white rice, as an accompaniment
chopped onion and lemon slices or chopped hard-cooked egg, for garnish

Soak black beans in water to cover for 4 to 6 hours or overnight. Drain. In a heavy stockpot, melt butter and sauté onion, celery and herbs over low heat for 10 minutes. Add ham bone, beans, broth, water, salt and pepper. Bring soup to a boil, reduce heat and simmer 3 to 4 hours, adding more liquid if necessary to keep the beans covered. Remove bouquet garni and discard. Remove ham bone; cut up ham and add to soup. Add dark rum and reheat. Season to taste with lemon juice, salt and pepper.

Serve Cuban-style with plain white rice and chopped raw onion on the side, or garnish with lemon slices and chopped hard-cooked egg.

8 TO 10 SERVINGS

Le Bourgeois Premium Claret 1 9 9 1 (Missouri)

BREADS

WINE WITH BREADS

*Bread and wine are both the
children of yeast. They go
marvelously together in many
combinations—for an intensely
spiced bread, look for a wine
with that spice; for an herbed
bread, choose a wine with an
herbal character, such as
Bordeaux, southern Italian
wines, Chinon from the Loire
Valley, or California Merlot,
Cabernet Franc or Monterey
Cabernet Sauvignon.*

CRANBERRY OATMEAL MUFFINS

Begin at least 2 hours before serving.

1 1/2   CUPS COARSELY CHOPPED FRESH
        CRANBERRIES
1/4   CUP GRANULATED SUGAR
1   CUP ROLLED OATS
1   CUP BUTTERMILK
1/3   CUP VEGETABLE SHORTENING
1/2   CUP LIGHT BROWN SUGAR
1   EGG
1   CUP SIFTED ALL-PURPOSE FLOUR
1   TEASPOON BAKING POWDER
1   TEASPOON SALT
1/2   TEASPOON BAKING SODA

In a small bowl, combine cranberries and granulated sugar. Set aside. In a second bowl, mix oats and buttermilk and let stand one hour. In a large bowl, mix shortening, brown sugar and egg until well blended. Sift together flour, baking powder, salt and baking soda. Stir dry ingredients into shortening mixture, alternating with oat-buttermilk mixture. Mix just until dry ingredients are moistened. Stir in cranberries. Fill greased muffin tins three-fourths full. Bake in a preheated 400 degree oven for 20 to 25 minutes or until cake tester inserted in center comes out clean.

These delicious cake-like muffins are naturally sweet and require no accompaniment. Make them during the holidays when cranberries are plentiful. They freeze well and can be enjoyed later in the season.

24 MUFFINS

RUSSIAN CHEESE BREAD
(KHACHAPURI)

1   POUND GOAT CHEESE (BUCHERON
        OR MONTRACHET), AT ROOM
        TEMPERATURE
8   OUNCES NEUFCHATEL CHEESE, AT
        ROOM TEMPERATURE
3   CUPS ALL-PURPOSE FLOUR
1/2   TEASPOON SALT
1   TEASPOON BAKING SODA
1   TABLESPOON BAKING POWDER
1 3/4   CUPS SOUR CREAM
1   EGG YOLK BEATEN WITH
        1 TEASPOON WATER

Blend together goat cheese and Neufchatel and set aside. Combine flour, salt, baking soda and baking powder in a large bowl. Add sour cream and stir until evenly blended and a dough is formed. Gently knead dough on a well-floured surface until smooth (20 to 30 turns). Roll two thirds of the dough into a 14-inch round. Fold in quarters for easy handling and place in a greased 10-inch springform pan. Unfold the dough and line pan, letting extra dough extend over rim. Spread cheese mixture evenly over dough.

Roll remaining dough into a 9-inch round and set on top of filling. Brush top of dough with egg yolk mixture. Fold extended edge of bottom layer over top, crimp, and brush with egg. Prick top with fork and bake in a preheated 400 degree oven until well browned, about 30 minutes. Let stand 5 minutes, then slip a knife between pan and bread to separate. Turn out of pan, then turn upright onto a wire rack. Cool at least 15 minutes.

Cut in wedges and serve warm or at room temperature.

8 TO 10 SERVINGS

JALAPEÑO PARMESAN MUFFINS

2 CUPS UNBLEACHED FLOUR
1 TABLESPOON SUGAR
1 TABLESPOON BAKING POWDER
1/2 TEASPOON SALT
1 CUP BEER
1 EGG, LIGHTLY BEATEN
1/4 CUP MELTED BUTTER, COOLED
1 SMALL JALAPEÑO PEPPER, SEEDED AND MINCED
1 CUP FRESHLY GRATED PARMESAN CHEESE

Sift flour together with sugar, baking powder and salt into a large mixing bowl. In another bowl, whisk together beer, egg and butter. Pour beer mixture over flour mixture and stir with a wooden spoon until ingredients are blended but still lumpy. Stir in minced pepper and cheese. Lightly grease 12 muffin cups. Fill three-fourths full with batter and bake in a preheated 400 degree oven for 20 minutes, or until lightly browned. Remove from pan to cool. Serve immediately.

12 MUFFINS

BAGUETTE WITH BRIE AND HERBS

Begin at least 5 hours before serving.
1/4 CUP OLIVE OIL
3 TABLESPOONS DRY WHITE WINE
1 TEASPOON COARSELY GROUND BLACK PEPPER
3 CLOVES GARLIC, CHOPPED
1 BAGUETTE
1/4 CUP SNIPPED FRESH CHIVES
1 CUP COARSELY CHOPPED FRESH BASIL
3/4 CUP COARSELY CHOPPED FRESH SAGE
3/4 CUP COARSELY CHOPPED FRESH SUMMER SAVORY
10 OUNCES RIPE BRIE CHEESE, RIND REMOVED, CUT INTO 1/4-INCH SLICES

Combine oil, wine, pepper and garlic. Cut baguette in half lengthwise and sprinkle both halves with oil mixture. In a small bowl, toss together chives, basil, sage and summer savory. Spread one half of herb mixture on bottom half of bread, layer Brie slices over herbs, then top with remaining herbs. Replace top half of bread, reforming the loaf. Press firmly together and roll tightly in plastic wrap, then in aluminum foil. Press the loaf between two baking sheets and refrigerate with a heavy weight on top for at least 5 hours.

Slice and serve at room temperature or warm briefly in the oven. If baguette is served warm, slice before heating and re-wrap in foil.

6 SERVINGS

BREAKFAST PRALINES

1	CUP LIGHT BROWN SUGAR
1/3	CUP MELTED UNSALTED BUTTER
2	EGGS, LIGHTLY BEATEN
1/2	CUP ALL-PURPOSE FLOUR
1	TEASPOON VANILLA
1	CUP CHOPPED PECANS

Combine sugar, butter and eggs in a small bowl. Stir in flour, vanilla and nuts. Grease and flour madeleine molds or tartlet pans. Fill each mold three-fourths full and bake in a preheated 350 degree oven for 15 to 18 minutes. Cool slightly and serve.

36 MADELEINES
24 TARTLETS

JONATHAN APPLE BREAD

2 2/3	CUPS ALL-PURPOSE FLOUR
1 1/2	TEASPOONS BAKING SODA
1/2	TEASPOON SALT
2	TEASPOONS CINNAMON
1	TEASPOON GROUND CLOVES
2	CUPS SUGAR
1	CUP VEGETABLE OIL
4	EGGS, BEATEN
2	TEASPOONS VANILLA EXTRACT
4	CUPS COARSELY CHOPPED JONATHAN APPLES
1	CUP RAISINS, IF DESIRED
1	CUP CHOPPED PECANS
1	TEASPOON SUGAR
	pecan halves, for garnish

In a mixing bowl, combine flour, baking soda, salt, cinnamon and cloves and set aside. Blend sugar and oil in a large bowl and stir in eggs and vanilla. Add apples, raisins and pecans, then add flour mixture, blending thoroughly. Grease three small loaf pans (approximately 7 by 3 1/2 by 2 inches) and line the bottoms with wax paper. Pour batter into pans and tap to settle. Bake 50 to 60 minutes in a preheated 325 degree oven. When loaves have baked for 20 minutes, sprinkle tops with sugar and press in pecan halves. Finish baking and cool 10 minutes before removing from pans.

3 SMALL LOAVES

APRICOT-ALMOND BREAKFAST CAKE

FILLING

6	OUNCES DRIED APRICOTS, CHOPPED AND SOAKED IN WARM WATER
1	CUP WATER
1/2	CUP SUGAR

Cook apricots and water in a small saucepan until thickened. Add sugar and continue cooking until mixture reaches jam-like consistency. Set aside.

CAKE

1/2	CUP SUGAR
1 1/2	CUPS ALL-PURPOSE FLOUR
1/2	TEASPOON BAKING POWDER
1/2	TEASPOON BAKING SODA
1/2	TEASPOON SALT
1/4	TEASPOON CINNAMON
5	TABLESPOONS BUTTER
1	EGG
1/2	CUP BUTTERMILK
1/2	TEASPOON ALMOND EXTRACT

In a large bowl, combine sugar, flour, baking powder, baking soda, salt and cinnamon. With a pastry cutter, cut in butter until mixture resembles fine crumbs. In a separate bowl, beat egg with buttermilk and almond extract. Add to dry ingredients and stir until moistened. Spread half of the batter in a buttered 8-inch springform pan. Cover with apricot filling and layer remaining batter over filling.

TOPPING

1	TABLESPOON BUTTER
3/8	CUP SUGAR
1/4	CUP ALL-PURPOSE FLOUR
1/4	CUP SHREDDED COCONUT
3/4	CUP SLIVERED ALMONDS

Combine butter, sugar, flour and coconut and sprinkle over batter. Top with almonds. Bake in a preheated 350 degree oven for 40 minutes. Cool before removing sides of pan and slicing.

16 TO 18 SERVINGS

BLUEBERRY THISTLE COFFEE CAKE

3/4	CUP SUGAR
1/4	CUP VEGETABLE SHORTENING
1	EGG, LIGHTLY BEATEN
1	TEASPOON VANILLA EXTRACT
1/2	CUP BUTTERMILK
2	CUPS ALL-PURPOSE FLOUR
2	TEASPOONS BAKING POWDER
1/2	TEASPOON SALT
2	CUPS FRESH OR FROZEN BLUEBERRIES

Combine sugar, shortening, egg and vanilla in a large bowl. Stir in buttermilk. Sift together flour, baking powder and salt and add to sugar mixture. Carefully fold in blueberries. Pour batter into a greased and floured 9-inch pie plate.

TOPPING

1/2	CUP SUGAR
1/3	CUP ALL-PURPOSE FLOUR
1/2	TEASPOON CINNAMON
1/4	CUP BUTTER, SOFTENED
	FLAKED COCONUT

Mix sugar with flour, cinnamon and butter and spread evenly on top of batter. Sprinkle on coconut and bake in a preheated 375 degree oven for 55 to 60 minutes. Increase baking time if frozen blueberries are used.

8 SERVINGS

ONION CHEESE BREADSTICKS

1	TABLESPOON ACTIVE DRY YEAST
1/3	CUP WARM WATER
1	CUP ALL-PURPOSE FLOUR
1	TABLESPOON DRIED PARSLEY FLAKES
1	TABLESPOON SHORTENING
1	TEASPOON SUGAR
1/2	TEASPOON SALT
1/8	TEASPOON GARLIC POWDER
1	EGG, BEATEN
1	TABLESPOON MINCED ONION
1/4	CUP PARMESAN CHEESE
1	TABLESPOON MELTED BUTTER
2	TABLESPOONS SESAME SEEDS

In a medium bowl, dissolve yeast in warm water and let stand until foamy, about 5 minutes. Add flour, parsley, shortening, sugar, salt, garlic powder and egg. With an electric mixer, beat at medium speed for 30 seconds, scraping bowl occasionally. Stir in onion and cheese and beat until well blended. With floured hands, spread dough evenly in a 9- by 13-inch pan. Let dough rise in a warm place until almost doubled in bulk, about 20 minutes. Cut dough into 1- by 3-inch sticks and place on an oiled baking sheet. Brush with butter and sprinkle with sesame seeds. Bake in a preheated 450 degree oven until edges are brown, 12 to 15 minutes.

MAKES ABOUT 3 DOZEN BREADSTICKS.

RED CHILI BRIOCHE

Begin 9 hours to 1 day before serving.

1	TABLESPOON ACTIVE DRY YEAST
1 1/2	TABLESPOONS SUGAR
3 1/2	CUPS ALL-PURPOSE FLOUR
1/2	TEASPOON CHILI POWDER
1 1/2	TEASPOONS SALT
1/2	TEASPOON FRESHLY GROUND BLACK PEPPER
2	TABLESPOONS MILK
1	TABLESPOON LUKEWARM WATER
1/2	CUP ROASTED, FINELY CHOPPED FRESH POBLANO CHILI (PAGE 177)
1/3	CUP ROASTED, FINELY CHOPPED RED BELL PEPPER (PAGE 177)
5	EGGS, AT ROOM TEMPERATURE
1	CUP PLUS 2 TABLESPOONS UNSALTED BUTTER, CUT INTO SMALL PIECES

Combine yeast, sugar, flour, chili powder, salt and black pepper in a large bowl. With an electric mixer, mix briefly at low speed. Add milk, water, poblano chili and bell pepper; increase speed to medium and mix well. Add eggs one at a time, blending well after each addition. Using a dough hook, knead mixture for 3 minutes. The dough will be very sticky. Add butter one piece at a time, and continue to knead until butter is thoroughly blended, 10 to 20 minutes.

Transfer dough to a buttered bowl, cover with plastic wrap, and let rise in a warm place until doubled in bulk, about 3 hours. Punch down dough and turn out onto a floured surface. Knead for 5 minutes, using additional flour to work the dough. Return dough to a buttered bowl and chill at least 6 hours or overnight in the refrigerator. Remove dough from refrigerator and shape into two loaves. Place in two buttered 4- by 9-inch loaf pans, cover with a towel and let rise in a warm place until the dough fills the pans, about 1 hour.

Bake in the middle of a preheated 375 degree oven for about 30 minutes, or until loaves are golden and sound hollow when tapped. Turn out onto wire racks to cool.

2 LOAVES

SALTY CARAWAY CRESCENTS

1	TABLESPOON ACTIVE DRY YEAST
1	CUP WARM WATER
1/2	CUP VEGETABLE OIL
1/2	CUP BEER
1	TEASPOON SALT
1	TABLESPOON CARAWAY SEEDS
4 1/2	CUPS BREAD FLOUR
1	EGG, BEATEN WITH 1 TABLESPOON WATER

sea salt or kosher salt, for garnish
cornmeal, for baking sheets

Dissolve yeast in warm water and let stand until foamy, about 5 minutes. In a large bowl, mix oil, beer, salt and caraway seeds. Add yeast mixture and most of the flour. Beat well. On a floured surface, knead dough until smooth and shiny, adding flour, a tablespoon at a time, as needed. Place dough in an oiled bowl, turning to coat evenly. Cover bowl with plastic wrap, a lid or a damp towel and let dough rise in a warm place until doubled in bulk, about 1 hour. Punch down dough and knead for 30 seconds to release air bubbles.

Dust baking sheets with cornmeal. Divide dough into 2 balls (for 24 rolls) or 4 balls (for 32 rolls). Roll each ball into a circle, 12 to 16 inches in diameter. Cut each circle into pie-shaped wedges—12 wedges each for 24 rolls or 8 wedges for 32 rolls. Roll up each wedge, starting at wide end, and place on baking sheet with the point down. Gently curve the ends forward and stretch slightly to make a crescent shape. Let rise in a warm place until doubled, about 30 minutes. Then brush with egg mixture and sprinkle with salt. Bake in a preheated 375 degree oven for 20 minutes or until golden brown, or at 400 degrees for 15 minutes for a crisper crust. Cool on wire rack.

Serve warm or store in a tightly covered container. Crescents freeze well. To reheat, place in a paper bag in a preheated 350 degree oven for 10 minutes, 20 minutes if rolls are still frozen.

To prepare in a food processor, place dry ingredients and caraway seeds in processor work bowl. Dissolve yeast in warm water and add beer and oil. Pour yeast mixture slowly over dry ingredients in food processor with machine running. After dough forms a shaggy ball, process for 1 minute to knead. Continue as directed above.

Serve as an accompaniment to Hearty Potato Chowder (page 69).

24 LARGE OR 32 SMALL ROLLS

HEARTY WHEAT BREAD

3	CUPS SCALDED MILK
1/3	CUP BUTTER
1/3	CUP BROWN SUGAR
1/4	CUP MOLASSES
1/4	CUP SESAME SEEDS
3	TABLESPOONS CORNMEAL
3	TABLESPOONS MILLET, IF DESIRED
2	EGGS, LIGHTLY BEATEN
1	TABLESPOON ACTIVE DRY YEAST
3/4	CUP WARM WATER
4 1/2	CUPS WHOLE WHEAT FLOUR
1	TABLESPOON SALT
4	CUPS UNBLEACHED FLOUR

Combine milk and butter, stirring until butter is melted. Add sugar, molasses, sesame seeds, cornmeal, millet and eggs and mix well. In a separate bowl, stir yeast into warm water and let stand until foamy, about 5 minutes. Add to milk and sugar mixture. Add whole wheat flour and stir to blend. Cover dough with a warm, damp towel and let rise in a warm place until doubled in bulk. Punch down and add salt and as much of the unbleached flour as possible. Knead in remaining flour and continue kneading until dough is elastic. Place in a greased bowl, cover with a warm, damp towel and let double again. Punch down dough and shape into three loaves. Place dough in greased loaf pans and set in cold oven. Bake at 375 degrees for 45 minutes, or until brown. Turn out on wire rack to cool.

Variation: Shape dough into rounds and slice an X across the top. Place on a preheated pizza stone or oven tile and bake in a preheated 375 degree oven for 45 minutes, or until brown.

3 LOAVES

POTATO BISCUITS

Begin at least 3 hours before serving.

1	LARGE POTATO, UNPEELED AND QUARTERED (8 OUNCES)
4	OUNCES PARMESAN CHEESE
1 1/2	CUPS UNBLEACHED ALL-PURPOSE FLOUR
1	CUP UNSALTED BUTTER, CUT IN PIECES
1 1/2	TEASPOONS SALT
1	LARGE EGG

Place potato in a saucepan with cold water to cover and bring to a boil. Cook uncovered until tender, about 10 minutes. Drain, cool and peel, then shred in a food processor and refrigerate until chilled. Using a metal blade, shred Parmesan cheese, then add flour, butter and salt, processing until mixture is coarsely crumbled. Add potato and egg and blend until dough holds together, but does not form a ball.

Place dough on a lightly floured surface and roll into a 6- by 16-inch rectangle. Fold shorter ends into the center and brush off excess flour. Fold over again at center to make 4 layers. Repeat, rolling into a 6- by 16-inch rectangle, and folding into the 4 layers again. Then wrap tightly in plastic and chill 30 minutes in refrigerator or 10 minutes in freezer. Repeat the entire procedure (rolling and folding twice, then chilling) twice more.

On a lightly floured surface, roll dough into an 8- by 14-inch rectangle, 3/8-inch thick. Cut into 1-inch squares and transfer to a lightly buttered baking sheet. Chill 10 minutes. Place another baking sheet underneath and bake on double pan for 10 minutes in a preheated 400 degree oven. Reduce oven temperature to 350 degrees and bake 10 to 15 minutes longer. Biscuits should be puffed and lightly browned. Serve warm.

Small cookie cutters may be used to make a variety of shapes.

Variations: Add 1 tablespoon chili powder or 1 tablespoon curry powder along with the flour.

MAKES ABOUT 65 SQUARES.

TWO-POTATO FOCACCIA

2 1/2	TEASPOONS ACTIVE DRY YEAST
1	CUP WARM WATER
4 1/2	CUPS ALL-PURPOSE FLOUR, DIVIDED
2	CUPS MASHED, COOKED BAKING POTATOES (ABOUT 1 1/4 POUNDS)
1	TABLESPOON SALT
3	CLOVES GARLIC, THINLY SLICED
1	TEASPOON DRIED THYME
2	TEASPOONS DRIED ROSEMARY
1/3	CUP OLIVE OIL
1 1/2	POUNDS SMALL RED OR NEW POTATOES, CUT INTO PAPER-THIN SLICES
	SALT, TO TASTE
	FRESHLY GROUND BLACK PEPPER, TO TASTE

In a small bowl, sprinkle yeast into water and let stand until foamy, about 5 minutes. Combine 4 cups flour with mashed potatoes and salt in a large bowl and stir until mixture resembles coarse meal. Add yeast and mix until dough is thoroughly blended. Place dough on a floured surface and knead, adding as much of the remaining flour as necessary to prevent sticking. Knead 8 to 10 minutes, or until dough is smooth and elastic. Shape dough into a ball, place in an oiled bowl, and turn to coat evenly. Cover dough with plastic wrap and let rise in a warm place until doubled in bulk, about 1 1/2 hours.

In a small bowl, combine garlic, thyme, rosemary and oil and set aside. Press dough evenly into a well-oiled 10 1/2- by 15 1/2-inch jelly-roll pan and let rise again, loosely covered, in a warm place for 45 minutes, or until almost doubled in bulk. Arrange potato slices on the dough, overlapping, and brush with the oil mixture, discarding the garlic. Season with salt and pepper to taste and bake in the bottom third of a preheated 400 degree oven for 40 to 50 minutes, or until potatoes are golden brown. Cool in the pan on a rack and serve warm or at room temperature.

12 SERVINGS

ITALIAN COUNTRY BREAD

Begin at least 6 hours to 1 day before serving.

2	TABLESPOONS ACTIVE DRY YEAST
1/2	CUP WARM WATER
1/2	CUP DRY WHITE WINE
1/4	CUP OLIVE OIL
1 1/2	CUPS WHOLE WHEAT FLOUR
1 1/4	CUPS UNBLEACHED FLOUR
1/4	CUP RYE FLOUR
1	TEASPOON SALT
1	EGG YOLK BEATEN WITH 1 TABLESPOON HEAVY CREAM
2/3	CUP COARSELY CHOPPED PINE NUTS

In a small bowl, dissolve yeast in warm water and let stand until foamy, about 5 minutes. Add wine and oil. Mix whole wheat flour, unbleached flour and rye flour with salt in a large mixing bowl; remove one cup and set aside. Pour in wine mixture and mix at low speed, using a dough hook. Gradually add reserved flour and knead with mixer until dough is shiny and elastic. If dough is too dry, knead in 1 tablespoon water; if it is very sticky, knead in 1 to 2 tablespoons flour.

Transfer dough to an oiled bowl and turn to coat evenly. Cover with a damp cloth and let rise in a warm place at least 3 hours or overnight, until doubled in bulk. Punch down dough and knead several times on a lightly floured surface. Shape into a smooth round loaf about 6 inches in diameter. Brush egg mixture over loaf, then roll loaf in chopped pine nuts. Set loaf on a greased baking sheet, cover with a damp cloth and let rise about 1 1/2 hours or until doubled in bulk.

Place a pan of water in bottom of oven to provide steam and preheat oven to 350 degrees. With a sharp knife, slash an X across top of loaf. Bake for about 45 minutes or until loaf sounds hollow when tapped on bottom. Serve warm or at room temperature.

1 LARGE LOAF

WILD RICE MUFFINS

3/4 CUP ALL-PURPOSE FLOUR
2 TEASPOONS SUGAR
1/2 TEASPOON SALT
1/4 TEASPOON FRESHLY GROUND
WHITE PEPPER
1 CUP COOKED WILD RICE
1/4 CUP TOASTED CHOPPED PECANS
3 TABLESPOONS MELTED BUTTER,
LIGHTLY BROWNED
1 CUP MILK
1 EGG, SLIGHTLY BEATEN
3 TABLESPOONS SNIPPED FRESH
CHIVES

Butter 12 muffin cups and warm in oven. In a small bowl, combine flour, sugar, salt and white pepper. In another bowl, combine wild rice, pecans and butter. Combine milk and egg. Add dry ingredients to rice, alternating with milk mixture, and blend. Pour batter into muffin cups and bake in a preheated 450 degree oven for 12 to 15 minutes. Serve hot.

The muffin batter may be made ahead and refrigerated. Bake just before serving.

12 MUFFINS

FRIED BREAD ROLLS

1 TABLESPOON ACTIVE DRY YEAST
1/4 CUP WARM WATER
3 TABLESPOONS VEGETABLE
SHORTENING
3 TABLESPOONS SUGAR
1 TABLESPOON SALT
1 CUP BOILING WATER
1 CUP MILK
6 CUPS ALL-PURPOSE FLOUR
APPROXIMATELY 1 1/2 CUPS
SHORTENING, FOR FRYING

Dissolve yeast in warm water and let stand until foamy, about 5 minutes. In a large bowl, combine shortening, sugar and salt. Add boiling water and milk, then stir in yeast mixture. Add flour and knead until elastic. Cover dough with a damp cloth and let rise in a warm place until doubled in bulk. Punch down dough, knead again and shape into walnut-sized balls. Cover with a damp cloth and let rise again until doubled.

Heat shortening in a heavy skillet; it should be about 1 inch deep. Place rolls in hot shortening and fry, turning often, until golden brown. Serve fresh, hot and crisp.

48 ROLLS

HERBED ROQUEFORT BISCUITS

2 CUPS ALL-PURPOSE FLOUR
1 TABLESPOON BAKING POWDER
1/2 TEASPOON SALT
1/4 TEASPOON BAKING SODA
3 OUNCES CRUMBLED ROQUEFORT CHEESE
2 TABLESPOONS MINCED GREEN ONION TOPS
1 TEASPOON DRIED BASIL
1/2 TEASPOON DRIED THYME
6 TABLESPOONS COLD UNSALTED BUTTER
3/4 CUP BUTTERMILK

In a large bowl, sift together flour, baking powder, salt and baking soda. Set aside. In a smaller bowl, combine cheese, green onion tops, basil and thyme. Using a pastry cutter, cut butter and the cheese mixture into dry ingredients until mixture resembles coarse crumbs. Add buttermilk and stir well. Transfer dough to a lightly floured surface and knead for about 30 seconds. Roll out dough 1-inch thick and cut out biscuits with a 2-inch biscuit cutter. Arrange biscuits about 1 inch apart on a lightly greased baking sheet. Bake in a preheated 425 degree oven until puffed and golden, about 15 minutes. Transfer biscuits to a wire rack to cool slightly. Serve immediately.

These versatile biscuits are delicious served with fresh or smoked ham. In a smaller size, they also make a savory accompaniment to cocktails, served plain or with meat as a tiny sandwich.

14 TO 16 BISCUITS

HERB BREAD WITH GREEN ONION

3 CUPS LUKEWARM WATER
1 TABLESPOON ACTIVE DRY YEAST
1 1/2 TEASPOONS SUGAR
1 TABLESPOON DRIED BASIL
1 TABLESPOON DRIED OREGANO
6 CUPS ALL-PURPOSE FLOUR
2 TEASPOONS SALT
1 1/2 TEASPOONS FRESHLY GROUND WHITE PEPPER
1 CUP CHOPPED GREEN ONION
6 TABLESPOONS OLIVE OIL, DIVIDED
3 CLOVES GARLIC, CHOPPED
COARSE SALT, TO TASTE
FRESHLY GROUND BLACK PEPPER, TO TASTE

Combine water, yeast, sugar, basil and oregano in a small bowl. Mix well, and let stand until foamy, about 5 minutes. In a large bowl, combine flour, salt, pepper and green onion. Stir 2 tablespoons of the olive oil into the yeast mixture and gradually add dry ingredients. If necessary, add a bit more water to fully blend all ingredients. The dough should be slightly wet and sticky. Turn out onto a floured surface, and knead until dough is smooth but not overly elastic, about 5 minutes. Place dough in a large oiled bowl, cover, and let rise in a warm place until doubled in bulk. Punch down dough, then transfer to an oiled 12- x 17-inch baking sheet. With fingertips, spread dough evenly. Cover and let it rise in a warm place until doubled in bulk.

In a small bowl, combine garlic and the remaining 4 tablespoons olive oil. When dough has doubled, drizzle the oil and garlic mixture over the top. Season with salt and pepper and bake in a preheated 450 degree oven about 20 minutes, or until golden brown. Cool slightly while still in the pan. Serve warm or at room temperature.

12 TO 15 SERVINGS

ONION BOARDS

1 TABLESPOON ACTIVE DRY YEAST
2 CUPS WARM WATER
2 TABLESPOONS SUGAR
2 TEASPOONS SALT
5 TO 5 1/2 CUPS ALL-PURPOSE FLOUR, DIVIDED
3/4 CUP INSTANT MINCED ONION
1 EGG YOLK BEATEN WITH
1 TABLESPOON WATER

In a large mixing bowl, dissolve yeast in warm water and let stand until foamy, about 5 minutes. Add sugar, salt and 2 cups flour and mix thoroughly. With a mixer, beat in 2 to 3 cups more flour to form a stiff dough. Turn out onto a well-floured surface and knead until smooth and elastic. Add more flour as needed to prevent sticking. Place dough in an oiled bowl and turn to coat evenly. Cover and let rise in a warm place until doubled in bulk, about 1 1/2 hours. Punch down dough. Divide into 6 equal parts, cover lightly and let stand 10 minutes.

Soak onion in water to cover for 10 minutes, then squeeze out excess moisture. On a lightly floured surface, roll and stretch each portion of dough into a 7- by 11-inch rectangle. Edges should be slightly raised. Lightly brush with egg yolk and water mixture. Place on a lightly greased baking sheet and sprinkle onions over top. Bake in a preheated 375 degree oven for 22 to 25 minutes, or until golden brown. Boards can stand, uncovered, until all are baked. Serve hot or warm, stacked on a large wooden platter. Tear off pieces to serve.

Serve as an accompaniment to Scallops with Three-Tomato Relish and Tomatillo Vinaigrette (page 147).

6 BOARDS

CORN THINS

3/4 CUP WHITE OR YELLOW CORNMEAL
1/4 TEASPOON SALT
1 CUP BOILING WATER
2 TABLESPOONS BUTTER

Coat two baking sheets with nonstick cooking spray. Mix cornmeal and salt in a medium bowl and stir in boiling water. Add butter and blend until smooth. Let stand for 5 minutes. Stir batter again, then spoon 1 tablespoon onto the oiled baking sheet. Batter should spread into a 3-inch circle. If mixture is too thin to hold its shape, stir in 1 tablespoon cornmeal. If it is too thick, add water by teaspoons. Continue to spoon remaining batter for each wafer onto the baking sheets. Bake thins in a preheated 425 degree oven for 20 minutes, or until crisp and golden brown around the edges. Serve with a crock of butter.

Serve with Tortilla Corn Soup (page 59).

16 CORN THINS

ONION CHEESE MUFFINS

4 OUNCES GRATED CHEDDAR CHEESE
3 CHOPPED GREEN ONIONS
1 CUP ALL-PURPOSE FLOUR
1/3 CUP YELLOW CORNMEAL
2 TEASPOONS BAKING POWDER
1/2 TEASPOON DRIED RED PEPPER
FLAKES
1/2 TEASPOON SALT
1 TABLESPOON SUGAR
3/4 CUP SOUR CREAM
1/3 CUP VEGETABLE OIL
2 EGGS

Combine cheese and green onion. In a separate bowl, combine flour, cornmeal, baking powder, red pepper flakes, salt and sugar. Add cheese and onion and blend thoroughly. In another bowl, mix sour cream, oil and eggs. Add dry ingredients and mix until just moistened. Fill greased mini muffin tins two-thirds full. Bake in a preheated 375 degree oven for 13 minutes. If using standard muffin tins, bake 18 minutes.

Decrease amount of pepper flakes for a milder taste. Muffins freeze and reheat well.

18 MINI MUFFINS

WINTER BREAD

2 TABLESPOONS ACTIVE DRY YEAST
1 1/2 CUPS WARM WATER, DIVIDED
3 TABLESPOONS LIGHT BROWN SUGAR
2 1/2 TEASPOONS SALT
1/3 CUP MOLASSES
1/2 CUP BUTTER
3/4 CUP MILK, SCALDED
1 CUP WHEAT GERM
2 CUPS UNBLEACHED WHITE FLOUR
2 CUPS WHOLE WHEAT FLOUR
1 CUP CORNMEAL
1 CUP WHEAT BRAN
MELTED BUTTER

Dissolve yeast in 1/4 cup warm water and let stand until foamy, about 5 minutes. In a saucepan, mix remaining water with sugar, salt, molasses and butter. Heat, stirring, until butter melts. Cool to lukewarm. In a large mixing bowl, pour milk over wheat germ and let stand until liquid is nearly absorbed and mixture is lukewarm. Combine yeast and molasses mixture, stir, and add to milk and wheat germ. Combine unbleached white flour, whole wheat flour, cornmeal and bran. Add half of flour mixture to liquid mixture, stir, then blend in remaining flour.

Turn out onto a floured surface and knead until smooth. Place dough in a well oiled bowl and turn to coat on all sides. Cover with a towel and let rise 30 minutes in a warm place. Punch down dough, shape into two loaves and place in two well-buttered 8-inch bread pans. Let rise in a warm place for 1 1/4 hours. Brush loaves with melted butter and bake in a preheated 400 degree oven for 20 minutes. Brush again with butter. Serve warm.

Any combination of flours can be used, but 2 cups must be unbleached white flour. Cornmeal gives the bread its crunchy texture.

2 LOAVES

ROLLED PESTO LOAVES

2 CUPS FRESH BASIL LEAVES
1/2 CUP FRESH PARSLEY
1/2 CUP OLIVE OIL
2 CLOVES GARLIC
1 TEASPOON SALT
1/2 CUP FRESHLY GRATED PARMESAN CHEESE
1 1/2 TABLESPOONS ACTIVE DRY YEAST
2 CUPS WARM WATER
1 1/2 TEASPOONS SALT
1 TABLESPOON SUGAR
6 TO 7 CUPS ALL-PURPOSE FLOUR
yellow or white cornmeal for baking sheet
sea salt, for garnish

In a food processor, purée basil, parsley, olive oil, garlic and salt. Stir in Parmesan cheese and set aside. In a large bowl, dissolve yeast in warm water and add salt and sugar. Stir thoroughly and let stand until foamy, about 5 minutes. With a wooden spoon, beat in flour, one cup at a time, to form a smooth dough. (This also can be done in a food processor.) Turn out dough onto a lightly floured surface; let stand a few minutes, then knead until dough is elastic. Place in a lightly oiled bowl, cover with a towel and let rise in a warm place until doubled in bulk, about 1 1/2 hours. Turn dough out onto a lightly floured surface, punch down and knead again.

Divide dough in half and pat into two rectangles, approximately 10 inches by 12 inches each. Spread a thin layer of pesto mixture over each, leaving a 1-inch border. Starting with a long side, roll each rectangle into a cylinder and shape into a loaf. Allow loaves to rise for 5 minutes. Sprinkle a baking sheet with cornmeal and set loaves on it. Brush each loaf with cold water and place in a cold oven. Place a pan of boiling water in the bottom of the oven and set oven temperature to 400 degrees. Bake for 35 to 40 minutes, or until loaves are browned and sound hollow when tapped on the bottom. Place on a rack to cool slightly. Brush warm bread with olive oil, sprinkle with sea salt and serve immediately.

2 LOAVES

CHEDDAR CHEESE AND CHIVE BISCUITS

2 CUPS ALL-PURPOSE FLOUR
1 TEASPOON SALT
1 TABLESPOON BAKING POWDER
1/4 CUP VEGETABLE SHORTENING
1 CUP GRATED SHARP CHEDDAR CHEESE
1/4 CUP SNIPPED FRESH CHIVES
1 CUP MILK
2 TABLESPOONS MELTED BUTTER

Combine flour, salt and baking powder in a large bowl. With a pastry cutter, cut in shortening until mixture resembles coarse crumbs. Add cheese and chives and mix well. Add milk, stirring just until mixture forms a soft dough that pulls away from the bowl. On a lightly floured surface, knead quickly to blend dough thoroughly. Roll out dough 1/2-inch thick and cut out biscuits with a 2 1/2-inch floured biscuit cutter. Place on an ungreased baking sheet and brush tops with melted butter. Bake in a preheated 450 degree oven for 12 to 15 minutes, or until golden brown. Serve immediately.

24 BISCUITS

RUSSIAN BLACK BREAD

3	CUPS RYE FLOUR
2	CUPS WHOLE BRAN CEREAL
2	TABLESPOONS ACTIVE DRY YEAST
2	TABLESPOONS CRUSHED CARAWAY SEEDS
2	TEASPOONS INSTANT COFFEE
2	TEASPOONS SALT
2	TEASPOONS SUGAR
1/2	TEASPOON CRUSHED FENNEL SEEDS
2 1/4	CUPS WATER
1/4	CUP BUTTER
1/4	CUP WHITE VINEGAR
1/4	CUP MOLASSES
1	OUNCE UNSWEETENED CHOCOLATE
3 1/2 TO 4	CUPS UNBLEACHED ALL-PURPOSE FLOUR
1/2	CUP WATER
1	TEASPOON CORNSTARCH

thinly sliced sweet red onion, for garnish

Combine rye flour, bran cereal, yeast, caraway seeds, coffee, salt, sugar and fennel seeds. Set aside. In a 2-quart saucepan, combine water, butter, vinegar, molasses and chocolate. Cook over medium heat, stirring until chocolate is almost melted, but mixture is still lukewarm. Turn into a mixing bowl and add rye flour mixture. Begin beating with dough hook. Gradually add unbleached flour, 1/2 cup at a time, to make a soft dough; beat about 3 minutes. Turn onto a lightly floured surface, cover with a bowl and allow to stand 10 to 15 minutes.

Knead dough until smooth and elastic, about 10 to 15 minutes, adding more flour as needed (a dough hook may be used). Place in a lightly greased bowl, turning to coat evenly. Cover dough with plastic wrap and a hot, damp towel and let rise in a warm place until doubled in bulk. Punch down and turn onto a lightly floured surface. Shape dough into two balls and place in two lightly greased 8-inch layer cake pans. Cover with plastic wrap and let rise in a warm place until doubled in bulk.

Bake in a preheated 350 degree oven for 40 minutes. Combine 1/2 cup water and cornstarch in a saucepan and boil over high heat for 1 minute. Brush lightly over bread, then return loaves to oven for 5 minutes, or until tops are glazed and loaves sound hollow when tapped. Remove from pans and let cool on racks.

Try this bread warm from the oven, thickly buttered and topped with thin slices of sweet red onion.

2 LOAVES

RICH CREAM BISCUITS

4   CUPS ALL-PURPOSE FLOUR
2   TABLESPOONS BAKING POWDER
1/2 TEASPOON SALT
1/2 CUP BUTTER
2   CUPS PLUS 2 TABLESPOONS HEAVY
     CREAM

In a large bowl, combine flour, baking powder and salt. Cut in butter, leaving it in coarse bits. Gradually add cream while stirring, then knead quickly to make a stiff dough. Do not overwork. Roll out dough 1/2-inch thick on a lightly floured surface. Cut into squares of desired size. Place on an ungreased baking sheet on lowest rack of a preheated 400 degree oven. Bake for 18 minutes and serve immediately.

These biscuits have a cloudlike texture and a unique shape. Try them as an accompaniment to Shrimp Quenelles with Shrimp-Herb Sauce (page 148).

THIRTY 2-INCH SQUARES

BLUE CHEESE SHORTBREAD

3/4 CUP BUTTER, SOFTENED
8   OUNCES BLUE CHEESE, SOFTENED
1/4 CUP SUGAR
     A PINCH OF SALT
2   CUPS SIFTED ALL-PURPOSE FLOUR
1/2 CUP SIFTED RICE FLOUR

Cream butter and cheese in a large bowl. Gradually add sugar and salt, then slowly beat in all-purpose flour and rice flour until just combined. Do not overbeat. Spread mixture evenly on a 9- by 12-inch baking sheet. Pierce holes in the surface with a fork. With the back of a knife, mark off single-serving size rectangles on the surface of the dough.

Bake in a preheated 350 degree oven for 25 minutes, or until golden brown. Remove from oven and immediately cut through surface of dough to mark off rectangles, but do not separate. Cool completely in pan. Cut into rectangles before serving.

The shortbread may be made up to 3 days ahead and stored in an airtight container.

4 1/2 DOZEN SQUARES

HERBED PEPPERCORN BREAD

Begin 1 day before serving.

1 TABLESPOON ACTIVE DRY YEAST
1/4 CUP SCALDED MILK, COOLED TO LUKEWARM
2 TABLESPOONS SUGAR
3 3/4 CUPS BREAD FLOUR
1 CUP UNSALTED BUTTER, SOFTENED AND CUT INTO PIECES
1 TEASPOON SALT
6 EGGS
3 TABLESPOONS CRACKED BLACK PEPPERCORNS
3/4 CUP CHOPPED FRESH BASIL OR TARRAGON

In a mixing bowl or food processor, mix yeast with milk and sugar until yeast dissolves. At low speed, beat in flour and add butter, one piece at a time. Beat in salt, eggs (one at a time), peppercorns and basil or tarragon. Continue mixing until dough pulls away from side of bowl. Place dough in a large, rinsed plastic storage bag; release air, seal and refrigerate overnight.

Halve the dough and knead on a floured surface into two flat rectangular loaves. Place dough, seam side down, in two lightly greased and floured 5- by 9-inch loaf pans. Cover with a cloth and let rise in a warm place until doubled in bulk, about 3 hours. Bake in a preheated 350 degree oven until golden brown, 35 to 40 minutes. Cool to room temperature before slicing.

Note: This brioche-like dough rises only once and should not be punched down.

Serve with Chesapeake Oyster Stew (page 153).

2 LOAVES

TUSCAN PEASANT BREAD

2 TABLESPOONS ACTIVE DRY YEAST
2 CUPS LUKEWARM WATER, DIVIDED
1 TEASPOON SUGAR
4 TO 4 1/2 CUPS UNBLEACHED WHITE FLOUR
1/2 CUP WHOLE WHEAT FLOUR
1 TEASPOON SALT
2 TABLESPOONS COARSELY CHOPPED FRESH ROSEMARY
2/3 CUP PITTED CHOPPED NIÇOISE OLIVES
2 TABLESPOONS CHOPPED FRESH BASIL OR THYME
1 TABLESPOON CHOPPED FRESH CILANTRO
OLIVE OIL

In a large bowl, stir yeast, 1/2 cup water and sugar together until yeast dissolves, then add remaining water and set aside until foamy, 5 to 10 minutes. Gradually stir in unbleached white flour, whole wheat flour, salt, rosemary, olives, basil or thyme and cilantro. Stir until mixture forms a dough, adding more flour if necessary. Knead dough on a lightly floured surface until smooth and elastic, about 10 minutes. Sprinkle with additional flour to prevent sticking.

Lightly grease a large bowl with olive oil; place dough in bowl and turn to coat evenly. Cover with a cloth and let rise in a warm place until doubled in bulk, about 1 hour. Punch down dough and shape into a round or oblong loaf. Place loaf on a baking sheet in the middle of a preheated 400 degree oven. A baking brick or stone or a small pan of water placed in the oven will give a crisper crust. Bake for 60 to 75 minutes or until bread is very crusty. Remove and place on a wire rack to cool.

Serve as an accompaniment to Basil Cream Minestrone (page 64).

1 LARGE LOAF

WHOLE WHEAT CORNBREAD

3/4	CUP YELLOW CORNMEAL
3/4	CUP WHITE CORNMEAL
1	CUP WHOLE WHEAT FLOUR
1	TABLESPOON BAKING POWDER
1	TEASPOON SALT
1 1/2	CUPS MILK
2	EGGS, LIGHTLY BEATEN
1/2	CUP HONEY
1/4	CUP VEGETABLE OIL
2/3	CUP SHREDDED CARROT
1/4	CUP SLICED GREEN ONION

Combine yellow and white cornmeal, whole wheat flour, baking powder and salt. Add milk, eggs, honey and oil and stir until blended. Stir in carrots and green onion. Pour into a greased 8- or 9-inch square pan and bake in a preheated 400 degree oven for 25 minutes. (If a glass pan is used, reduce oven temperature to 375 degrees). Serve with honey and butter.

9 SERVINGS

ROZZELLE COURT SCONES

1 2/3	CUPS HEAVY CREAM
4	EGGS
3/4	CUP CURRANTS
1	POUND UNSALTED BUTTER, SOFTENED
4	CUPS ALL-PURPOSE FLOUR
2	TABLESPOONS BAKING POWDER
1/2	CUP SUGAR
1/2	TEASPOON SALT
1	EGG YOLK, BEATEN WITH 3 TABLESPOONS WATER

Pour cream into a small mixing bowl and add eggs and currants, stirring gently to break egg yolks. Set aside. Using a dough hook, briefly cream butter in a large mixing bowl. Add flour, baking powder, sugar and salt. Mix until butter is the size of small peas and mixture is crumbly. Add egg mixture, beating just until ingredients are moist. Do not overbeat. Pour batter onto a heavily floured surface and lightly sprinkle the top with flour. Pat out slightly, flour again, then pat to a 2 1/2-inch thickness. Working from the outside toward the center, cut scones in 2-inch circles and place on an ungreased baking sheet. (The scones can be frozen at this point.) Brush with egg glaze and bake in a preheated 350 degree oven for 20 minutes.

TWENTY 2-INCH SCONES

BRUSCHETTA

BASIC BRUSCHETTA

12 PIECES DENSELY TEXTURED BREAD,
    CUT 1/2-INCH THICK
1/3 TO 1/2 CUP OLIVE OIL
2   CLOVES GARLIC, PEELED AND
    HALVED LENGTHWISE

Toast bread slices over a grill or in a preheated 425 degree oven until lightly browned on both sides. Remove from heat and generously brush tops with olive oil. Rub warm bruschetta with garlic and serve immediately—or continue with some of the toppings suggested below.

RED ONION AND PARMESAN CHEESE

12 PIECES BASIC BRUSCHETTA
1/4 CUP OLIVE OIL
3   SMALL RED ONIONS, PEELED AND
    THINLY SLICED
    SALT, TO TASTE
    FRESHLY GROUND BLACK PEPPER,
    TO TASTE
3   TABLESPOONS SNIPPED FRESH
    CHIVES
6   OUNCES PARMESAN CHEESE, CUT IN
    PAPER-THIN SLICES

In a sauté pan, heat olive oil over medium-low heat. Add onions and sauté until very tender. Add salt and pepper and stir in chives. Spread onion mixture on top of warm bruschetta and top with sliced Parmesan cheese. Place on a baking sheet and heat under a broiler until cheese softens.

TOMATO, FRESH HERB AND MOZZARELLA RELISH

12 PIECES BASIC BRUSCHETTA
2   POUNDS FRESH PLUM TOMATOES,
    PEELED AND SEEDED
4   CLOVES GARLIC, MINCED
6   TABLESPOONS FINELY CHOPPED
    FRESH BASIL OR 3 OUNCES YOUNG,
    TENDER ARUGULA
2   TABLESPOONS FINELY CHOPPED
    FRESH ITALIAN PARSLEY
4   TABLESPOONS OLIVE OIL
1   TEASPOON SALT
1   TEASPOON FRESHLY GROUND
    BLACK PEPPER
1/2 POUND FRESH MOZZARELLA
    CHEESE, SHREDDED OR GRATED
    ADDITIONAL OLIVE OIL, TO TASTE

Cut tomatoes into 1/2-inch pieces and drain over a bowl for 30 minutes to remove excess liquid. Combine tomatoes with garlic, basil, parsley, olive oil, salt and pepper in a small nonreactive bowl. Stir well and taste for seasoning. Just before serving, add mozzarella cheese to tomato mixture and heap onto warm bruschetta. Sprinkle with pepper and drizzle with olive oil. Heat topped bruschetta in a preheated 350 degree oven until cheese melts.

MATCHSTICK PEPPER STRIPS

12 PIECES BASIC BRUSCHETTA
2   GREEN BELL PEPPERS
2   YELLOW BELL PEPPERS
2   RED BELL PEPPERS
2   SMALL ONIONS, THINLY SLICED
6   TABLESPOONS OLIVE OIL
4   TABLESPOONS CAPERS
    SALT, TO TASTE
    FRESHLY GROUND BLACK PEPPER,
    TO TASTE
6   ANCHOVIES, COARSELY CHOPPED
12 FRESH BASIL LEAVES, TORN

Slice green, yellow and red peppers into thin strips. Sauté with sliced onions in olive oil until tender. Remove from heat and add capers, salt and pepper. Spoon mixture on warm bruschetta and top with anchovies and basil.

SMOKED SALMON

12	PIECES BASIC BRUSCHETTA
3	TABLESPOONS TOASTED PINE NUTS
2	MEDIUM TOMATOES, DICED
4	OUNCES FRESH MOZZARELLA CHEESE, FINELY DICED
4	OUNCES FINELY CHOPPED SMOKED SALMON
3	TABLESPOONS OLIVE OIL
8	FRESH BASIL LEAVES, CUT IN THIN STRIPS

Combine pine nuts, tomatoes, cheese, salmon and olive oil. Scoop heaping portions of the mixture on warm bruschetta. Garnish with basil leaves.

AVOCADO AND GREEN ONION

12	PIECES BASIC BRUSCHETTA
6	RIPE AVOCADOS
	FRESHLY SQUEEZED LEMON JUICE, TO TASTE
	SALT, TO TASTE
6	THINLY SLICED GREEN ONIONS
	OLIVE OIL

Peel avocados and mash, adding lemon juice and salt, to taste. Heap avocado mixture on warm bruschetta and sprinkle with green onion. Drizzle olive oil over the tops.

Serve Bruschetta as a versatile appetizer or light lunch, or as an accompaniment to soups and salads. Try them with Oven Vegetable Chowder (page 66).

12 SERVINGS EACH

1	PACKAGE ACTIVE DRY YEAST
1	CUP LUKEWARM WATER
2 3/4	CUPS BREAD FLOUR
3	TABLESPOONS RYE FLOUR
4	TABLESPOONS OLIVE OIL, DIVIDED, PLUS ADDITIONAL OIL TO BRUSH ON AFTER BAKING
2	TEASPOONS SALT
1	TABLESPOON MINCED GARLIC
2	TABLESPOONS DRIED ROSEMARY KOSHER SALT, TO TASTE
2	TEASPOONS COARSELY GROUND BLACK PEPPERCORNS UNSALTED BUTTER, IF DESIRED

In a small bowl, dissolve yeast in lukewarm water and let stand until foamy, about 5 minutes. In a large bowl, combine bread flour, rye flour, 2 tablespoons oil, salt and the yeast mixture, and stir to blend. Turn dough onto a lightly floured surface and knead for 8 to 10 minutes, until smooth and elastic. Transfer dough to a lightly oiled bowl, turning to coat well. Let dough rise, covered, in a warm place until doubled in bulk.

With fingertips, press the dough into a well-oiled 6- by 12- inch jelly-roll pan. A larger pan may be used to make a thinner focaccia. Brush dough with the remaining 2 tablespoons of oil and sprinkle with garlic, rosemary, kosher salt and peppercorns. Bake in the middle of a preheated 375 degree oven for 20 to 30 minutes—20 minutes for a chewy, soft texture; longer, for a crisper golden focaccia. Brush with additional olive oil. Cut the focaccia into wedges or tear apart and serve with butter or olive oil.

EIGHT 3-INCH SQUARES

PASTA

&

GRAINS

WINE WITH PASTA

Combinations of wine and pasta, traditionally considered, are narrowly defined. In Italian cuisine, as each type of pasta has its appropriate sauce (fettuccine with white clam sauce, gnocchi with its traditional fork marks that serve to hold a sauce with finely ground meat), so too does each region have an indigenous dish and a locally produced wine. Italian food and wine are meant to go together, but Italian-inspired food requires only an awareness of and respect for the types of wines that are Italian. Somewhat broadly, these are wines which emphasize intense fruits and high acidity.

Even more broadly, Italian wines, whether white or red, fall into two categories—traditional or modern (international style). Good traditional reds are intense, older-tasting, perhaps leathery, leafy, woody and/or earthy, with acidity, or tartness, as their structuring element. Good modern reds are intense, very young-tasting, full of fruit, almost chocolatey, with tannin, or dustiness, as their structuring element.

Traditional whites are generally to be avoided. They are often products of enormous cooperatives producing wines of little character and much oxidation. Modern whites are either squeaky clean and pleasant, or may have an unidentifiable aroma of minerals that seems without purpose until they are accompanied by food. Then their marvelous acidity holds its own with almost any food.

If the pasta dish is an accompaniment to an entrée or a meat dish, drink a wine that goes well with the entrée or meat. If pasta with tomatoes is a single course, remember that tomatoes are very high in acid and hard on wine. The only white wine that will work is Italian, or perhaps a French or American Sauvignon Blanc.

Do not assume that tomato and spaghetti mean Chianti. If the tomatoes are simply a small part of a many-ingredient dish, white wine, as above, is possible. If it is a heavy tomato sauce, choose a wine with a lot of fruit, such as a young Barbera or Zinfandel, and with plenty of acidity (to combat the acid in the dish), such as very young Vino Nobile di Montepulciano or Dolcetto d'Alba.
When tomatoes are absent, choosing a wine is simpler. With a heavy cream sauce, consider an acidic French Chardonnay such as Chablis or St. Véran. An abundance of herbs suggests an herbal wine such as Sauvignon Blanc.

As always, test the wine while cooking to see if it goes with the dish. One can always add some of the wine to the dish to bring the food and wine closer together.

WINE WITH GRAINS

Grains are endless in variety and flavors. They range from rice (sweet) to corn (fatty) to barley (earthy). However interesting, they all reflect the four flavors—sweet, sour, salt and bitter. Find their character in their simple, unadorned flavor—a basic component in the food/wine matching process.

 Preceding page: Pesto Tortellini Salad, page 102

VEGETABLE PASTA SALAD

1	SMALL RED BELL PEPPER, CUT INTO JULIENNE
1	SMALL GREEN BELL PEPPER, CUT INTO JULIENNE
1	MEDIUM ZUCCHINI, CUT INTO JULIENNE
2	TABLESPOONS BUTTER
1/2	POUND PASTA—SPIRAL, BOW TIE OR TORTELLINI—COOKED AL DENTE, DRAINED AND RINSED IN COLD WATER
1/2	CUP SUN-DRIED TOMATOES, SOAKED IN WATER 40 MINUTES AND CUT INTO SMALL PIECES
1/2	HEAD BROCCOLI, CUT INTO FLOWERETS AND BLANCHED
4	OUNCES THINLY SLICED MOZZARELLA CHEESE
1/2	CUP OLIVE OIL
3	TABLESPOONS RED-WINE VINEGAR
1	CLOVE GARLIC, MINCED SALT, TO TASTE FRESHLY GROUND BLACK PEPPER, TO TASTE
1/4	CUP MINCED FRESH BASIL
1/2	CUP FRESHLY GRATED PARMESAN CHEESE
	fresh basil leaves, for garnish

Sauté red and green peppers and zucchini in butter and combine with pasta. Add sun-dried tomatoes, broccoli and mozzarella cheese. In a food processor, slowly add olive oil to red-wine vinegar. Add garlic, salt, pepper, basil and Parmesan cheese, blending well. Pour over pasta and toss. Refrigerate. Garnish with fresh basil leaves.

This salad can be served as a main dish or as an accompaniment to Cold Summer Pork (page 113) or Charcoaled Lemon Chicken (page 239).

6 TO 8 SERVINGS

ORZO SALAD

2	CUPS ORZO, COOKED AL DENTE, DRAINED AND RINSED WITH COLD WATER
1	CUP CRUMBLED FETA CHEESE
2/3	CUP MINCED FRESH PARSLEY
2/3	CUP MINCED FRESH DILL
3	TOMATOES, PEELED, SEEDED AND COARSELY CHOPPED
1/4	CUP FRESHLY SQUEEZED LEMON JUICE
1/3	CUP OLIVE OIL SALT, TO TASTE FRESHLY GROUND BLACK PEPPER, TO TASTE

In a large bowl, combine orzo, feta, parsley, dill and tomatoes. In a small bowl, whisk together lemon juice, olive oil, salt and pepper. Pour dressing over orzo mixture and toss well. Chill.

This rice-shaped pasta makes a delicious and unusual pasta salad.

8 SERVINGS

Tiefenbrunner 1 9 9 0 Pinot Grigio (Alto Adige)

FUSILLI
WITH CHEESE AND HAM

6   TABLESPOONS BUTTER, DIVIDED
1   TABLESPOON PLUS 1 TEASPOON
     FLOUR
2   CUPS SCALDED MILK
1/2 POUND GRATED SHARP CHEDDAR
     CHEESE
1/4 TEASPOON FRESHLY GRATED
     NUTMEG
1/4 TEASPOON FRESHLY GROUND BLACK
     PEPPER
1/8 TEASPOON CAYENNE PEPPER
1/2 CUP FINELY CHOPPED ONION
1/2 TO 3/4 POUND SLICED FRESH MUSHROOMS
3/4 POUND SMOKED HAM (ABOUT 2
     CUPS), CUT INTO JULIENNE
1   CUP HEAVY CREAM
1/2 POUND FUSILLI, COOKED AL DENTE
     AND DRAINED
     SALT, TO TASTE
3   TABLESPOONS FRESHLY GRATED
     PARMESAN CHEESE

Melt 2 tablespoons of the butter in a saucepan
and add flour. Cook, stirring, about 1 minute.
Add milk, stirring rapidly with a whisk. Simmer
for 1 minute, then add cheddar cheese, nutmeg,
black pepper and cayenne and heat, stirring until
cheese melts. Set aside.

Heat remaining butter in a separate skillet and
add onions and mushrooms. Sauté until onions
are wilted and slightly golden. Add ham and
sauté about 1 minute. Stir in the cheese sauce
and heavy cream and heat. Combine the sauce
with fusilli and add salt to taste. Pour into a
buttered 10-cup baking dish, sprinkle with
Parmesan cheese, and bake in a preheated 425
degree oven until bubbling. Remove dish from
oven and place under broiler until top is
browned, 2 to 3 minutes. Let cool 5 to 10
minutes and serve.

4 SERVINGS

Taurino 1 9 9 0 Salice Salentino Rosato (Apulia)

RATATOUILLE WITH PASTA

3   CLOVES GARLIC
2   MEDIUM EGGPLANTS, CUBED
4   TABLESPOONS OLIVE OIL, DIVIDED
1   LARGE ONION, DICED
1   RED BELL PEPPER, DICED
1   GREEN BELL PEPPER, DICED
1   YELLOW BELL PEPPER, DICED
10   FRESH MUSHROOMS, SLICED
3   TABLESPOONS BALSAMIC VINEGAR
1   TABLESPOON DIJON-STYLE
     MUSTARD
1/2 CUP CHILI SAUCE
1/2 TEASPOON DRIED BASIL
     SALT, TO TASTE
     FRESHLY GROUND BLACK PEPPER,
     TO TASTE
3/4 POUND PENNE OR RIGATONI,
     COOKED AL DENTE AND DRAINED
1/4 CUP TOASTED PINE NUTS
3/4 CUP CRUMBLED FETA CHEESE OR 1/2
     CUP FRESHLY GRATED PARMESAN
     CHEESE
1/2 CUP SLICED BRINE-CURED BLACK
     OLIVES
1/2 CUP FRESHLY GRATED PARMESAN
     CHEESE
10   WHOLE BRINE-CURED BLACK OLIVES,
     PITTED

Wrap garlic in foil and roast in a preheated 325
degree oven for 45 minutes. Slip garlic cloves
out of skins and mash. In a large skillet, sauté
eggplant in 3 tablespoons olive oil for 10
minutes. Add onion, red, green, and yellow
peppers and mushrooms and sauté about 10
minutes or until eggplant and onion are
translucent. In a large bowl, combine vinegar, 1
tablespoon oil, mustard, chili sauce, basil, salt,
pepper and roasted garlic, mixing well. Toss
pasta, vegetables and dressing together, adding
pine nuts, feta cheese, and sliced olives. Transfer
to a large casserole and sprinkle with Parmesan
cheese and whole black olives. Bake 40 minutes
in a preheated 350 degree oven until heated
through.

8 SERVINGS AS A SIDE-DISH
4 SERVINGS AS A MAIN DISH

Robert Mondavi Fumé Blanc 1 9 8 9 (Napa)

BOW TIES
WITH CURRIED MUSHROOM SAUCE

1	POUND LARGE FRESH MUSHROOMS, SLICED 1/4-INCH THICK
1 1/2	TEASPOONS CURRY POWDER
12	TABLESPOONS BUTTER
2	TABLESPOONS ALL-PURPOSE FLOUR
1 1/2	CUPS LIGHT CREAM
1/2	CUP DRY SHERRY
3	TABLESPOONS FRESHLY GRATED PARMESAN CHEESE, DIVIDED
1 1/2	TEASPOONS SALT
1/8	TEASPOON CAYENNE PEPPER
3/4	POUND BOW TIE PASTA, COOKED AL DENTE AND DRAINED
1	POUND GRATED SWISS CHEESE, DIVIDED

In a large skillet, sauté mushrooms and curry powder in butter. Cook for about 5 minutes, or until mushrooms are soft and beginning to brown. Remove mushrooms with a slotted spoon, draining well, and set aside. Add flour to butter remaining in the skillet and cook for about 1 minute over low heat. Slowly add cream, stirring constantly. Add sherry, stirring, and bring just to the point of thickening. Do not simmer. Remove from heat and add 2 tablespoons Parmesan cheese, salt, and cayenne pepper. Combine hot pasta, mushrooms, and all but 1/2 cup sauce. Place half of the pasta mixture in a square glass dish and sprinkle with half of the Swiss cheese. Repeat layering with remaining pasta and cheese. Spread with reserved sauce and top with remaining tablespoon of Parmesan cheese. Bake in a preheated 350 degree oven for 30 minutes, then brown briefly under the broiler.

4 SERVINGS

Moriette 1 9 8 9 Vouvray (Loire)

FRESH SUMMER SPAGHETTI

Begin at least 3 hours before serving.

8 TO 12	MEDIUM, FIRM RIPE TOMATOES, PEELED, SEEDED AND HALVED
2 TO 3	TABLESPOONS CHOPPED FRESH PARSLEY
10 TO 20	CHOPPED FRESH BASIL LEAVES
3 TO 6	CLOVES GARLIC, CRUSHED
1	TEASPOON SALT
1/2	TEASPOON FRESHLY GROUND BLACK PEPPER
1/4	CUP FRESHLY SQUEEZED LEMON JUICE
3 TO 4	TABLESPOONS OLIVE OIL
1 TO 4	TEASPOONS TOMATO PASTE, IF DESIRED
1	POUND SPAGHETTI, COOKED AL DENTE AND DRAINED
2	TABLESPOONS BUTTER OR OLIVE OIL FRESHLY GRATED PARMESAN OR ROMANO CHEESE

Purée one-fourth of the tomatoes in a food processor and combine with parsley, basil, garlic, salt, pepper, lemon juice and olive oil. Chop remaining tomatoes, then combine with tomato purée in a bowl. Cover and refrigerate at least 3 hours. Taste and adjust the seasonings. The sauce will become juicier. Add tomato paste for a slightly thicker sauce that will adhere to the spaghetti.

Toss hot spaghetti with butter or olive oil and divide evenly among warmed soup bowls or high-rimmed plates. Top with cold sauce and sprinkle with grated cheese.

Variations: Fresh oregano or thyme can be substituted for the basil; black olives, marinated artichoke hearts or anchovies can be added to the sauce; cooked, shelled shrimp or lobster can be served on top of the pasta and sauce.

4 TO 6 SERVINGS

Vescovo 1 9 9 0 Pinot Grigio (Friuli - Venezia)

PASTA PUTTANESCA WITH SHRIMP AND PROSCIUTTO

2   TABLESPOONS OLIVE OIL
2   CLOVES GARLIC, MINCED
8   ANCHOVIES, CHOPPED
4 1/2   CUPS FRESH PLUM TOMATOES, PEELED AND SEEDED
8   STUFFED GREEN OLIVES, SLICED
8   BRINE-CURED BLACK OLIVES, SLICED
1   TEASPOON CAPERS
1/2   CUP CHOPPED FRESH BASIL LEAVES
A PINCH OF DRIED RED PEPPER FLAKES, TO TASTE
FRESHLY GROUND BLACK PEPPER, TO TASTE
1   POUND ANGEL HAIR PASTA, COOKED AL DENTE AND DRAINED
16   LARGE SHRIMP, SHELLED AND COOKED
16   SLICES PROSCIUTTO, SLIVERED

Heat oil in a skillet and sauté garlic until browned. Add anchovies and tomatoes and simmer over high heat for 5 minutes. Stir in green and black olives, capers, basil, red pepper flakes and black pepper. Simmer over low heat until slightly thickened. Gently toss hot pasta, shrimp and prosciutto with the sauce in a large serving bowl.

4 TO 6 SERVINGS

Silverado Sauvignon Blanc 1 9 9 1 (Napa)

LAYERED LINGUINE PRIMAVERA

1/3   CUP BUTTER
1/3   CUP CHOPPED ONION
1   MEDIUM GREEN BELL PEPPER, THINLY SLICED
4   MEDIUM TOMATOES, CUT INTO WEDGES
2   MEDIUM ZUCCHINI, QUARTERED LENGTHWISE AND CUT INTO 3-INCH PIECES
1/4   CUP CHOPPED FRESH PARSLEY
3/4   POUND LINGUINE, BROKEN INTO 1-INCH PIECES, COOKED AL DENTE AND DRAINED
1/2   CUP FRESHLY GRATED PARMESAN CHEESE, DIVIDED
GARLIC SALT, TO TASTE
FRESHLY GROUND BLACK PEPPER, TO TASTE
DRIED OREGANO, TO TASTE

Melt butter in a saucepan and sauté onion until translucent. Add green pepper and sauté 5 minutes longer. Combine tomatoes, zucchini and parsley in a medium bowl and stir in onions and green peppers. Lightly butter a 2-quart casserole. Spread half of the cooked linguine on the bottom and cover with half of the vegetable mixture. Sprinkle with half the cheese. Layer remaining pasta, vegetables and cheese. Sprinkle with garlic salt, pepper and oregano to taste. Cover and bake in a preheated 350 degree oven for 40 minutes.

4 SERVINGS

La Rocca 1 9 9 0 Gavi (Piedmont)

ANGEL HAIR PASTA
WITH VEGETABLES

3 TO 4	TABLESPOONS OLIVE OIL, DIVIDED
6	SMALL ZUCCHINI AND/OR YELLOW ZUCCHINI, SLICED 3/4-INCH THICK
1	LARGE ONION, CHOPPED
2	CLOVES GARLIC, MINCED
1/2	POUND LARGE MUSHROOMS, SLICED 1/2-INCH THICK
ONE	16-OUNCE CAN STEWED TOMATOES, PARTIALLY DRAINED
1	CUP TINY FROZEN PEAS, THAWED
1	TABLESPOON MINCED FRESH BASIL, OR 1 TEASPOON DRIED
1/2	CUP PORT WINE OR CHICKEN BROTH
	SALT, TO TASTE
	FRESHLY GROUND BLACK PEPPER, TO TASTE
3/4	POUND ANGEL HAIR PASTA, COOKED AL DENTE AND DRAINED
	FRESHLY GRATED ROMANO OR PARMESAN CHEESE

Heat half of the olive oil in a large sauté pan over high heat. When sizzling, add zucchini and sauté, tossing until browned. Remove with a slotted spoon to a warmed bowl. Add oil to sauté pan if needed, then add onion, garlic and mushrooms. Reduce heat to medium-high and cook until vegetables are tender but firm. Stir in zucchini and tomatoes (broken up with the edge of a spoon), peas, basil, wine or chicken broth, salt and pepper. Cook, uncovered, 4 to 6 minutes until vegetables are tender and liquid is slightly reduced. Divide hot pasta among four heated plates and top with vegetable sauce. Sprinkle grated cheese over each dish.

4 SERVINGS

San Quirico 1 9 9 0 Vernaccia di San Gimignano (Tuscany)

FETTUCCINE
WITH SMOKED TURKEY

2	TABLESPOONS BUTTER
2	TABLESPOONS MINCED SHALLOT
2	TEASPOONS COARSELY GROUND BLACK PEPPERCORNS
2/3	CUP DRY WHITE WINE
2	CUPS HEAVY CREAM
1/4	TEASPOON NUTMEG
3/4	POUND SMOKED TURKEY BREAST, CUT INTO JULIENNE
3/4	POUND FETTUCCINE, COOKED AL DENTE AND DRAINED
2	TABLESPOONS CHOPPED FRESH CHIVES
	FRESHLY GRATED PARMESAN CHEESE

Melt butter in a heavy skillet over medium heat and sauté shallots until soft, about 3 to 4 minutes. Add peppercorns and sauté 30 seconds. Add wine and boil until almost no liquid remains in skillet, about 2 minutes. Stir in cream, nutmeg and turkey and heat for about 5 minutes until sauce thickens. Do not boil. Combine hot fettuccine with sauce and toss to mix thoroughly. Serve on warmed plates and sprinkle with chives. Pass Parmesan cheese separately.

4 SERVINGS

Pfeffingen Ungsteiner Herrenberg Spätlese 1 9 9 0 (Rheinpfalz)

SICILIAN PASTA

1/2 CUP OLIVE OIL
1 CUP PINE NUTS
6 CLOVES GARLIC, MINCED
3 LARGE TOMATOES, SEEDED AND CHOPPED
18 OUNCES MARINATED ARTICHOKE HEARTS, DRAINED
1 CUP CHOPPED FRESH BASIL
1 1/2 TABLESPOONS CHOPPED FRESH OREGANO OR 1 TEASPOON DRIED SALT, TO TASTE FRESHLY GROUND BLACK PEPPER, TO TASTE
1 POUND ANGEL HAIR PASTA, COOKED AL DENTE AND DRAINED FRESHLY GRATED PARMESAN CHEESE COARSELY GROUND BLACK PEPPER

Heat oil in a heavy skillet over medium-high heat. Sauté pine nuts and garlic until golden, about 3 minutes. Stir in tomatoes, artichoke hearts, basil and oregano. Season with salt and pepper and heat through. Pour sauce over hot pasta and toss gently. Sprinkle with Parmesan cheese, black pepper, and serve.

4 TO 6 SERVINGS

Zenato 1 9 9 0 Lugana di San Benedetto (Lombardy)

PESTO TORTELLINI SALAD

SALAD

18 OUNCES CHEESE TORTELLINI, COOKED AL DENTE, DRAINED AND RINSED
5 PLUM TOMATOES, PEELED, SEEDED AND CUT INTO EIGHTHS
ONE 15-OUNCE CAN BLACK OLIVES, SLICED
1/4 POUND THINLY SLICED PEPPERONI
1/2 CUP LIGHTLY SALTED WHOLE ALMONDS

In a large bowl, combine tortellini, tomatoes, black olives, pepperoni and almonds. Set aside.

PESTO SAUCE

1 CUP FRESH BASIL
1/4 CUP OLIVE OIL
1 LARGE CLOVE GARLIC, CRUSHED
1 1/2 TABLESPOONS WALNUTS OR PINE NUTS
1/4 CUP GRATED PARMESAN CHEESE
2 TABLESPOONS RICOTTA CHEESE SALT, TO TASTE, IF DESIRED

Purée basil, olive oil, garlic and nuts in a blender or food processor. Fold in Parmesan and ricotta cheeses. Add salt, to taste, if desired. While pasta is still warm, toss with pesto sauce. Chill. Serve cold or at room temperature. The salad may be made one day before serving.

This is a good main dish salad, or it may be served as an accompaniment to Grilled Southwestern Lamb Chops (page 1 1 5). To save time, or if fresh basil is not available, use a 7-ounce container of prepared pesto sauce.

6 TO 8 SERVINGS

La Viarte 1 9 8 9 Sauvignon Blanc (Friuli - Venezia)

CHICKEN PASTA SALAD

DRESSING
1/2 CUP FRESHLY SQUEEZED LEMON
JUICE
2/3 CUP GRATED PARMESAN CHEESE
3/4 CUP MAYONNAISE

Whisk together lemon juice, Parmesan cheese and mayonnaise. Cover and chill until ready to use.

SALAD
1 POUND FETTUCINI, COOKED
AL DENTE, DRAINED AND CHILLED
1 POUND CHICKEN BREASTS, BONED,
SKINNED, COOKED AND CUT INTO
1/2-INCH PIECES
1/2 CUP CHOPPED CELERY
1/2 CUP PEELED, CHOPPED CUCUMBER
1/4 CUP CHOPPED GREEN ONION
1 CUP GREEN GRAPES
SALT, TO TASTE
FRESHLY GROUND WHITE PEPPER,
TO TASTE
kiwi slices and mandarin orange sections, for garnish
pistachio nuts, for garnish, if desired

In a large bowl, combine fettucini, chicken, celery, cucumber, onion and grapes. Toss with dressing. Season to taste with salt and white pepper. Garnish with kiwi and mandarin oranges. Sprinkle with pistachio nuts, if desired.

4 SERVINGS

Terruzi & Puthod 1 9 9 0 Terre di Tufo (Tuscany)

SHRIMP CAPELLINI

Begin at least 3 hours before serving.
1/2 CUP BUTTER, SOFTENED
1/4 CUP HEAVY CREAM
1/2 CUP GRATED PARMESAN CHEESE
2 TO 3 CLOVES GARLIC, MINCED
1 1/2 TABLESPOONS CHOPPED FRESH
PARSLEY OR CILANTRO
1 1/2 TABLESPOONS CHOPPED PIMIENTO
SALT TO TASTE
FRESHLY GROUND BLACK PEPPER,
TO TASTE
1 POUND CAPELLINI, COOKED
AL DENTE AND DRAINED
1 POUND MEDIUM SHRIMP, SHELLED
AND COOKED
1/2 CUP SLICED FRESH MUSHROOMS
2 FRESH RIPE TOMATOES, CHOPPED
AND BRIEFLY SAUTÉED
2 CUPS FRESH SUGAR PEA PODS,
COOKED UNTIL TENDER

Cream butter until fluffy, then beat in cream and Parmesan cheese. Stir in garlic, parsley or cilantro, pimiento, salt and pepper. Chill for several hours or overnight to blend flavors. Before serving, allow mixture to come to room temperature. Place cooked pasta in a large saucepan and add butter mixture, tossing well. Add shrimp, mushrooms, tomatoes and pea pods. Toss again and heat through.

4 TO 6 SERVINGS

La Viarte 1 9 8 9 Liende (Fruili - Venezia)

PASTA
WITH ITALIAN SAUSAGE

2	TABLESPOONS OLIVE OIL
4	ITALIAN SAUSAGES
4	CLOVES GARLIC, MINCED
1	CUP HEAVY CREAM
4	FRESH RIPE TOMATOES, PEELED, SEEDED AND CUBED
2	CUPS CHICKEN STOCK, PREFERABLY HOMEMADE
1	TABLESPOON FRESH TARRAGON, OR 1 TEASPOON DRIED FRESHLY GROUND BLACK PEPPER, TO TASTE
1	POUND FRESH PASTA, COOKED AL DENTE AND DRAINED
	fresh basil leaves, for garnish

Heat olive oil in a skillet and cook the sausages over medium heat until done. Remove sausages from pan and set aside. In the same pan, sauté garlic briefly, then add cream and tomatoes. Reduce the cream mixture as the tomatoes cook, adding chicken stock as needed. Stir in tarragon and pepper. Cut the sausages into small pieces. In a serving dish, toss the hot pasta with sausages and cream mixture until thoroughly mixed. Garnish with fresh basil leaves.

4 SERVINGS

Ojai Syrah 1 9 8 8 (Southern California)

SPAGHETTI
WITH FRESH TOMATOES AND PINE NUTS

Begin at least 1 hour before serving.

3/4	CUP OLIVE OIL, DIVIDED
3	CLOVES GARLIC, PEELED AND THINLY SLICED
1/2	CUP PINE NUTS
6	LARGE RIPE TOMATOES, DICED
1	CUP CHOPPED FRESH BASIL
1/4 TO 1/2	POUND BRINE-CURED BLACK OLIVES, PITTED AND HALVED SALT, TO TASTE FRESHLY GROUND BLACK PEPPER, TO TASTE
1	POUND SPAGHETTI, COOKED AL DENTE AND DRAINED FRESHLY GRATED PARMESAN CHEESE

In a large skillet, heat 1/4 cup olive oil and sauté garlic. Add pine nuts and sauté briefly until golden brown, being careful not to burn them. Remove skillet from heat and let cool. In a small bowl, combine tomatoes, basil, olives, salt, pepper and 1/2 cup olive oil. Add the cooled pine nut mixture and mix well. Set aside for 1 hour at room temperature.

To serve, toss hot spaghetti with tomato mixture in a serving bowl. Sprinkle with Parmesan cheese.

4 SERVINGS

Giacosa 1 9 9 0 Dolcetto d'Alba (Piedmont)

DILLED LEMON RICE

2 1/2   CUPS CHICKEN BROTH, PREFERABLY
       HOMEMADE
1/2   TEASPOON SALT
1   CLOVE GARLIC, SLIGHTLY CRUSHED
1   CUP LONG-GRAIN RICE
1   TABLESPOON FINELY GRATED
     LEMON ZEST
2   TABLESPOONS CHOPPED FRESH DILL
2   TABLESPOONS UNSALTED BUTTER
     FRESHLY GROUND BLACK PEPPER,
     TO TASTE

fresh dill and lemon wedges, for garnish

Combine broth, salt and garlic in a heavy saucepan, heat and bring to a boil. Stir in rice, cover and simmer over low heat until liquid is absorbed, about 20 minutes, lifting lid only near end of cooking time to see if rice is done. Remove from heat. Stir in lemon zest and let stand, covered, for 5 minutes. Remove garlic and gently stir in dill and butter. Season to taste with pepper and garnish with dill and lemon. Serve immediately.

*Serve as an accompaniment to Duck with
Fresh Raspberry Sauce (page 141).*

4 SERVINGS

FLINT HILLS WILD RICE

1   CUP WILD RICE
1/2   CUP OLIVE OIL
1/4   POUND GRATED CHEDDAR CHEESE
1   CUP COARSELY CHOPPED BLACK
     OLIVES
ONE   16-OUNCE CAN TOMATOES,
     DRAINED AND CHOPPED
1   CUP COARSELY CHOPPED FRESH
     MUSHROOMS
1   CUP CHOPPED ONION
1 1/2   CUPS BOILING WATER
     SALT, TO TASTE
     FRESHLY GROUND BLACK PEPPER,
     TO TASTE

Soak rice in cold water to cover for 1 hour. Drain. Add olive oil, cheese, olives, tomatoes, mushrooms and onion, and pour into a 2-quart casserole. Add boiling water and season with salt and pepper. Bake uncovered in a preheated 350 degree oven for 2 hours. The rice may be prepared one day ahead; add boiling water just before baking.

8 TO 10 SERVINGS

Regaleali 1 9 9 0 Bianco (Sicily)

COUSCOUS
WITH BELL PEPPERS

2 TABLESPOONS VEGETABLE OIL
1/2 RED BELL PEPPER, CUT INTO SMALL
  SQUARES
1/2 YELLOW BELL PEPPER, CUT INTO
  SMALL SQUARES
4 GREEN ONIONS, THINLY SLICED
1/2 CUP CURRANTS
3 CUPS CHICKEN BROTH, PREFERABLY
  HOMEMADE
1/2 TEASPOON TURMERIC
2 CUPS COUSCOUS

Heat vegetable oil in a saucepan and add red and yellow peppers and green onions. Sauté for about 2 minutes. Stir in currants, chicken broth and turmeric and bring to a boil. Add the couscous and stir until well blended. Cover the pan and turn off the heat. Let stand for about 10 minutes. To serve, fluff with a fork.

4 TO 6 SERVINGS

*Minet 1 9 8 9 Pouilly Fumé Vieille Vignes
(Loire)*

CORN AND WILD RICE SAUTÉ

2 TABLESPOONS UNSALTED BUTTER
2 TABLESPOONS OLIVE OIL
1 TABLESPOON GARLIC, PRESSED OR
  MINCED
6 EARS WHITE CORN, STEAMED, WITH
  KERNELS REMOVED FROM COB, OR 3
  CUPS FROZEN CORN, THAWED
2 CUPS COOKED WILD RICE
3 TABLESPOONS SUN-DRIED
  TOMATOES IN OIL, MINCED AND
  WELL DRAINED
1/3 CUP MINCED FRESH CILANTRO OR
  BASIL, OR A COMBINATION
  SALT, TO TASTE
  FRESHLY GROUND BLACK PEPPER,
  TO TASTE

Melt butter and olive oil in a large, heavy saucepan. Add garlic and sauté for 30 seconds. Stir in corn, rice and tomatoes. Sauté until corn is heated through, about 4 to 8 minutes. Stir in cilantro and season with salt and pepper.

6 TO 8 SERVINGS

Fausto Maculan 1 9 9 0 Chardonnay (Northern Italy)

FRENCH RICE CASSEROLE

1 1/2	CUPS WILD RICE
1	CUP LONG-GRAIN WHITE RICE
4 1/4	CUPS CHICKEN BROTH, PREFERABLY HOMEMADE
1	LARGE ONION, CHOPPED
1	GREEN BELL PEPPER, CHOPPED
8	TABLESPOONS BUTTER
1	CUP SLICED FRESH MUSHROOMS, SPRINKLED WITH FRESHLY SQUEEZED LEMON JUICE
2	CUPS HEAVY CREAM
1/2	TEASPOON SALT
1	TEASPOON FRESHLY GROUND BLACK PEPPER
1/2 TO 3/4	CUP FRESHLY GRATED PARMESAN CHEESE, DIVIDED

Place wild and white rice in a 3-quart saucepan and pour in broth. Cover and cook over medium heat until done, about 45 to 60 minutes. Sauté onion and green pepper in butter and add to cooked rice. Add mushrooms, cream, salt, pepper and half of Parmesan cheese, mixing well. Spoon rice mixture into a buttered 9- by 13-inch casserole and sprinkle remaining cheese on top. Bake, covered, in a preheated 350 degree oven until bubbly, about 20 minutes. Uncover and continue baking until slightly browned, about 10 minutes longer.

This recipe is easily halved. One cup sliced carrots or 1 cup sugar pea pods may be substituted for the mushrooms.

Serve as an accompaniment to Braised Quail with Hunter's Sauce (page 143).

12 SERVINGS

MEAT

POULTRY

&

FISH

WINE WITH MEATS

There is no reason to be afraid of violating rules as broad as that of white wine with white meat, and red wine with red meat, an often accurate but gross generalization. History provides many exceptions— Sauternes and foie gras, Spätlese and pork loin, Dao and grilled sardines, Pinot Noir and grilled salmon, Tavel and ham, Pinot Gris and duck, Sancerre and boar. What all of the aforementioned wines have in common is that they are, in their finest examples, very rich. Red meat has tremendous flavor, is rarely subtle, and needs a high-fruit, high-acid wine to overcome it if the wine is white.

Beef and some game meats are always safe with a big red wine. These meats are usually high in fat content and can taste fatty without a rich tannic red to balance them. Tannin, present in most good red wines, is a dusty component that leaches from the skin, seeds and stems of red grapes when they are crushed and the juice and solids are allowed to steep. That dustiness, which can seem almost bitter by itself, cuts through the fats of red meats and the fat cancels the tannin. Young California Cabernet, Merlot and Zinfandel, Australian Cabernet or Shiraz, Bordeaux and wines of the Rhône Valley in France, and just about any big Italian red, are all safe choices.

A classic combination in the wine world is Bordeaux and lamb, but the lamb should be relatively straightforward (Dill Roasted Leg of Lamb, for example) if it is to allow the wine any breathing space. Lamb is often served with mint or jalapeño jelly, rendering it useless for most wine purposes. When lamb is accompanied by an abundance of herbs, spices and earthy vegetables, try a big, fruity American Zinfandel to overcome the many flavors.

Pork offers a different set of choices. Often a dry rosé, such as the Tavel mentioned above, has enough fruit to handle a ham's saltiness. Pork with Chinese seasonings can be exciting when paired with a great German Spätlese, a wine with great mineral and fruit power and tremendous acidity. For a pork roast, try a Pinot Noir, lighter, more subtle, and soft enough in tannins to handle the leaner character of most pork. Pork and chicken are somewhat alike in their malleability; they may be big and rich, or light and clean. With pork, however, there is always an earthiness that responds well to European wines (which are often earthy), and some saltiness. This saltiness is best dealt with by using an acidic wine, such as German Riesling, Sancerre, young Burgundy (Pinot Noir) or Italian red wines.

 Preceding page: Ceramic Hamburger and Utensil, Creative Arts Center

BRAISED PORK
WITH ORANGE-MUSTARD SAUCE

1 1/2	POUNDS BONELESS PORK LOIN, TRIMMED AND CUT INTO 6 SLICES
1/4	TEASPOON SALT
1/8	TEASPOON FRESHLY GROUND BLACK PEPPER
1	TABLESPOON VEGETABLE OIL
2 TO 3	TEASPOONS FINELY CHOPPED FRESH GINGER
1/2	CUP ORANGE JUICE
3	TABLESPOONS SOY SAUCE
2	TABLESPOONS HONEY
1	TABLESPOON DIJON-STYLE MUSTARD
2	CLOVES GARLIC, PRESSED

sliced oranges and sprigs of fresh watercress, for garnish

Season pork slices with salt and pepper. Heat oil in a large skillet and brown pork slices over medium heat, 3 to 4 minutes per side. Remove and drain well, wiping skillet to remove excess oil. Return pork slices to pan. In a small bowl, blend ginger, orange juice, soy sauce, honey, mustard and garlic. Pour mixture over pork slices and simmer, uncovered, over low heat 10 to 12 minutes, or until pork is tender.

To serve, arrange pork slices on a warm platter. Spoon half of the Orange-Mustard Sauce over pork and garnish with orange slices and watercress. Serve with remaining sauce, accompanied by Baked Vidalia Onions (page 170).

6 SERVINGS

von Simmeren Hattenheimer Nussbrunnen Spätlese 1 9 9 0 (Rheingau)

BALSAMIC PORK TENDERLOIN
WITH FRESH THYME

1 1/2	POUNDS PORK TENDERLOIN
1/2	CUP FLOUR
1	TEASPOON SALT
1/2	TEASPOON FRESHLY GROUND BLACK PEPPER
1	TABLESPOON UNSALTED BUTTER
1	TABLESPOON OLIVE OIL
2	TABLESPOONS MINCED SHALLOT
2/3	CUP BALSAMIC VINEGAR
1/4	CUP CHICKEN STOCK, PREFERABLY HOMEMADE
2	TABLESPOONS CHOPPED FRESH THYME OR 1 TEASPOON DRIED

Slice the tenderloin into 1 1/4-inch medallions. (Freeze the small ends of the tenderloin for later use.) With the flat side of a large knife, lightly pound each slice to flatten to about 1/2-inch thickness. Combine flour, salt and pepper on a sheet of wax paper and coat medallions with the seasoned flour, shaking off the excess.

Melt butter and oil in a large, heavy sauté pan over medium-high heat. Sauté the shallots until softened, about 3 minutes, then remove and set aside. In the same pan, brown medallions 2 to 3 minutes per side. Remove, cover with foil and keep warm.

Add vinegar to the sauté pan and cook over medium-high heat to reduce by half. Add the shallots, chicken stock, thyme and any juices that have accumulated around the pork and cook for 1 to 2 minutes, reducing the sauce until it is dark and shiny. Return the medallions to the pan to coat with sauce and serve.

Depending upon availability, other fresh herbs, such as sage, rosemary or tarragon, may be used in place of thyme.

3 TO 4 SERVINGS

Blachon St. Joseph 1 9 9 0 (Northern Rhône)

INDONESIAN PORK KEBABS

Begin 1 day before serving.

1/4	CUP SOY SAUCE
1	CLOVE GARLIC, PRESSED
2	TABLESPOONS LIGHT BROWN SUGAR
2	TABLESPOONS FRESHLY SQUEEZED LEMON JUICE
1/4	TEASPOON FRESHLY GROUND BLACK PEPPER
1	PORK TENDERLOIN, CUBED
	PEARL ONIONS
	YELLOW BELL PEPPER, CUT INTO CHUNKS

In a small bowl, combine soy sauce, garlic, brown sugar, lemon juice and pepper. Pour over tenderloin and refrigerate overnight. When ready to broil or grill, thread meat on wooden skewers, alternating with pearl onions and bell pepper chunks. Broil 2 1/2 inches from heat for 10 to 15 minutes, or grill 8 to 10 minutes over medium-hot coals, turning often.

4 SERVINGS

Trimbach 1 9 9 0 Pinot Gris (Alsace)

ORIENTAL PORK CHOPS

1/4	CUP RICE OR WHITE VINEGAR
3	TABLESPOONS SOY SAUCE
2	TABLESPOONS HONEY
4 TO 6	DROPS HOT PEPPER SAUCE
2	TEASPOONS VEGETABLE OIL
2	TEASPOONS SESAME OIL
4	BONELESS PORK LOIN CHOPS (1 INCH THICK), TRIMMED
6	CLOVES GARLIC, CRUSHED
1	TABLESPOON GRATED FRESH GINGER
	chopped fresh cilantro, for garnish

Whisk together vinegar, soy sauce, honey and hot pepper sauce in a small bowl. Set aside. Heat vegetable oil and sesame oil in a heavy skillet over medium-high heat. Add pork chops and cook until browned, about 2 minutes per side. Add garlic and ginger and cook, stirring, for 3 minutes. Reduce heat to low and add vinegar mixture. Cover skillet and cook until chops are tender, about 10 minutes. Remove cover and cook an additional 2 to 3 minutes or until sauce is slightly thickened. Garnish with chopped cilantro.

4 SERVINGS

Karthäusershofberg Eitelsbacher Karthäusershofberg Kabinett 1 9 9 0 (Mosel - Saar - Ruwer)

ROSEMARY PORK MEDALLIONS WITH MUSHROOMS

2 PORK TENDERLOINS, EACH TRIMMED AND CUT INTO 8 SLICES
2 TABLESPOONS BUTTER
2 CUPS SLICED FRESH MUSHROOMS
4 TABLESPOONS FINELY CHOPPED ONION
6 TEASPOONS CHOPPED FRESH ROSEMARY
1/2 TEASPOON CELERY SALT
1/2 TEASPOON FRESHLY GROUND BLACK PEPPER
2 CLOVES GARLIC, PRESSED
2 TABLESPOONS DRY VERMOUTH

sprigs of fresh rosemary and fresh mushrooms, for garnish

Pound each tenderloin slice to 1-inch thickness. In a heavy skillet, melt the butter and brown the pork quickly over medium-high heat, about 1 minute on each side. Remove pork slices. Add mushrooms, onion, rosemary, celery salt, pepper and garlic to the drippings. Cook for about 2 minutes over low heat, stirring often. Add vermouth and return pork slices to the skillet. Spoon mushroom mixture over the slices. Cover and simmer 3 to 4 minutes.

Arrange the pork and mushrooms on a warm serving plate and garnish with sprigs of rosemary and fresh mushrooms.

4 SERVINGS

Lassarat 1 9 8 9 St. Véran "Fournaise"
(Mâcon - France)

COLD SUMMER PORK

Prepare 1 day before serving.

ONE 4-POUND ROLLED PORK LOIN ROAST
3 CLOVES GARLIC, SLIVERED AND PLACED UNDER SKIN OF ROAST
1 CUP SOUR CREAM
1 CUP MAYONNAISE, PREFERABLY HOMEMADE
FRESHLY SQUEEZED JUICE OF 1 LEMON
8 LETTUCE LEAVES, BIBB OR GREENLEAF
9 OUNCES CAPERS, DRAINED

tomato, avocado or lemon wedges, for garnish

Place pork roast, fat side up, in a preheated 400 degree oven for 15 minutes. Reduce oven temperature to 375 degrees; add water to cover bottom of pan and bake for a total of 30 minutes per pound (including first 15 minutes). Cool and refrigerate overnight, tightly wrapped to prevent drying. Slice the roast in 1/2- to 1/4-inch slices.

Whisk together sour cream, mayonnaise and lemon juice until smooth. Arrange pork slices on lettuce leaves. Spread sour cream mixture on individual pork slices, covering the top completely. Generously sprinkle capers on each slice. Garnish platter with fresh tomato, avocado or lemon wedges.

Serve with Vegetable Pasta Salad (page 97) or Red Onion Compote (page 169).

8 SERVINGS

Calera Central Coast Pinot Noir 1 9 9 0 (Central Coast)

MEDITERRANEAN PORK ROAST

    5   CLOVES GARLIC
    2   TABLESPOONS FENNEL SEEDS
1 1/2   TEASPOONS COARSE SALT
  1/2   TEASPOON FRESHLY GROUND BLACK
         PEPPER
  1/4   CUP OLIVE OIL
    1   PORK LOIN (3 TO 4 POUNDS),
         TRIMMED

With food processor running, drop in garlic
cloves to mince. Add fennel seeds, salt and
pepper. With a sharp knife, make small incisions
in the pork and fill with the garlic mixture. Rub
remaining mixture over the meat along with the
olive oil. Place pork in a shallow roasting pan
and bake uncovered in a preheated 325 degree
oven for 1 1/2 hours, or until meat thermometer
registers 170 degrees.

*Serve with Sherried Sweet Potatoes and Apples (page 168)
or with Grilled Polenta (page 117).*

6 TO 8 SERVINGS

*Ridge Cabernet Sauvignon Santa Cruz 1 9 8 9
(Santa Cruz Mountains)*

CROWN PORK ROAST
WITH CORNBREAD STUFFING

  ONE   15-POUND CROWN PORK ROAST,
         FRENCHED, WITH ENDS TIED

Place roast in a large roasting pan upside down,
so that bone tips rest on bottom of pan. Bake,
uncovered, in a preheated 325 degree oven for
2 1/2 hours. Remove from oven. Drain
drippings into a measuring cup, skimming fat off
the top, and reserve for stuffing. Turn roast over
so the bone tips are up.

STUFFING
    2   CUPS CHOPPED CELERY
    2   CUPS CHOPPED ONION
    8   TABLESPOONS BUTTER
    1   POUND DRY CORNBREAD STUFFING
    1   LARGE GRANNY SMITH APPLE,
         SHREDDED
    2   EGGS, LIGHTLY BEATEN
  1/2   CUP BREADCRUMBS
  1/2   CUP SESAME SEEDS
    1   TEASPOON DRIED SAGE
  1/2   TEASPOON DRIED THYME
  1/2   TEASPOON BAKING POWDER
  1/2   TEASPOON BAKING SODA
    1   TEASPOON SALT
  1/2   TEASPOON FRESHLY GROUND BLACK
         PEPPER
    2   CUPS PORK DRIPPINGS FROM ROAST

In a saucepan, sauté celery and onion in butter.
In a large mixing bowl, combine the cornbread
stuffing, apple, eggs and celery-onion mixture.
Add breadcrumbs, sesame seeds, sage, thyme,
baking powder, baking soda, salt and pepper.
Pour the drippings over the mixture and stir
well. Fill the center of the crown roast with the
stuffing. Bake uncovered in a preheated 325
degree oven for 1 hour or until stuffing is done.
The bone tips may be covered with aluminum
foil to keep them from burning.

Remove roast from pan and place on a serving
platter. Slice between each bone before serving.

*This elegant roast goes well with Balsamic Carrots
(page 174) and Zucchini Flan (page 176).*

15 TO 20 SERVINGS

Matrot 1 9 8 9 Meursault (White Burgundy)

PORK TENDERLOIN WITH CHAMPAGNE MUSTARD SAUCE

Begin at least 4 hours before serving.

1/4	CUP SOY SAUCE
1/4	CUP BOURBON
2	TABLESPOONS BROWN SUGAR
2	PORK TENDERLOINS

Blend soy sauce, bourbon and brown sugar. Pour over pork and marinate, covered, at room temperature for 3 hours, turning occasionally. Remove tenderloins from marinade, reserving liquid. Place in a shallow pan and bake in a preheated 325 degree oven for 60 to 75 minutes, basting often with reserved marinade.

CHAMPAGNE MUSTARD SAUCE

1/3	CUP SOUR CREAM
1/3	CUP MAYONNAISE
1	TABLESPOON CHAMPAGNE MUSTARD
1	TABLESPOON FINELY CHOPPED GREEN ONION
1 1/2	TEASPOONS JALAPEÑO-GARLIC VINEGAR

In a small bowl, mix sour cream, mayonnaise, mustard, green onion and vinegar. Set aside.

To serve, thinly slice pork on the diagonal and top with Champagne Mustard Sauce.

4 SERVINGS

Emilia Lustau Dry Oloroso (Sherry - Spain)

GRILLED SOUTHWESTERN LAMB CHOPS

4	LOIN LAMB CHOPS, CUT 1-INCH THICK
1	TEASPOON SALT, DIVIDED
1/2	TEASPOON FRESHLY GROUND BLACK PEPPER
1/2	TEASPOON GROUND CINNAMON
1/2	CUP JALAPEÑO PEPPER JELLY
1/4	CUP FRESHLY SQUEEZED LEMON JUICE
1	TABLESPOON PREPARED MUSTARD
1	CUP PAPAYA OR TOMATILLO, MASHED

Sprinkle lamb chops with a mixture of 1/2 teaspoon salt, pepper and cinnamon. Combine jelly, lemon juice, mustard, 1/2 teaspoon salt and papaya or tomatillo in small saucepan. Bring to a boil, stirring until jelly is melted. Grill lamb chops 4 inches from hot coals for 10 minutes, turning once, or broil in oven. Spoon sauce over lamb during the last 5 minutes of cooking time.

Serve with Pesto Tortellini Salad (page 102) and fresh sliced tomatoes for a summer meal.

4 SERVINGS

Marques des Caceres 1 9 8 9 Rioja Tinto (Rioja)

DILL ROASTED LEG OF LAMB

ONE 8-POUND LEG OF LAMB,
     BUTTERFLIED
     SALT, TO TASTE
     FRESHLY GROUND BLACK PEPPER,
     TO TASTE
2 TABLESPOONS FRESH DILL, DIVIDED
     FRESHLY SQUEEZED JUICE OF 3
     LEMONS, DIVIDED
1 STALK CELERY, MINCED
1 CLOVE GARLIC, MINCED
1 SHALLOT, MINCED
1 TABLESPOON BUTTER
2 TABLESPOONS OLIVE OIL
1/2 CUP DRY SAUTERNES
sprigs of fresh dill, lemon slices and yellow lilies,
for garnish

Season inside (lean) part of the lamb by rubbing with salt and pepper, 1 tablespoon dill and juice of 2 lemons. Sauté celery, garlic and shallot in butter until soft, about 20 minutes, and spread mixture inside lamb. Roll up the lamb, fat side out, and skewer at bottom or tie with heavy string. Place in baking pan and rub well with olive oil. Season top and sides of roast with salt, pepper and remaining dill. Pour wine into the pan and bake in a preheated 400 degree oven for 20 minutes. Reduce heat to 350 degrees and bake about 1 hour, or until temperature on a meat thermometer registers 150 degrees, basting two or three times during cooking.

To serve, squeeze juice of one lemon over top of roast. Garnish with sprigs of fresh dill, lemon slices and yellow lilies, if available.

The lamb may be prepared up to the trussing point 24 hours in advance. Serve with Potatoes Gruyère (page 172) and English Peas with Sherry (page 174).

8 SERVINGS

Whitehall Lane Cabernet Sauvignon 1 9 8 9 (Napa)

HERB-CRUSTED RACK OF LAMB

4 CLOVES GARLIC, PRESSED
2 TEASPOONS FRESHLY GROUND
     BLACK PEPPER
4 TEASPOONS CHOPPED FRESH
     ROSEMARY OR 3 TEASPOONS DRIED
2 RACKS OF LAMB, TRIMMED AND
     FRENCHED
1 CUP FRESH BREADCRUMBS
1/2 CUP CHOPPED FRESH PARSLEY
2 TEASPOONS PAPRIKA
1/2 CUP BEEF BROTH, PREFERABLY
     HOMEMADE

Combine garlic, pepper and rosemary and rub over lamb. Place lamb on rack of a shallow roasting pan, meaty side down, and roast in a preheated 475 degree oven for 10 minutes. Remove from oven and reduce oven temperature to 400 degrees. Turn lamb over, return to oven and roast an additional 15 minutes for medium-rare. While lamb is roasting, combine breadcrumbs, parsley and paprika in a small bowl. Moisten mixture with beef broth so that breadcrumbs are saturated and all liquid is absorbed. Add more broth if necessary. When lamb is done, remove from oven. Preheat broiler. Press crumb mixture firmly onto meaty side of the lamb, covering completely. Broil 4 inches from heat until the crumbs are browned, about 3 minutes. Remove from oven and let stand 5 minutes. Slice ribs individually and serve.

Serve with Baked Swiss Cauliflower (page 171) and a fresh green vegetable.

4 SERVINGS

Stag's Leap Vintner's Merlot 1 9 8 9
(Napa)

BUTTERFLIED LEG OF LAMB
WITH GRILLED POLENTA

Begin 1 day before serving.

3 TO 4   POUNDS BONELESS LEG OF LAMB, BUTTERFLIED

4   LARGE CLOVES GARLIC, PEELED

1   TABLESPOON FINELY CHOPPED ROSEMARY, FRESH OR DRIED

1   SMALL BUNCH FINELY CHOPPED FRESH PARSLEY

2   TEASPOONS FINELY CHOPPED THYME, FRESH OR DRIED

1   TEASPOON COARSELY GROUND BLACK PEPPER

Place meat fat side down and open flat. Make shallow cuts near the center to allow meat to lie flat, but do not cut all the way through. Combine garlic, rosemary, parsley, thyme and pepper. Place the meat flat in a large glass dish and rub the herb mixture on both sides. Cover and refrigerate overnight.

Remove from refrigerator one hour before grilling. Grill meat 4 to 5 inches from hot coals, about 15 minutes per side for medium rare.

Carve across the grain in 1/4- to 1/2-inch thick slices and serve with Grilled Polenta and Red Onion Compote (page 169).

6 TO 8 SERVINGS

Fattoria Baggiolino 1 9 8 6 Poggio Brandi (Tuscany)

GRILLED POLENTA

Begin 1 day before serving.

6   CUPS WATER

1   TEASPOON SALT

2   CUPS COARSELY GROUND YELLOW CORNMEAL

3   TABLESPOONS BUTTER, IF DESIRED OLIVE OIL

pesto, blue cheese or goat cheese, as an accompaniment

Bring water and salt to a boil. Reduce heat to low and very gradually whisk in the polenta. Cook, stirring constantly with a wooden spoon until mixture is thick. The spoon will stand upright and the polenta will pull away from the sides of the pan. Add butter if desired. Pour into a greased 8- by 4- by 2-inch loaf pan and refrigerate overnight. To grill, unmold polenta and slice 3/4-inch thick. Brush with olive oil on both sides. Grill over medium heat until lightly toasted, about 8 to 10 minutes per side. Serve as is or top with pesto, blue cheese or goat cheese.

10 SERVINGS

TANDOORI LAMB

Begin 1 day before serving.

3 TO 4 POUNDS BONELESS LEG OF LAMB, BUTTERFLIED
2 CUPS PLAIN YOGURT
1/4 CUP HEAVY CREAM
1/4 TEASPOON GRATED FRESH GINGER
3 CLOVES GARLIC, PRESSED
1/4 TEASPOON GROUND CLOVES
1/4 TEASPOON CINNAMON
3 TABLESPOONS WHITE VINEGAR
1/2 TEASPOON CHILI POWDER
2 TABLESPOONS FRESHLY SQUEEZED LEMON JUICE
1 TEASPOON CORIANDER
1 TEASPOON CUMIN
SALT, TO TASTE
FRESHLY GROUND BLACK PEPPER, TO TASTE

Place yogurt, cream, ginger, garlic, cloves and cinnamon in a blender or food processor. Add vinegar, chili powder, lemon juice, coriander, cumin, salt and pepper and blend until frothy. Place lamb in a 9- by 13-inch pan and pour on marinade. Cover and refrigerate overnight, turning at least once.

Remove from refrigerator at least 45 minutes before cooking. Grill lamb over hot coals approximately 15 minutes per side for medium rare.

Serve this unusual main dish with Curry of Potatoes and Cauliflower (page 173), or slice into strips and serve in pita halves with cucumber slices and a sauce of yogurt, mint, dill and garlic.

6 SERVINGS

Pesquera Tinto 1 9 8 9 (Ribera del Duero - Spain)

SAUTÉED SUNFLOWER LAMB CHOPS

1 3/4 CUPS GROUND SUNFLOWER SEEDS
1 3/4 CUPS DRIED BREADCRUMBS
1 3/4 CUPS FRESHLY GRATED PARMESAN CHEESE
8 RIB LAMB CHOPS, 1 INCH THICK, FRENCHED AND WELL-TRIMMED
2 TABLESPOONS FLOUR
1 EGG, LIGHTLY BEATEN
7 TABLESPOONS BUTTER
1 TABLESPOON VEGETABLE OIL

Combine sunflower seeds, breadcrumbs and Parmesan cheese in a shallow bowl. Dust each lamb chop with flour, dip in egg and coat with sunflower seed mixture. Press the coating onto both sides so that it will adhere. Place chops on a plate and refrigerate for 30 minutes.

Heat butter and oil in a heavy skillet over medium-high heat. Remove lamb chops from refrigerator and cook, turning frequently to prevent burning, about 4 minutes per side. Chops should be crisp on the outside but pink in the center. Remove from pan as they are done and drain on paper towels until ready to serve. The lamb chops may be served warm or at room temperature.

Serve with Vegetable Sauté (page 177).

4 SERVINGS

Château Le Gay 1 9 8 3 Pomerol (Bordeaux)

TENDERLOIN SLICES
ON SALAD GREENS

2   POUNDS BEEF TENDERLOIN

Place tenderloin in a roasting pan. Bake in a preheated 400 degree oven until the tenderloin is medium-rare to medium, 150 to 160 degrees on a meat thermometer. Remove from oven and thinly slice on the diagonal.

VINAIGRETTE
1/2   CUP OLIVE OIL
1   CLOVE GARLIC, PRESSED
1 1/2   TABLESPOONS WORCESTERSHIRE SAUCE
2   TABLESPOONS RED-WINE VINEGAR
1   TABLESPOON COUNTRY-STYLE MUSTARD
2   TABLESPOONS HONEY
SALT, TO TASTE
FRESHLY GROUND BLACK PEPPER, TO TASTE

Whisk together olive oil, garlic, Worcestershire sauce, vinegar, mustard, honey, salt and pepper. Set aside.

BAGUETTE
8   TABLESPOONS BUTTER
1   SHALLOT, MINCED
1   BAGUETTE, SLICED

Melt butter in a small saucepan and lightly sauté shallot. Brush baguette slices lightly with shallot butter on both sides. Broil until golden brown, turning once.

SALAD
1   RED BELL PEPPER, SLICED IN RINGS
1   YELLOW BELL PEPPER, SLICED IN RINGS
1/2   POUND RED CHERRY TOMATOES
1   RED ONION, SLICED IN RINGS
1 1/2   POUNDS MIXED SALAD GREENS

In a salad bowl, gently toss together red and yellow peppers, cherry tomatoes, red onion and salad greens.

To serve, arrange salad on individual dinner plates. Top with slices of beef and spoon vinaigrette over the top. Place a baguette slice on the side and serve.

6 SERVINGS

Caves Velha 1 9 8 5 Garrafeira (Portugal)

NEAPOLITAN FLANK STEAK

1/2   POUND FRESH SPINACH, WASHED
       AND TRIMMED
1/2   CUP ITALIAN BREADCRUMBS
1/2   CUP FRESHLY GRATED PARMESAN
       CHEESE
1/4   CUP OLIVE OIL
2   CLOVES GARLIC
1 1/2   POUNDS FLANK STEAK, BUTTERFLIED
       SALT, TO TASTE
       FRESHLY GROUND BLACK PEPPER
3   RED BELL PEPPERS, ROASTED AND
       HALVED (PAGE 177)
       CHERRY PEPPERS OR HOT RED
       PEPPERS, MINCED
       spinach leaves, for garnish

Place spinach in a saucepan with just the water that clings to the leaves. Cover and cook over medium heat until wilted, about 5 minutes. Transfer to a colander and press out excess moisture with the back of a spoon. Combine spinach, breadcrumbs, cheese, olive oil and garlic in a food processor and purée until thick and smooth. Open the butterflied steak on a flat surface and season with salt and pepper. Spread spinach purée over steak, then layer roasted red peppers on top. Sprinkle with cherry peppers or hot red peppers. Roll up steak from the shorter end and tie with heavy string. Brush with olive oil, season with salt and pepper and place in a shallow baking pan. Bake 40 minutes in a preheated 350 degree oven for medium rare.

Cool steak slightly before slicing. Serve on a bed of spinach leaves.

4 TO 6 SERVINGS

Altesino 1 9 8 8 Palazzo Altesi (Tuscany)

SPLENDID BEEF TENDERLOIN

3 TO 3 1/2   POUNDS BEEF TENDERLOIN,
       TRIMMED
1/2   CUP CHOPPED ONION
1 1/2   TABLESPOONS BUTTER
1   CUP DRY SHERRY
3   TABLESPOONS SOY SAUCE
2   TEASPOONS DRY MUSTARD
1/8   TEASPOON SALT
1/8   TEASPOON FRESHLY GROUND BLACK
       PEPPER

Place tenderloin in large shallow baking pan and bake uncovered in a preheated 400 degree oven for 15 minutes. Sauté onion in butter until tender. Add sherry, soy sauce, mustard, salt and pepper, and bring to a boil. Pour over tenderloin. Reduce oven temperature to 325 degrees and bake 45 minutes, or until meat thermometer registers 140 degrees for rare to 160 degrees for medium. Baste often with drippings. Slice tenderloin and serve with remaining sauce.

Serve with Polenta Pizza (page 47) or Layered Summer Vegetables (page 171).

6 TO 8 SERVINGS

Sorrel Hermitage 1 9 8 9 (Northern Rhône)

MUSHROOM STUFFED BEEF TENDERLOIN

Begin 8 hours to 1 day before serving.

1	POUND SLICED FRESH MUSHROOMS
1	CUP CHOPPED GREEN ONIONS
4	TABLESPOONS BUTTER
1/4	CUP CHOPPED FRESH PARSLEY
5 1/2	POUNDS BEEF TENDERLOIN, TRIMMED
1/2	TEASPOON SEASONED SALT
1/4	TEASPOON LEMON PEPPER
4	OUNCES CRUMBLED BLUE CHEESE
1	CUP RED-WINE VINEGAR AND OIL DRESSING
1/4 TO 1/2	CUP CRUSHED BLACK PEPPERCORNS

fresh mushrooms and watercress, for garnish

In a large skillet, sauté sliced mushrooms and green onions in butter until tender. Drain. Stir in parsley and set aside to cool. Cut tenderloin in half lengthwise to within 1/4 inch of the other edge, leaving one long side connected. Sprinkle the inside with seasoned salt and lemon pepper. Spoon mushroom mixture into opening of tenderloin and sprinkle with blue cheese. Fold top half over stuffing and tie with heavy string at 2-inch intervals. Place in a large, shallow dish and pour dressing over tenderloin. Cover and refrigerate 8 hours or overnight, basting occasionally.

Remove tenderloin from marinade and press crushed peppercorns onto each side. Grill over medium-hot coals, covered or tented with foil, for 35 minutes, or until meat thermometer registers 140 degrees for rare to 160 degrees for medium. Garnish with whole mushrooms and watercress. The tenderloin may also be baked in a preheated 350 degree oven for 40 minutes, or until meat thermometer registers desired temperature.

Asparagus in Lemon Vinaigrette (page 172) provides a simple accompaniment to this elegant dish.

8 TO 10 SERVINGS

Verset 1 9 8 7 Cornas (Northern Rhône)

PESTO MEAT LOAF WITH FRESH TOMATO SAUCE

MEAT LOAF

1/3	CUP PINE NUTS
1	POUND LEAN GROUND BEEF
1	POUND LEAN GROUND PORK
1	CUP FINE BREADCRUMBS
1	EGG, LIGHTLY BEATEN
1/2	CUP FRESHLY GRATED PARMESAN CHEESE
2	TABLESPOONS OLIVE OIL
2	TABLESPOONS FINELY CHOPPED GARLIC
1/2	CUP FINELY CHOPPED FRESH BASIL
1/4	CUP FINELY CHOPPED FRESH PARSLEY
	SALT, TO TASTE
	FRESHLY GROUND BLACK PEPPER, TO TASTE

Brown pine nuts quickly in a dry skillet and cool. In a large mixing bowl, combine ground beef, ground pork, breadcrumbs, egg and Parmesan cheese. Add the olive oil, garlic, basil, parsley, pine nuts, salt and pepper and mix thoroughly. Shape into an oval loaf and bake on a broiler pan or rack of a shallow roasting pan in a preheated 350 degree oven for 1 1/2 to 2 hours until done.

FRESH TOMATO SAUCE

1/2	CUP FINELY CHOPPED ONION
1	TEASPOON FINELY MINCED GARLIC
2	TABLESPOONS OLIVE OIL
2	CUPS FRESH TOMATOES, PEELED AND CHOPPED
1	TABLESPOON MELTED BUTTER
1/4	CUP CHOPPED FRESH BASIL
1	TABLESPOON CHOPPED FRESH THYME OR 1/2 TEASPOON DRIED
	SALT, TO TASTE
	FRESHLY GROUND BLACK PEPPER, TO TASTE

In a heavy saucepan, sauté onion and garlic in olive oil until soft. Just before serving, add tomatoes, butter, basil, thyme, salt and pepper and heat. Slice meat loaf and spoon tomato sauce over each serving.

8 SERVINGS

Sausal Zinfandel 1 9 8 8 (Alexander Valley)

HIBACHI BEEF

Begin 4 to 5 days before serving.

1   ROUND STEAK, 2 1/2 INCHES THICK,
    WITH BONE
1 1/4   CUPS SOY SAUCE
ONE   2-INCH PIECE PEELED FRESH GINGER
8   LARGE CLOVES GARLIC, PEELED
1/2   CUP DRY SHERRY

In a blender, purée soy sauce, ginger, garlic and sherry. Place steak in a container that can be tightly sealed and pour on marinade. Cover well and refrigerate for 4 to 5 days, turning the meat each morning and evening. Remove steak from marinade and grill over hot coals, 12 minutes per side, for medium-rare. Let stand for 10 minutes, then slice across the grain.

Serve with Scalloped Potatoes Baked in Cream (page 173) and fresh steamed broccoli with lemon.

8 SERVINGS

Au Bon Climat Pinot Noir 1 9 8 9 (Santa Barbara)

TENDERLOIN WITH ROASTED SHALLOTS

1   WHOLE TENDERLOIN OF BEEF
    (3 TO 4 POUNDS), TRIMMED
2   TABLESPOONS MELTED UNSALTED
    BUTTER
2   TABLESPOONS SOY SAUCE
1   MEDIUM SHALLOT, FINELY CHOPPED

Prepare the roast by tucking the tail under the meat so that roast is of uniform thickness. Tie meat tightly with heavy string, lengthwise and crosswise, and place on a roasting rack in a preheated 400 degree oven. Roast for 45 to 50 minutes, or until a meat thermometer registers 140 degrees for rare or 160 degrees for medium. Check temperature after 25 minutes. Remove beef and let stand for 10 minutes.

ROASTED SHALLOTS

18   LARGE SHALLOTS, PEELED, WITH TIPS
    OF ROOT END REMOVED
1   TABLESPOON BUTTER
1/2   CUP HEAVY CREAM
2   TABLESPOONS MADEIRA WINE
1 1/2   TEASPOONS CHOPPED FRESH
    TARRAGON
1/4   TEASPOON SALT
    FINELY GROUND WHITE PEPPER,
    TO TASTE

Bring water to a boil in a medium saucepan; add shallots, boil 2 minutes and drain. Place shallots in a small baking dish and dot with butter. Roast in a preheated 400 degree oven for 10 minutes. In a small bowl, mix cream with Madeira, tarragon, salt and pepper and pour over shallots. Return shallots to oven and roast 30 to 35 minutes. Watch carefully to see that cream does not separate. Stir gently and reduce heat if necessary.

To serve, slice tenderloin diagonally and spoon 3 shallots with a little sauce onto each serving. Serve immediately.

Turnip Potato Gratinée (page 167) provides an interesting accompaniment to the roast.

4 SERVINGS

Canalicchio di Sopra 1 9 8 6 Brunello di Montelcino (Tuscany)

CURRY GRILLED FLANK STEAK

Begin 3 hours to 1 day before serving

2	FLANK STEAKS, ABOUT 1 1/4 POUNDS EACH
3	TABLESPOONS LIGHT BROWN SUGAR
1	TABLESPOON CURRY POWDER
3	TABLESPOONS WORCESTERSHIRE SAUCE
2	TABLESPOONS SHERRY
2	TABLESPOONS OLIVE OIL
4	TABLESPOONS MINCED FRESH CORIANDER
1	TABLESPOON MINCED GARLIC
2	TEASPOONS MINCED FRESH GINGER
4	GREEN ONIONS, THINLY SLICED
1/4	TEASPOON FRESHLY GROUND BLACK PEPPER

Score flank steaks at regular intervals with a sharp knife, making slits 1/8-inch deep on both sides of the meat. In a small bowl, combine sugar, curry powder, Worcestershire sauce, sherry, olive oil, coriander, garlic, ginger, onions and pepper. Place steaks in a shallow glass dish and marinate 3 hours or overnight in the refrigerator.

Return steaks to room temperature before grilling. Remove from marinade and grill over hot coals, 3 minutes per side for rare, 5 minutes per side for medium. Halfway through grilling time for each side, rotate the meat 90 degrees, to form a grill pattern. To serve, carve across grain of meat into thin slices.

Serve with Curried Tomatoes (page 176) and grilled potatoes.

4 TO 6 SERVINGS

Shafer Merlot 1 9 9 0 (Napa)

SIRLOIN STUFFED BUTTERNUT SQUASH

3	MEDIUM BUTTERNUT SQUASH, CUT LENGTHWISE, WITH SEEDS REMOVED
6	TABLESPOONS BUTTER, DIVIDED
1/2	CUP HONEY, DIVIDED
4	CUPS CUBED BEEF SIRLOIN (ABOUT 2 POUNDS), TRIMMED
2	MEDIUM ONIONS, THINLY SLICED
1/4	CUP WATER
1/2	CUP APPLE CIDER VINEGAR
1/3	CUP KETCHUP
1/2	CUP DARK RAISINS
1 1/2	TEASPOONS SALT
1/4	TEASPOON FRESHLY GROUND BLACK PEPPER

In a small saucepan, melt 4 tablespoons butter and mix with 1/4 cup honey. Pour into two or three casserole dishes and place squash, cut side down, in butter and honey. Cover and bake in a preheated 325 degree oven for 1 hour.

Brown meat in 2 tablespoons butter, reduce heat to low and add onions and water. Combine 1/4 cup honey, vinegar, ketchup, raisins, salt and pepper and pour over meat mixture. Cover and cook over low heat, adding more water if necessary, until squash is done. Remove squash from oven, fill the centers with meat and serve.

6 SERVINGS

La Rioja Alta Rioja 1 9 8 7 (Rioja)

STEAKS WITH GREEN PEPPERCORNS AND COGNAC

4   BONELESS BEEF STRIP STEAKS, ABOUT
      8 OUNCES EACH
8   TEASPOONS GREEN PEPPERCORNS
4   CLOVES GARLIC
1   TABLESPOON OLIVE OIL
1   TABLESPOON BUTTER
      SALT, TO TASTE
2   TABLESPOONS COGNAC, WARMED

Using a mortar and pestle, mash the peppercorns and garlic into a thick paste. Spread the mixture on both sides of the steaks and let stand for 1 to 2 hours. Heat the oil and butter in a heavy sauté pan large enough to cook the steaks without crowding. Sprinkle the steaks with salt and sear over medium-high heat. Cook 1 to 2 minutes per side for rare, or 3 to 4 minutes per side for medium-rare. Remove steaks from pan and keep warm.

Pour the cognac into the juices in the pan and ignite, shaking pan until flames subside. Stir sauce with a wire whisk until blended, scraping up browned bits from the bottom of the pan. Pour sauce over steaks and serve immediately.

4 SERVINGS

Château Haut Marbuzet 1 9 8 9 St. Estèphe (Bordeaux)

TENDERLOIN FILLETS WITH TARRAGON MUSTARD SAUCE

4   BEEF TENDERLOIN FILLETS, ABOUT 8
      OUNCES EACH
3   TABLESPOONS BUTTER, SOFTENED
2   TABLESPOONS DIJON-STYLE
      MUSTARD
1   CUP DRY WHITE WINE
1/4 CUP MINCED SHALLOTS
2   TABLESPOONS CHOPPED FRESH
      TARRAGON
2   TABLESPOONS HEAVY CREAM
4   TABLESPOONS CORNICHONS,
      CHOPPED

Grill fillets over hot coals, about 6 minutes per side for medium-rare. Cover the grill during the last 4 minutes of cooking time on the second side. Meanwhile, blend butter and mustard until smooth and set aside. Combine wine, shallots and tarragon in a small saucepan and cook over medium-high heat until wine is reduced to 4 tablespoons. Reduce heat to low and stir in cream and cornichons. Cook until sauce is slightly thickened, about 3 minutes. Do not boil. Gradually whisk in mustard butter, spoon sauce sparingly over fillets and serve.

4 SERVINGS

Konocti Cabernet Franc 1 9 8 9 (Mendocino)

POULTRY

WINE WITH POULTRY

Chicken is an extremely flexible entrée staple. Sautéed with butter and vegetables, its light, moist flavors are great with a bright, tart Chardonnay. Grilled and simply presented with grilled vegetables, it is delicious with red wines ranging from French Pinot Noir to American Merlot. Nevertheless, at its heaviest, chicken is only a medium-weight dish, so a medium-weight red wine such as Merlot is as big a wine as it can handle. Chicken can be quite oily and is often cooked with pungent herbs and vegetables, such as rosemary, thyme, garlic and onion. A pungent red wine is allowable, but the dusty, almost bitter tannins of most Cabernet Sauvignon or Bordeaux are appropriate only to the big flavors and fat of red meat. However, the fruit and lighter body of Pinot Noir is well matched to almost all chicken dishes.

Turkey and turkey dinners are usually all sweetness—yams, cranberries, dressings—and combine well with slightly sweet German wines. Take care, however, to avoid the insipid, sweet wines, and choose instead a rich, crisp Spätlese from a great producer (J.J. Prum, Zilliken, Pfeffingen, or any producer affiliated with the VDP or Charta groups).

Duck and other game fowl require richer and richer wine. If white wine is desired, choose the richest available that have great acidity as well. Loire wines such as Coulée de Serrant, Savennières and Vouvray Demi-Sec are all brilliant examples of richness, veritable sweetness and dryness, all from the same bottle. But, as with pork, almost any great German Spätlese will do, especially if young. Most duck is so fatty, however, that red wine is much safer. Pinot Noir again has the right lightness of body, almost as airborne as the duck, and in excellent vintages has big, ripe, delicious fruits, no harsh tannins and a citric acidity that cuts the fat of the duck.

Pheasant generally has more earthiness to it, although it resembles chicken in the rest of its flavors. Pinot Noir or fruity Italian medium-bodied reds like Dolcetto d'Alba or Barbera d'Asti match up well. A lighter Cabernet Franc, such as French Chinon or Merlot can work, but Pinot Noir is the safest.

Quail is also oily, giving it a certain affinity to Merlot, but the meat underneath works most often with Pinot Noir or the aforementioned fruity, medium-bodied Italian red wines.

Because chicken goes with everything, it is generally combined with everything. As a go-with-everything meat, it often seems somewhat neutral; consider the sauce with chicken dishes and remember that most tomato-based dishes need wines with a lot of fruit and acidity.

CHICKEN DELLA ROBBIA

ONE   5 1/2-POUND ROASTING CHICKEN,
         AT ROOM TEMPERATURE
2   TABLESPOONS OLIVE OIL

Preheat oven to 375 degrees. Remove giblets from chicken. Wash inside and out and pat dry. Rub outside of chicken with olive oil and tie legs together. Set aside while preparing dressing.

DRESSING

8 TO 10   RED PLUMS (3 OR 4 CUT IN QUARTERS)
1   BUNCH RED GRAPES (1/4 CUP HALVED)
1   TABLESPOON FRESH ROSEMARY OR 1/2 TEASPOON DRIED
1   TABLESPOON FRESH TARRAGON OR 1/2 TEASPOON DRIED
1   TABLESPOON FRESH BASIL OR 1/2 TEASPOON DRIED
1/3   TEASPOON CURRY POWDER
1/4   TEASPOON CINNAMON
1   MEDIUM ONION, CHOPPED
2   CLOVES GARLIC, CHOPPED
1/3   CUP PECAN HALVES
1/3   CUP SHREDDED CARROTS
1 1/2   CUPS DRIED BREADCRUMBS
2   CUPS COOKED WHITE RICE
3   OUNCES TOMATO PASTE
2   CUPS CHICKEN STOCK, PREFERABLY HOMEMADE, DIVIDED

fresh leaf lettuce and unshelled pecans, for garnish

In a large bowl, combine cut-up plums and grapes with rosemary, tarragon, basil, curry powder and cinnamon, mixing well. Blend in onion, garlic, pecans, carrots, breadcrumbs and rice. In a separate bowl, mix tomato paste with 1 cup chicken stock, and add to dressing. Pour in remaining stock, stirring just until mixture holds together. Fill chicken cavity with dressing. Place the chicken breast-side down in a baking dish and arrange remaining dressing around chicken. Roast uncovered until the back is brown, approximately 20 minutes. Turn breast side up, and continue to cook until done about 1 1/2 to 2 hours. To test for doneness, pierce thigh with a knife to see that juices run clear.

Remove chicken from baking dish and place on a carving tray. Let stand for 10 minutes and remove string. Garland with fresh lettuce, remaining plums, small grape clusters, and unshelled pecans.

4 TO 6 SERVINGS

*Robert Arnoux 1 9 8 8 Bourgogne Rouge
(Red Burgundy)*

ZESTY LEMON CHICKEN
WITH MINT CHIFFONADE

6 LARGE CHICKEN BREAST HALVES,
   BONED AND SKINNED
2 TABLESPOONS BUTTER
2 TABLESPOONS VEGETABLE OIL
   SALT, TO TASTE
3/4 CUP DRY WHITE WINE

Sauté chicken on both sides in butter and oil over low heat until slightly firm. Place in a single layer in a 9- by 13-inch baking dish, sprinkle with salt and add wine. Cover the dish with foil and bake in a preheated 300 degree oven for about 20 minutes, or until done. Remove and let cool in baking dish. Pour off cooking juices and reserve. Set chicken aside.

MINT CHIFFONADE SAUCE

3 TABLESPOONS BUTTER
3 TABLESPOONS ALL-PURPOSE FLOUR
2 CUPS HALF-AND-HALF
   SALT, TO TASTE
   COARSELY GROUND WHITE PEPPER,
   TO TASTE
   ZEST OF 1 LARGE LEMON
2 TABLESPOONS FRESHLY SQUEEZED
   LEMON JUICE
1/2 CUP LOOSELY PACKED FRESH MINT
   OR LEMON MINT LEAVES, SHREDDED
lemon zest or lemon slices and sprigs of fresh mint,
for garnish

In a large skillet, melt butter and add flour, whisking until smooth, about 3 minutes. Add cream and reserved cooking juices. Cook, stirring often, until the sauce thickens and comes to a boil. Season to taste with salt and white pepper. Add lemon zest and lemon juice and return to a boil. The sauce should coat a spoon lightly. If sauce is too thick, thin it with additional cream or chicken broth.

When ready to serve, reheat the sauce over low heat; do not boil. Just before serving, add the chicken breasts to the sauce, cover, and warm until chicken is heated through. Add the chiffonade of mint to the warm sauce just before serving.

To serve, place one breast on each plate, top with a spoonful of sauce and garnish with mint sprigs, lemon zest or lemon slices.

6 SERVINGS

Mitchelton Marsanne 1 9 8 8 Reserve
(Victoria - Australia)

GRILLED CHICKEN, SZECHUAN-STYLE

Begin 1 day before serving.

8   CHICKEN BREAST HALVES, BONED AND SKINNED

MARINADE

1/3   CUP SESAME OIL
1/2   CUP SOY SAUCE
1/2   CUP APPLE JUICE
4   LARGE CLOVES GARLIC, MINCED
1   TABLESPOON GRATED FRESH GINGER
1   TEASPOON COARSELY GROUND FRESH BLACK PEPPER

Combine sesame oil, soy sauce and apple juice. Add garlic, ginger and pepper. Place chicken breasts in a container and pour on marinade. Seal tightly and refrigerate overnight. When ready to serve, remove breasts from marinade and grill over hot coals, about 5 minutes per side.

SZECHUAN PEANUT SAUCE

1   CUP SMOOTH PEANUT BUTTER
1/2   CUP SOY SAUCE
2/3   CUP CHICKEN STOCK, PREFERABLY HOMEMADE
1/2   CUP SESAME OIL
4   LARGE CLOVES GARLIC, CRUSHED
4   TEASPOONS SUGAR
2   TEASPOONS CHINESE HOT PEPPER OIL, MORE IF DESIRED, TO TASTE
4   TEASPOONS GRATED FRESH GINGER
4   TEASPOONS RED-WINE VINEGAR
1/2   CUP HALF-AND-HALF, MORE IF DESIRED
24 TO 32   OUNCES CHINESE NOODLES, COOKED AL DENTE AND DRAINED
1 large red bell pepper, cut into julienne, for garnish
fresh chives, cut in 3-inch strips, for garnish

In a heavy saucepan, melt peanut butter with soy sauce, chicken stock and sesame oil. Add garlic, sugar, hot pepper oil, ginger and vinegar. Stir in cream. If sauce stands for any length of time, add more cream and whisk to thin.

Toss a small amount of the sauce with cooked Chinese noodles. Slice grilled chicken breasts and arrange over noodles. Drizzle Szechuan Peanut Sauce over chicken and garnish with red pepper julienne, crossed with pieces of chive. Serve with colorful stir-fried vegetables.

8 SERVINGS

Josmeyer Riesling 1 9 8 9 (Alsace)

CHICKEN PROVENÇAL

PROVENÇAL SAUCE

3/4	CUP FRESH TOMATOES, SEEDED AND CHOPPED
4	TABLESPOONS FINELY CHOPPED FRESH BASIL
2	TABLESPOONS FINELY CHOPPED FRESH PARSLEY
1	SMALL CLOVE GARLIC, MINCED
1/4	CUP FINELY CHOPPED SHALLOTS
1/4	CUP FINELY CHOPPED PINE NUTS
2	TABLESPOONS WHITE WINE
1	TABLESPOON TARRAGON VINEGAR
1/4	TEASPOON SALT
1/8	TEASPOON FRESHLY GROUND BLACK PEPPER

Mix tomatoes, basil, parsley, garlic, shallots and pine nuts. Add wine and vinegar, salt and pepper. Let stand at room temperature for 30 minutes before serving. The sauce may be refrigerated for several hours.

CHICKEN

2/3	CUP ALL-PURPOSE FLOUR
2	TEASPOONS SALT
2 1/2	TEASPOONS FRESHLY GROUND BLACK PEPPER, DIVIDED
8	CHICKEN THIGHS
8	CHICKEN BREAST HALVES
3	TABLESPOONS OLIVE OIL, DIVIDED
6	SHALLOTS, THINLY SLICED
3	CLOVES GARLIC, CRUSHED
4	RED BELL PEPPERS, CUT INTO 1/4-INCH STRIPS
4	YELLOW BELL PEPPERS, CUT INTO 1/4-INCH STRIPS
2	POUNDS SMALL GREEN AND YELLOW ZUCCHINI, QUARTERED LENGTHWISE AND SLICED INTO 1/3-INCH PIECES
3/4	CUP PESTO, PREFERABLY HOMEMADE
1 1/2	CUPS CRÈME FRAÎCHE (PAGE 198)
1	CUP FRESHLY GRATED PARMESAN CHEESE (ABOUT 4 OUNCES)
1 1/2	CUPS FRESH BREADCRUMBS
1	TEASPOON DRIED THYME
1	TEASPOON DRIED OREGANO
1/4	TEASPOON CAYENNE PEPPER

Combine flour, salt, and 2 teaspoons of the black pepper. Dredge chicken pieces in the flour mixture and shake off excess. Set on rack until ready to cook. In a large ovenproof casserole, heat 2 tablespoons of the olive oil over medium-high heat. Add chicken in batches and cook, turning often, until evenly browned, about 15 minutes. Drain on paper towels. Wipe the excess oil from the casserole.

Heat remaining oil in a skillet over medium-high heat. Add shallots and sauté until translucent, 2 to 3 minutes. Add garlic and cook for 1 minute more, then add red and yellow bell peppers and zucchini and cook until tender, stirring frequently, about 5 to 7 minutes. Remove from heat.

In a small bowl, combine pesto and crème fraîche and whisk until blended. In another bowl, toss Parmesan cheese with breadcrumbs, thyme, oregano, cayenne and the remaining 1/2 teaspoon black pepper. Return chicken to the large casserole and spread the vegetable mixture evenly on top. Spread pesto cream over the vegetables. The recipe can be prepared to this point up to 2 days ahead and refrigerated. Return to room temperature before continuing.

Sprinkle the Parmesan mixture evenly over the casserole and bake in the middle of a preheated 375 degree oven for 45 minutes. Heat under the broiler for 2 to 3 minutes to brown. Serve hot, directly from the casserole. Pass the Provençal Sauce in a separate bowl.

8 SERVINGS

Cloudy Bay Sauvignon Blanc 1 9 9 0 (New Zealand)

RED-WINE CHICKEN
WITH GREEN PEPPERCORNS

2   LARGE FRYING CHICKENS (ABOUT
    6 POUNDS IN ALL), EACH CUT INTO
    8 SERVING PIECES
2   TEASPOONS SALT
    FRESHLY GROUND BLACK PEPPER,
    TO TASTE
3   TABLESPOONS UNSALTED BUTTER
3   TABLESPOONS VEGETABLE OIL

Season chicken pieces with salt and pepper. In a large, heavy skillet, melt butter in oil over medium-high heat. Place half of the chicken pieces skin side down in skillet and cook for about 5 minutes, until browned. Turn and brown the other side, about 10 minutes longer. Repeat until all chicken has been browned. Set chicken aside and pour off oil from skillet.

RED-WINE SAUCE

12   LARGE SHALLOTS, PEELED
 3   LARGE CLOVES GARLIC, PEELED
1/2   TABLESPOON CHOPPED FRESH
      OREGANO
1/2   TABLESPOON CHOPPED FRESH
      THYME
 2   CUPS DRY RED WINE
1/4   CUP RED-WINE VINEGAR
 1   BAY LEAF
 3   LARGE TOMATOES, PEELED, SEEDED
      AND COARSELY CHOPPED
1/4   CUP OIL-PACKED SUN-DRIED
      TOMATOES, DRAINED AND
      CHOPPED
 1   CUP BEEF BROTH, PREFERABLY
      HOMEMADE
 1   CUP CHICKEN STOCK, PREFERABLY
      HOMEMADE
1 1/2 TABLESPOONS TOMATO PASTE
 1   TEASPOON SUGAR
1 TO 2 TABLESPOONS GREEN PEPPERCORNS,
      DRAINED
 4   TABLESPOONS UNSALTED BUTTER,
      CUT INTO PIECES

With food processor running, drop in shallots, garlic, oregano and thyme and process until finely minced, stopping once to scrape the bowl. Over medium heat, deglaze the skillet with wine and vinegar, stirring with a wooden spoon to loosen particles. Stir in shallot mixture and bay leaf. Simmer, uncovered, until liquid is reduced to 2/3 cup.

Add tomatoes, sun-dried tomatoes, beef broth, chicken stock, tomato paste and sugar to the skillet, mixing well. Add dark meat chicken pieces and simmer, uncovered, for 20 minutes. Add white meat and cook 10 to 15 minutes longer. Remove chicken to a warmed serving platter.

Strain the liquid into a small saucepan and boil until reduced to 1 1/2 cups. Stir in green peppercorns, then add butter piece by piece, stirring constantly. Adjust seasonings, pour sauce over the chicken and serve immediately.

6 TO 8 SERVINGS

Babich Sauvignon Blanc 1 9 8 9 (New Zealand)

TUSCAN CHICKEN

Begin 1 day before serving.

TUSCAN BEANS

2 CUPS TUSCAN BEANS (CANNELLINI OR GREAT NORTHERN), SOAKED OVERNIGHT IN COLD WATER, RINSED AND DRAINED
3 OUNCES COARSELY CHOPPED PANCETTA OR PROSCIUTTO
4 TABLESPOONS OLIVE OIL
3 CLOVES GARLIC, PEELED
3 TABLESPOONS FRESH ROSEMARY LEAVES
SALT, TO TASTE
FRESHLY GROUND BLACK PEPPER, TO TASTE

Place beans, pancetta and olive oil in a deep casserole and cover with cold water by 1 inch. Add garlic, rosemary, salt and pepper. Cover and bake 1 1/2 hours in a preheated 375 degree oven.

STUFFING

4 CHICKEN THIGHS, BONED AND ROUGHLY CHOPPED
2 EGGS
3/4 POUND ITALIAN SAUSAGE, PARTIALLY GRILLED
3/4 CUP RICOTTA CHEESE
1/2 CUP CHOPPED FRESH ITALIAN PARSLEY
1/4 CUP TOASTED PINE NUTS
SALT, TO TASTE
FRESHLY GROUND BLACK PEPPER, TO TASTE

In a food processor, blend chopped chicken and eggs. Add sausage and cheese, pulsing until lightly blended. Remove to a bowl and fold in parsley, pine nuts, salt and pepper. Chill for 30 minutes.

CABBAGE

4 TABLESPOONS OLIVE OIL
3 TABLESPOONS COARSELY CHOPPED GARLIC
8 WILD MUSHROOMS (SHIITAKE, OYSTER OR PORCINI), CUT INTO QUARTERS
1/4 CUP CHOPPED PANCETTA OR PROSCIUTTO
1 CUP COARSELY CHOPPED SAVOY CABBAGE
3 CUPS TUSCAN BEANS, FROM ABOVE
2 CUPS CHICKEN STOCK, PREFERABLY HOMEMADE
Italian parsley, for garnish

Heat oil in a sauté pan and sauté garlic for 1 to 2 minutes. Stir in mushrooms, pancetta and cabbage. Then add cooked bean mixture and toss. Pour in chicken stock and bring to a light simmer. Do not boil.

CHICKEN

SIX 7-OUNCE CHICKEN BREASTS, BONED, WITH SKIN INTACT
OLIVE OIL

Pound chicken breasts lightly, then brush with olive oil. Place about 2 ounces of the stuffing in the center of each breast. Roll the breast around stuffing and secure with cotton kitchen twine. Chill. Grill chicken rolls over hot coals for about 20 to 30 minutes, turning to brown evenly. Remove, slice and keep warm.

Divide the cabbage mixture among six soup plates or bowls. Top the cabbage with the sliced chicken and garnish with Italian parsley leaves.

6 SERVINGS

Au Bon Climat Chardonnay Reserve 1 9 9 0 (Santa Barbara)

CHICKEN BREASTS
WITH YOGURT-TOMATO SAUCE

4	CHICKEN BREAST HALVES
1	TEASPOON MINCED FRESH THYME OR 1/4 TEASPOON DRIED
1/4	TEASPOON SALT FRESHLY GROUND BLACK PEPPER, TO TASTE
4	TEASPOONS OLIVE OIL, DIVIDED
1	TEASPOON UNSALTED BUTTER
1	MEDIUM ONION, FINELY CHOPPED
1	POUND SPINACH, WASHED, STEMMED AND COARSELY CHOPPED
1/2	CUP RICOTTA CHEESE
1/2	CUP FRESHLY GRATED PARMESAN CHEESE
1	TEASPOON MINCED FRESH BASIL OR 1/2 TEASPOON DRIED FRESHLY GROUND BLACK PEPPER, TO TASTE

YOGURT-TOMATO SAUCE

1	CUP PLAIN YOGURT
1	TABLESPOON TARRAGON VINEGAR
1/4	TEASPOON SALT
1	LARGE RIPE TOMATO, PEELED, SEEDED AND CHOPPED
4	LARGE BASIL LEAVES, THINLY SLICED FRESHLY GROUND BLACK PEPPER, TO TASTE

Combine yogurt, vinegar, salt, tomato, basil leaves and pepper. Let stand at room temperature. Serve spooned over chicken breasts.

4 SERVINGS

Groth Sauvignon Blanc 1 9 9 1 (Napa)

Preheat oven to 375 degrees. Prepare chicken breasts by rubbing thyme, salt and pepper into the skin. Drizzle 1/4 teaspoon olive oil over the skin of each breast. In a large heavy skillet over medium heat, melt 3 teaspoons olive oil and the butter. Add chicken breasts and brown, about 5 minutes per side; transfer to a dish.

In the same skillet, sauté onion slowly, until translucent and soft. Add spinach to the pan and cook until it is wilted and the moisture has evaporated, about 6 minutes longer. Remove from heat and stir in ricotta cheese, Parmesan cheese, basil and pepper. Spread the spinach mixture in the bottom of a 10- to 12-inch shallow, oiled roasting pan and place chicken breasts on top. Bake for 40 minutes or until golden brown.

CHICKEN
IN THREE-PEPPER SAUCE

Begin 8 hours to 1 day before serving.

8   CHICKEN BREAST HALVES, BONED AND SKINNED

MARINADE

1/2 CUP OLIVE OIL
1/4 CUP MINCED FRESH BASIL
3   TABLESPOONS FRESHLY SQUEEZED LEMON JUICE
1   TABLESPOON DRIED RED PEPPER FLAKES
2   TEASPOONS MINCED GARLIC

In a shallow dish, combine olive oil, basil, lemon juice, red pepper flakes and garlic. Add chicken and turn to coat. Cover and refrigerate 8 hours or overnight.

Remove chicken from marinade and broil or grill, cooking until tender, approximately 5 minutes per side. Cut chicken into 1/2-inch strips. Cover and keep warm.

THREE-PEPPER SAUCE

3   TABLESPOONS UNSALTED BUTTER
1   MEDIUM RED BELL PEPPER, CUT INTO JULIENNE
1   MEDIUM YELLOW BELL PEPPER, CUT INTO JULIENNE
1   MEDIUM GREEN BELL PEPPER, CUT INTO JULIENNE
1/2 CUP DRY WHITE WINE
1/2 CUP CHICKEN BROTH, PREFERABLY HOMEMADE
2   CUPS HEAVY CREAM
1   CUP SLICED MUSHROOMS
2   TABLESPOONS UNSALTED BUTTER
1/2 TEASPOON SALT
3/4 CUP FRESHLY GRATED PARMESAN CHEESE
1/4 CUP MINCED FRESH BASIL
12 OUNCES SPINACH FETTUCINE, COOKED AL DENTE AND DRAINED

In a large skillet, melt 3 tablespoons butter and sauté red, yellow and green peppers over medium heat for 2 minutes. Remove peppers and set aside. Stir in wine and chicken broth. Increase heat to high and boil until sauce is reduced to 2 tablespoons, about 5 minutes. Add cream and cook until sauce is reduced by half, about 4 minutes.

In another skillet, sauté mushrooms in butter over medium-high heat until lightly browned. Add cream sauce, sautéed peppers and salt. At this point the pepper sauce can be refrigerated for up to 24 hours.

Reheat pepper sauce and stir in Parmesan cheese and basil. On a warm serving platter, arrange chicken on top of hot fettucine and pour sauce over all.

6 TO 8 SERVINGS

Jordan Chardonnay 1 9 8 8 (Sonoma)

HERBED CHICKEN SCALLOPS
WITH ROASTED RED PEPPER SAUCE

Begin 6 hours to 1 day before serving.

4 TO 6   CHICKEN BREAST HALVES, BONED, SKINNED AND POUNDED TO FLATTEN

MARINADE

1 1/2   TABLESPOONS CHOPPED FRESH BASIL
1 1/2   TABLESPOONS CHOPPED FRESH OREGANO
1 1/2   TABLESPOONS CHOPPED FRESH ROSEMARY
1 1/2   TABLESPOONS CHOPPED FRESH THYME
1/3   CUP OLIVE OIL
ZEST OF 1 LEMON
FRESHLY SQUEEZED JUICE OF 1 LEMON
1/8   TEASPOON ALLSPICE
1/8   TEASPOON CAYENNE PEPPER

In a medium bowl, combine basil, oregano, rosemary and thyme. Add olive oil, lemon zest and juice, allspice and cayenne and mix well. Add chicken breasts, cover and marinate in the refrigerator 6 hours or overnight.

ROASTED RED PEPPER SAUCE

2   TABLESPOONS OLIVE OIL
6   SHALLOTS, THINLY SLICED
A PINCH OF DRIED RED PEPPER FLAKES
1   CUP WHITE WINE
1   CUP DRY VERMOUTH
2   CUPS CHICKEN STOCK, PREFERABLY HOMEMADE
1   CUP HEAVY CREAM
2   LARGE ROASTED RED BELL PEPPERS (PAGE 177), CUT INTO JULIENNE
1/2   TABLESPOON DIJON-STYLE MUSTARD
1   CUP KALAMATA OLIVES, PITTED AND SLICED
1 1/2   TABLESPOONS CAPERS, DRAINED
4   TABLESPOONS CHOPPED FRESH BASIL
sprigs of fresh basil or oregano, for garnish

Heat oil in a large heavy skillet. Sauté shallots until soft, about 10 minutes. Stir in red pepper flakes and cook 1 or 2 minutes longer. Increase heat to high and add wine and vermouth. Reduce sauce by half, to about 1 cup, and add the chicken stock. Reduce by half to about 1 1/2 cups, then add cream, reducing by half again. There should be about 1 1/4 cups sauce.

While the liquids are cooking, prepare the roasted peppers. After the liquids have been reduced, add mustard to the sauce. Cook a minute or two, then add roasted peppers, olives and capers, cooking just to blend flavors. Add basil and remove from heat. The sauce may be prepared several hours in advance and reheated. If sauce is made ahead, reserve fresh basil and add after the sauce has been reheated. If sauce is too thick, add a few tablespoons of wine or stock when reheating.

Just before serving, remove chicken breasts from marinade and grill over hot coals, about 5 minutes per side. Try to avoid flare-ups by banking the coals to either side of the cooking area of the grill. Reheat the sauce.

Serve chicken topped with Roasted Red Pepper Sauce and garnished with a sprig of fresh basil or oregano.

4 TO 6 SERVINGS

Talosa 1 9 8 6 Vino Nobile di Montepulciano Riserva (Tuscany)

GRILLED HERB GARDEN CHICKEN

Begin 2 to 4 hours before serving.

8   LARGE CHICKEN BREAST HALVES,
      BONED AND SKINNED

MARINADE

1/2   CUP FRESHLY SQUEEZED LEMON
      JUICE
1   TABLESPOON CHOPPED LEMON
      ZEST
1/4   CUP DIJON-STYLE MUSTARD
1   TABLESPOON CHOPPED FRESH
      ROSEMARY
1   TABLESPOON CHOPPED FRESH
      THYME
1   TABLESPOON CHOPPED FRESH BASIL
1   TABLESPOON CHOPPED FRESH
      OREGANO
3/4   TEASPOON SALT
1/4   TEASPOON COARSELY GROUND
      BLACK PEPPER

lemon slices and whole fresh herb leaves, for garnish
Basil Tsatziki, as an accompaniment

In a small bowl, combine lemon juice, lemon zest and mustard. Add rosemary, thyme, basil, oregano, salt and pepper. Blend well.

Arrange chicken breasts in a large glass baking dish and pour on marinade. Cover and refrigerate 2 to 4 hours or overnight. Remove chicken from marinade and grill over medium-hot coals about 3 inches from flame, 6 to 8 minutes per side.

Place chicken on individual plates or on a platter and top with Basil Tsatziki. Garnish with lemon slices and fresh herb leaves.

Served chilled, this chicken makes elegant picnic fare. Serve with Vegetable Strata (page 170).

8 SERVINGS

Arrowood Chardonnay 1 9 9 0 (Sonoma)

Begin at least 2 hours before serving.

BASIL TSATZIKI

1/2   CLOVE GARLIC
1/4   CUP PINE NUTS
1   TABLESPOON TARRAGON VINEGAR
1   TEASPOON DIJON-STYLE MUSTARD
2   TABLESPOONS CHOPPED FRESH
      BASIL
1/2   CUP SOUR CREAM
1/2   CUP PLAIN YOGURT
      SALT, TO TASTE
1/2   TEASPOON LEMON ZEST

Chop garlic and pine nuts in a food processor. Add vinegar, mustard and basil and process until blended. Add the sour cream and blend. Remove to a small bowl and mix in yogurt, salt and lemon zest. Refrigerate for 2 hours or more and serve with Herb Garden Chicken.

MAKES 1 1/4 CUPS.

POULET
EN PERSILLADE

4 HALF-BROILERS OR 6 WHOLE
    CHICKEN BREASTS
4 TABLESPOONS DIJON-STYLE
    MUSTARD
1 TABLESPOON CHOPPED FRESH
    TARRAGON OR 1 TEASPOON DRIED
4 CLOVES GARLIC
3/4 CUP FRESH ITALIAN PARSLEY SPRIGS,
    LOOSELY PACKED
1/2 CUP FRESH BASIL, LOOSELY PACKED
1 CUP CHICKEN BROTH, PREFERABLY
    HOMEMADE
4 TABLESPOONS RED-WINE VINEGAR
1/2 CUP HEAVY CREAM
1/2 TEASPOON CORNSTARCH
    fresh basil leaves, for garnish

Coat the chicken with mustard and tarragon and place in a baking dish large enough to hold chicken in one layer. In a food processor, chop garlic, parsley and basil to make a persillade. Top chicken with persillade. Combine broth and vinegar and pour the mixture around chicken. Bake in a preheated 375 degree oven for 1 hour.

Remove chicken to a warm platter and pour the baking liquid into a saucepan. Add cream and boil until reduced, thickened and flavorful. Reduce heat. Combine a little of the hot sauce in a small bowl with the cornstarch, whisk, and return to sauce. Whisk again. Spoon sauce over chicken and serve.

4 TO 6 SERVINGS

Mountadam Chardonnay 1 9 8 9
(Adelaide Hills - Australia)

CHICKEN BREASTS
WITH CAPERS, PINE NUTS AND RAISINS

1/2 CUP PINE NUTS
4 CHICKEN BREAST HALVES, BONED
    AND SKINNED
    ALL-PURPOSE FLOUR
    SALT, TO TASTE
    FRESHLY GROUND BLACK PEPPER,
    TO TASTE
2 TABLESPOONS OLIVE OIL
1 CUP WHITE WINE
3 TABLESPOONS FRESHLY SQUEEZED
    LEMON JUICE
2 TABLESPOONS CAPERS, DRAINED
6 TABLESPOONS UNSALTED BUTTER,
    CHILLED AND CUT INTO SMALL
    PIECES
1/4 CUP DARK OR GOLDEN RAISINS

Toast pine nuts in a 400 degree oven for 4 minutes. Set aside. Season flour with salt and pepper and coat chicken breasts lightly, shaking off excess. Heat oil in a sauté pan and brown chicken breasts for 5 minutes. Do not crowd the pan. Turn, and cook 3 to 5 minutes more, or until done. Set aside and cover with foil to keep warm.

Add wine to the sauté pan, bring to a boil, and cook for about 3 to 4 minutes to reduce by half. Add the lemon juice and capers. Remove from heat and whisk in chilled butter, 1/2 tablespoon at a time. Add raisins to sauce and whisk. Return chicken breasts to the pan and heat, spooning the sauce over the breasts.

To serve, place chicken breasts on individual plates and top with sauce. Divide pine nuts evenly and sprinkle over the chicken breasts.

Serve with buttered orzo or rice and Kalamata Broccoli
with Feta Cheese (page 169).

4 SERVINGS

Domaine Joly Coulée de Serrant 1 9 8 6 (Loire)

CURRY GLAZED CHICKEN

- 8   CHICKEN BREAST HALVES, BONED AND SKINNED
- 1/3   CUP FLOUR, SEASONED WITH SALT, PEPPER AND PAPRIKA
- 2   TABLESPOONS OLIVE OIL

Pat chicken breasts dry and coat with seasoned flour, shaking off excess. Heat 2 tablespoons oil in a heavy, non-stick skillet and brown the chicken breasts on each side, four at a time. Cook about 3 to 4 minutes per side. Add more oil, if necessary, and brown remaining breasts. Arrange in one layer in an ovenproof 9- by 13-inch baking dish.

CURRY GLAZE

- 1/3   CUP HONEY
- 3   TABLESPOONS DIJON-STYLE MUSTARD
- 1 1/2   TEASPOONS INDIAN CURRY POWDER
- 3/4   TEASPOON CUMIN
- 3/4   TEASPOON TURMERIC
- 4   TABLESPOONS OLIVE OIL
- 1/3   CUP BLANCHED SLIVERED ALMONDS
- 1/3   CUP DATES, SLIVERED TO RESEMBLE ALMONDS

Combine honey, mustard, curry powder, cumin, turmeric and olive oil. Drizzle over chicken breasts. Top breasts with almonds and dates. Chicken may be prepared several hours in advance up to this point and refrigerated until baking time. Bake in a preheated 350 degree oven for 15 to 20 minutes, or longer if chicken has been refrigerated.

Serve with Papaya-Mango Relish (page 202) and Couscous with Bell Peppers (page 106).

Wynn's Coonawarra Chardonnay 1 9 8 8 (Coonawarra - Australia)

SAVORY MAHOGANY CHICKEN

Begin 3 hours before serving.

- 8   CHICKEN BREAST HALVES, SKINNED
- 2   CUPS DRY RED WINE
- 1/2   CUP OLIVE OIL
- 1/2   CUP SOY SAUCE
- 1/4   CUP LIGHT BROWN SUGAR
- 2   TEASPOONS GROUND GINGER
- 1   TEASPOON DRIED OREGANO
- 1/2   TEASPOON DRIED THYME
- 2   CLOVES GARLIC, MINCED

Arrange chicken in a large, shallow glass baking dish. Combine red wine, olive oil and soy sauce. Stir in brown sugar, ginger, oregano, thyme and garlic. Pour the marinade over chicken. Cover and refrigerate 2 hours.

Bake chicken in marinade in a preheated 350 degree oven until done, about 40 to 45 minutes, basting twice with marinade. Remove to a platter and cover with foil to keep warm. Strain the marinade into a heavy saucepan, and boil until liquid is reduced to 2 cups, about 20 minutes.

Pour half of marinade over chicken and serve. Pass the remaining marinade.

Serve with Asparagus in Lemon Vinaigrette (page 172).

8 SERVINGS

Foreau 1 9 8 9 Vouvray Demi-Sec (Loire)

CHICKEN IN PEAR BRANDY CREAM

4	LARGE CHICKEN BREAST HALVES
2	TABLESPOONS COARSELY CHOPPED, TOASTED HAZELNUTS OR WALNUTS
2	TABLESPOONS MINCED FRESH PARSLEY
2 1/2	TEASPOONS LEMON ZEST
	GROUND CORIANDER, TO TASTE
	GROUND CARDAMOM, TO TASTE
	FRESHLY GROUND WHITE PEPPER, TO TASTE
	FRESHLY GROUND BLACK PEPPER, TO TASTE
	SALT, TO TASTE
2	TABLESPOONS UNSALTED BUTTER
1	TABLESPOON VEGETABLE OIL
1/3	CUP THINLY SLICED GREEN ONIONS, WHITE PART ONLY
1	MEDIUM CLOVE GARLIC, MINCED
1/3	CUP PEAR-FLAVORED BRANDY OR PLAIN BRANDY

In a small mixing bowl, combine hazelnuts or walnuts, parsley and lemon zest. Set aside. In another bowl, mix coriander, cardamom, white pepper, black pepper and salt. Sprinkle chicken on both sides with the coriander mixture. Cover and set aside for 30 minutes. Melt butter with oil in a large skillet over medium-high heat. Add chicken, skin side down. Cook until brown, about 10 minutes, then turn and cook 5 minutes longer. Add the green onions and garlic and cook for another 5 minutes. Pour brandy into the pan and ignite, shaking skillet until flames subside. Remove chicken to a warm plate and cover.

PEARS

2	BOSC OR ANJOU PEARS, PEELED, CORED AND CUT LENGTHWISE INTO 8 SLICES EACH
1/2	CUP PEAR NECTAR
1/3	CUP DRY WHITE WINE
1 1/2	TABLESPOONS FRESHLY SQUEEZED LEMON JUICE
	2 red pears, for garnish

In a heavy, nonreactive skillet, combine pears, pear nectar, wine and lemon juice. Simmer about 15 minutes until pears are tender, yet crisp. Remove from heat, cover to keep warm, and set aside.

PEAR BRANDY CREAM

1	CUP HEAVY CREAM
	SALT, TO TASTE
	FRESHLY GROUND WHITE PEPPER, TO TASTE

Pour cooking liquid from pears into the skillet used for the chicken. Boil over high heat until liquid is reduced by half, about 7 minutes. Add cream and boil until reduced by half again, about 7 minutes more. Season with white pepper and salt. Return chicken to the sauce and reheat for about 10 minutes.

Arrange chicken on a serving platter; slice 2 red pears in half lengthwise and garnish. Pour sauce over or around chicken and sprinkle with hazelnut mixture.

Prepare this beautiful dish in the fall when pears are at their best. Serve with Golden Vegetable Purée (page 166).

4 SERVINGS

Tualatin Chardonnay Reserve 1 9 8 8 (Oregon)

FLOUR TORTILLAS
WITH CHICKEN AND SPINACH FILLING

4   WHOLE CHICKEN BREASTS, BONED
    AND SKINNED

Place chicken breasts in a saucepan with water to cover and poach until done, about 15 to 20 minutes. Drain and cool. Shred chicken into bite-sized pieces. Set aside.

FILLING

4   TABLESPOONS UNSALTED BUTTER
1   LARGE WHITE ONION, FINELY
    CHOPPED
1   POUND FRESH SPINACH, WASHED
    AND STEMMED
3   CUPS SOUR CREAM
ONE 8-OUNCE CAN CHOPPED GREEN
    CHILIES, DRAINED, OR 6 GREEN
    CHILIES, ROASTED AND CHOPPED
    (PAGE 177)
1   TEASPOON GROUND CUMIN
1/4 CUP MILK
    SALT, TO TASTE
12 FLOUR TORTILLAS
6   OUNCES GRATED MONTEREY JACK
    CHEESE

In a small skillet, melt butter and sauté onion until tender; set aside. Steam spinach and drain, reserving 1/2 cup of the cooking liquid. Let spinach cool and chop coarsely. In a medium bowl, combine onion, spinach, sour cream, chilies, cumin, reserved spinach liquid, and milk; mix well and season to taste. Add half the sauce to the shredded chicken and mix well.

Place tortillas in a preheated 350 degree oven to soften (2 to 3 minutes) and remove. Fill tortillas with equal amounts of filling and roll up. Lightly butter a large baking dish and place tortillas seam side down in one layer. Cover with half the grated cheese and top with the remaining sauce. Sprinkle with remaining cheese. Bake until heated through, about 30 minutes, then broil 2 to 3 minutes to brown.

Variations: Substitute turkey for chicken, and sautéed mushrooms for chilies.

6 SERVINGS

Hippolyte Reverdy 1 9 8 9 Sancerre (Loire)

DUCK
WITH FRESH RASPBERRY SAUCE

DUCK STOCK

	NECKS, HEARTS, GIZZARDS AND LOWER WINGS OF DUCKS
1	SMALL ONION, SLICED
1	CARROT, SLICED
1 1/2	TABLESPOONS COOKING OIL
1	CUP BEEF STOCK, PREFERABLY HOMEMADE
1	CUP CHICKEN STOCK, PREFERABLY HOMEMADE
2	SPRIGS FRESH PARSLEY
1/2	BAY LEAF
1	SMALL SPRIG FRESH THYME

Chop duck parts into uniform pieces, about 1 1/2 inches long. Brown with carrot and onion in hot oil. Pour off oil and add beef and chicken stocks, parsley, bay leaf, thyme and enough water to cover, if necessary. Simmer 40 to 60 minutes, to allow flavors to develop, skimming occasionally. Strain out herbs and use stock to make the Fresh Raspberry Sauce.

2	MEDIUM DUCKS, WINGS AND TAILS REMOVED
2	TABLESPOONS GARLIC POWDER
1	TEASPOON SALT

Preheat oven to 425 degrees. Rub the skin of each duck with garlic powder and salt. Place ducks in a roasting pan, breast side up, and cook for 45 minutes. Remove from oven; ducks should be slightly rare. Carve off the leg/thigh pieces at the joint and remove breasts by slipping a sharp knife between the meat and the breastbone. Discard carcasses. Finish cooking on the grill over medium-hot coals, about 5 to 10 minutes, or until crispy and cooked through. Remove skin from breasts. Slice the breast meat into slender strips and fan strips out, keeping the shape.

FRESH RASPBERRY SAUCE

1	CUP DUCK STOCK
2/3	CUP CHAMBORD, OR OTHER RASPBERRY LIQUEUR
3	TABLESPOONS RASPBERRY VINEGAR
3	TABLESPOONS BROWN SUGAR
8	TABLESPOONS BUTTER, CUT INTO 8 PIECES, AT ROOM TEMPERATURE
1	PINT FRESH RASPBERRIES, LIGHTLY RINSED

While the ducks are cooking, place duck stock, Chambord, vinegar and brown sugar in a saucepan and cook over medium heat. Reduce to a syrup, approximately 2/3 cup, skimming sauce occasionally. Transfer sauce to a large skillet and heat reduced syrup to the boiling point. Add butter, whisking each addition thoroughly before adding the next. Add fresh raspberries to finish sauce and heat thoroughly, stirring gently so that berries keep their shape.

Arrange duck pieces on a platter and pour on Fresh Raspberry Sauce. Serve immediately.

Served with Baked Asparagus (page 240) and Dilled Lemon Rice (page 105), the duck makes a delicious and elegant dinner.

4 SERVINGS

Mongeard-Mugneret 1 9 8 9 Echézeaux (Red Burgundy)

DUCK WITH BLACK PEPPER
AND BOURBON SAUCE

Begin 3 days before serving.

3   DUCKS, NECKS AND WING TIPS REMOVED AND RESERVED

1/4   CUP HU KWA (OR OTHER LAPSANG SOUCHONG TYPE) TEA LEAVES

Three days ahead, trim ducks of all fat. Place ducks on racks over a drip pan and refrigerate, uncovered, for three days.

MARINADE

2   CLOVES GARLIC

ZEST OF 1 ORANGE

1 1/2   TEASPOONS WHOLE BLACK PEPPERCORNS

2   TABLESPOONS HONEY

Three days ahead, combine garlic, orange zest, peppercorns and honey in a jar and shake. Refrigerate. Bring to room temperature before using.

DUCK STOCK

1   TABLESPOON VEGETABLE OIL

DUCK NECKS AND WING TIPS

1   STALK CELERY, CHOPPED

1   ONION, CHOPPED

1   BAY LEAF

2   TABLESPOONS DRIED MUSHROOM PIECES (ANY VARIETY)

4   CLOVES GARLIC

6   WHOLE CLOVES

1 1/2   TABLESPOONS CRUSHED BLACK PEPPERCORNS

2   TABLESPOONS ALL-PURPOSE FLOUR

2   CUPS WATER

2   CUPS CHICKEN BROTH, PREFERABLY HOMEMADE

2   CUPS BEEF BROTH, PREFERABLY HOMEMADE

One day ahead, sauté duck necks and wing tips in hot oil in a large skillet for 10 minutes until brown. Add celery and onion and sauté. Place duck pieces and vegetables in a stockpot and stir in bay leaf, dried mushrooms, garlic, cloves, peppercorns, flour, water, chicken and beef broth.

Simmer, partially covered, for 2 hours or until reduced by half. Strain out solids and refrigerate stock. When stock is completely cold, skim off fat. Reserve stock for use in sauce.

Three hours before cooking, gently pierce duck skin with the tip of a knife. Do not pierce meat. Strain marinade and brush on ducks. Spoon remaining marinade into duck cavities.

At roasting time, adjust oven racks to lowest and second lowest position and preheat oven to 350 degrees. Fill a shallow roasting pan with water, stir in tea leaves and place on lowest rack. Place ducks directly on the rack above, breast side down. Roast for 20 minutes, then turn breast side up and roast for 1 hour and 10 minutes more. It may be necessary to place a tent of foil over the ducks to prevent burning.

Carefully remove ducks from rack and pour cavity juices into a bowl. Allow ducks to cool 10 minutes before carving.

BOURBON SAUCE

COOKING JUICES FROM DUCK CAVITIES

DUCK STOCK

1 1/2   CUPS BOURBON

3   TABLESPOONS UNSALTED BUTTER

1   TABLESPOON CRUSHED PEPPERCORNS

Combine duck juices and reserved stock and heat. Stir in bourbon, butter and peppercorns. Heat to simmering and taste for seasoning. Arrange carved duck slices on individual plates and pass Bourbon Sauce separately.

The use of a smoky tea accents the unusual taste of this beautifully colored entrée. Refrigerating the ducks uncovered dries out the skin and makes it very crisp when cooked. Serve with Cranberry Chutney (page 202).

8 SERVINGS

*Storybook Mountain Vineyard Zinfandel
1 9 9 0 (Napa)*

BRAISED QUAIL
WITH HUNTER'S SAUCE

Begin 1 day before serving.

MARINADE

1/4	CUP OLIVE OIL
1/4	CUP FRESHLY SQUEEZED LEMON JUICE
1/4	CUP DRY WHITE WINE
1	CLOVE GARLIC, CRUSHED
2	TEASPOONS DRIED TARRAGON

Combine oil, lemon juice, wine, garlic and tarragon and blend well.

QUAIL

12 TO 14	QUAIL
1/2	CUP ALL-PURPOSE FLOUR
1	TEASPOON SALT
1	TEASPOON FRESHLY GROUND BLACK PEPPER
1	TEASPOON SEASONED SALT
4	TABLESPOONS BUTTER, DIVIDED
2	TABLESPOONS OLIVE OIL, DIVIDED
3	TABLESPOONS BRANDY
1 TO 1 1/2	CUPS CHICKEN STOCK, PREFERABLY HOMEMADE
1 TO 1 1/2	CUPS BEEF STOCK, PREFERABLY HOMEMADE

Place quail in a large, shallow glass dish and pour on marinade. Cover and refrigerate 24 hours or longer, turning once every 12 hours. Mix flour with salt, pepper and seasoned salt. Pat quail dry and roll in seasoned flour, shaking off excess. Melt half the butter and half the oil in a large skillet and sauté 6 to 7 of the quail, browning all four sides—back, top of breast, and each side. Set aside and repeat the procedure with the remaining quail. Place the browned quail in a heavy, ovenproof casserole with a tight-fitting lid.

Deglaze the sauté pan with brandy, and add chicken and beef stocks. Bring to a boil and reserve. Quail may be prepared ahead up to this point. Pour stock mixture over quail in casserole. Cover and braise quail for 1 to 1 1/2 hours in a preheated 350 degree oven until cooked through.

Serve with Hunter's Sauce, French Rice Casserole (page 107) and Cognac Carrots (page 242).

HUNTER'S SAUCE

1	CUP CURRANT JELLY
1/2	CUP MADEIRA OR PORT WINE
2	TABLESPOONS RED-WINE VINEGAR
4	TABLESPOONS BUTTER
3/4	CUP TOMATO PURÉE
	A PINCH OF ALLSPICE
	A PINCH OF GROUND GINGER
	SALT, TO TASTE
1	TABLESPOON WORCESTERSHIRE SAUCE
	FRESHLY SQUEEZED JUICE OF 1/2 LEMON

Combine jelly, Madeira or port wine, vinegar, butter, tomato purée, allspice, ginger, salt, and Worcestershire sauce in a heavy saucepan. Bring to a boil, reduce heat and boil slowly for 5 minutes. Turn off heat. Add lemon juice, bring to a boil again, and cook for 1 minute. Remove from heat. Sauce may be made in advance and reheated.

MAKES 2 CUPS.

6 TO 7 SERVINGS

Le Bacco Chianti Classico 1 9 8 8 (Chianti)

GAME HENS
WITH WILD MUSHROOMS

Begin 4 hours to 1 day before serving.

DRESSING

1 CUP PORT OR MADEIRA WINE, DIVIDED

3/4 CUP DRIED MUSHROOMS—CÈPES, PORCINI, MOREL, OR OYSTER (ABOUT .8 OUNCE)

2 OUNCES DRIED BING CHERRIES (IF NOT AVAILABLE, SUBSTITUTE 1 CUP SEEDLESS RED GRAPES, HALVED)

1/2 CUP DRIED FRENCH BREAD CRUMBS

1 TEASPOON CHOPPED FRESH THYME

1 TABLESPOON CHOPPED FRESH OREGANO

1/4 TEASPOON SALT

1/4 TEASPOON FRESHLY GROUND BLACK PEPPER

1 TABLESPOON CHOPPED PECANS

8 TABLESPOONS UNSALTED BUTTER, AT ROOM TEMPERATURE, DIVIDED

Soak mushrooms and cherries in 2/3 cup of the port or Madeira for at least 2 hours, preferably overnight. Remove cherries from marinade, reserving the mushrooms in marinade. Combine cherries, breadcrumbs, thyme, oregano, salt, pepper, pecans and half of the butter in a mixing bowl and mix gently but thoroughly.

GAME HENS

4 CORNISH GAME HENS, RINSED AND PATTED DRY
SALT, TO TASTE
FRESHLY GROUND BLACK PEPPER, TO TASTE

1/3 CUP WHITE WINE

1 TABLESPOON BALSAMIC OR RED-WINE VINEGAR

Fill each hen cavity with the dressing and two or three of the wild mushrooms. Return remaining mushrooms to marinade and set aside until ready to make the sauce. Place birds in a roasting pan, spread with remaining butter and season with salt and pepper. Pour 1/3 cup of the reserved wine and 1/3 cup white wine into the roasting pan. Bake for 1 hour in a preheated 375 degree oven, basting occasionally.

Remove hens from oven and pour accumulated liquid from the roasting pan into a heavy saucepan. Cover hens and keep warm. Hens can be prepared up to this point and held, covered, for half an hour, until ready to serve. Add mushrooms in wine marinade and the vinegar to roasting liquid in the saucepan. Cook, stirring, over low heat until slightly reduced, about 5 minutes. Pour 1 or 2 tablespoons of sauce over the hens and serve. Pass remaining sauce.

Serve these game hens for a special dinner. They are elegant, yet simple to prepare.

4 SERVINGS

François Jobard 1 9 8 9 Meursault (White Burgundy)

FISH
&
SHELLFISH

WINE WITH FISH AND SHELLFISH

In the examples mentioned at the beginning of this section, two of the red wines matched with fish—Pinot Noir and Portuguese Dao—are characteristically more acid than tannic. Almost without exception, tannic red wines are inappropriate to fish and should never be served with shellfish. The tannin in them combines with the proteins in the fish to form an unappetizing metallic flavor. Red wines which are often low in tannin and high in acidity are Pinot Noir, Côtes de Beaune reds (made from the same grape), Portuguese reds (like the Dao), Sancerre rouge (Pinot Noir again), German Trollinger and Lemberger. The best examples of these can be quite thrilling along with a rich grilled fillet of salmon or tuna, but it is the treatment of the fish that should direct the use of red or white wine. If the fish is grilled, the grill marks add a fatty-to-bitter flavor that the strong fruit of red wine helps control.

Still, there is no point in taking this option too far. Most fish goes wonderfully with Sauvignon Blanc, Sancerre, white Bordeaux, Riesling, and any German, Alsatian or Italian white wine. Shellfish make one of these wines obligatory. The combination of white Bordeaux and oysters, or Muscadet and mussels is an absolutely no-fail match. But dishes with fish and shellfish often contain other ingredients as well, so the weight of the dish should be matched with a wine of similar weight. If the dish is a simple, light presentation of mussels in a broth, then by all means serve Muscadet, a light dry white from the port of Nantes on the Loire River. If the dish is rich and intense, with mushrooms, butter and saffron, consider a wine of heavier weight, such as Chardonnay. America's favorite cocktail wine, Chardonnay is not as flexible a grape as Sauvignon Blanc or Riesling, but there are times when it is perfect.

A heavier, more steak-like fish such as swordfish or tuna goes well with a good quality Chardonnay, especially one from France. American and Australian Chardonnays are delicious, rich wines, but are better suited to chicken than to most fish. German Riesling and its northern European neighbors, Alsatian Pinot Gris, Pinot Blanc and Riesling, are particularly wonderful with fresh-water fish such as trout and catfish.

SCALLOPS
WITH THREE-TOMATO RELISH
AND TOMATILLO VINAIGRETTE

THREE-TOMATO RELISH

5   TABLESPOONS RED TOMATO,
    PEELED, SEEDED AND DICED
4   TABLESPOONS YELLOW TOMATO,
    PEELED, SEEDED AND DICED
3   TABLESPOONS DICED TOMATILLO
2   TABLESPOONS DICED YELLOW
    ONION
1   TABLESPOON COARSELY CHOPPED
    FRESH CILANTRO
    FRESHLY SQUEEZED JUICE OF 1/2
    LIME
    SALT, TO TASTE
    FRESHLY GROUND WHITE PEPPER,
    TO TASTE

Combine red and yellow tomatoes, tomatillo and onion. Add cilantro and lime juice and season with salt and pepper. Let stand 30 minutes at room temperature.

TOMATILLO VINAIGRETTE

1 1/2   CUPS TOMATILLOS, QUARTERED
1   SERRANO PEPPER WITH SEEDS,
        CHOPPED (WEAR GLOVES)
2   SHALLOTS, CHOPPED
1   TEASPOON ROASTED GARLIC,
        MINCED
1 1/2   CUPS WATER
1   TEASPOON HONEY
2   TABLESPOONS WHITE WINE VINEGAR
2   TABLESPOONS FRESH BASIL LEAVES
1/2   CUP VEGETABLE OIL
        SALT, TO TASTE
        FRESHLY GROUND BLACK PEPPER,
        TO TASTE

Combine tomatillos, serrano pepper, shallots, garlic and water. Bring to a boil, reduce heat and simmer about 5 minutes, or until soft. Drain. In a food processor, combine tomatillo mixture, honey, vinegar and basil and purée until smooth. Slowly drizzle in oil and blend thoroughly. Season with salt and pepper.

SCALLOPS

16   JUMBO SEA SCALLOPS
     KOSHER SALT, TO TASTE
2   TABLESPOONS VEGETABLE OIL
watercress or arugula leaves, for garnish

Dry scallops and salt lightly. In a large non-stick pan, heat oil over high heat. Add scallops and sear until cooked half through, about 1 to 2 minutes. Turn and sear the other sides, being careful not to overcook. Scallop centers will be slightly translucent.

To serve, spoon Tomatillo Vinaigrette onto warm plates. Spoon Three-Tomato Relish in center and arrange four scallops around outside of each plate. Garnish with greens.

This makes a beautiful first course or luncheon entrée. Serve accompanied by Onion Boards (page 85).

4 SERVINGS

Crusius Traiser Rotenfels Auslese 1 9 8 9 (Nahe)

SALMON SORREL

SIX   6-OUNCE SALMON FILLETS, SCORED
ON SKIN SIDE
SALT, TO TASTE
FRESHLY GROUND BLACK PEPPER,
TO TASTE
1/2   CUP DRY VERMOUTH OR WHITE
WINE

Season salmon with salt and pepper and place skin side down in a buttered baking dish large enough to hold fillets in one layer. Pour vermouth around fish and cover with buttered wax paper. Braise 12 to 15 minutes on lower middle rack of a preheated 350 degree oven, basting several times.

SORREL SAUCE

1   TABLESPOON UNSALTED BUTTER
1   BUNCH FINELY SHREDDED FRESH
SORREL LEAVES
1/4   CUP HEAVY CREAM
SALT, TO TASTE
FRESHLY GROUND BLACK PEPPER,
TO TASTE
fresh sorrel, for garnish

Melt butter in a medium skillet. Add sorrel leaves and sauté until limp, about 2 minutes. Stir in cream, season to taste with salt and pepper, and heat through. Keep sauce warm until ready to serve.

Remove fillets from baking dish and carefully scrape off skin. Arrange salmon on a heated platter or individual plates, top with sauce, and garnish with fresh sorrel.

Serve accompanied by pan-roasted potatoes and Snow Peas with Carrots and Red Pepper (page 165).

6 SERVINGS

Pecorari Pinot Grigio 1 9 9 0 (Friuli - Venezia)

SHRIMP QUENELLES WITH SHRIMP-HERB SAUCE

QUENELLES

1   POUND MEDIUM SHRIMP, SHELLED
2   EGG WHITES
3/4   TEASPOON SALT
1/4   TEASPOON FRESHLY GROUND
WHITE PEPPER
1/8   TEASPOON CAYENNE PEPPER
1   CUP HEAVY CREAM
FISH STOCK, PREFERABLY
HOMEMADE, or see EASY FISH STOCK
(PAGE 149)

Reserve 3 to 5 shrimp. Place raw shrimp in a food processor with egg whites, salt, white pepper and cayenne. Purée the mixture while slowly adding the cream. When the mixture is smooth, place container in a large bowl of ice. Form quenelles by dipping a large soup spoon into hot water and scooping a tablespoon of the shrimp mixture. Use another spoon to round it off. Place finished quenelles in a buttered sauté pan or fireproof dish. Do not crowd; cook in two or three batches, if necessary. Heat fish stock to simmering and pour over quenelles to cover. Quenelles will float on surface. Cover the pan or dish and simmer for 3 minutes. With a slotted spoon, turn quenelles, cover and cook 3 minutes longer. Drain quenelles on paper towels.

SHRIMP-HERB SAUCE

3 TO 5	SHRIMP, SHELLED
4	TABLESPOONS UNSALTED BUTTER, DIVIDED
1	LARGE CLOVE GARLIC, MINCED
1 1/2	TABLESPOONS ONION, FINELY DICED
1 1/2	TABLESPOONS RED BELL PEPPER, FINELY DICED
1	CUP FISH STOCK
1	TABLESPOON FINELY CHOPPED FRESH BASIL
1	TABLESPOON FINELY CHOPPED FRESH CHIVES
1	TABLESPOON FINELY CHOPPED FRESH TARRAGON
1	TABLESPOON FINELY CHOPPED FRESH PARSLEY
1	CUP HEAVY CREAM
	SALT, TO TASTE
	FRESHLY GROUND BLACK PEPPER, TO TASTE
	A HANDFUL OF WILD MUSHROOMS, IF DESIRED
	sprigs of fresh basil, for garnish

Sauté reserved shrimp in 2 tablespoons of butter until pink and cooked through. Remove and place in food processor with remaining 2 tablespoons butter. Process until smooth and set aside. Add garlic, onion and red pepper to sauté pan and simmer until soft. Add fish stock, basil, chives, tarragon and parsley and cook until liquid is reduced to 1/4 cup. Slowly add cream, stirring constantly. Beat shrimp-butter mixture into cream mixture, one tablespoon at a time. Season with salt and pepper. Add mushrooms, if desired, and simmer gently.

To serve, coat a large platter or individual plates with sauce. Top with quenelles and garnish with a sprig of fresh basil.

The quenelles make an elegant first course, or serve as a luncheon entrée, accompanied by a green salad and Rich Cream Biscuits (page 89).

6 SERVINGS

Boudry Sancerre les Romains "Fouassier" 1 9 9 0 (Loire)

EASY FISH STOCK

1	CUP CLAM JUICE
1	CUP DRY VERMOUTH OR WHITE WINE, OR A COMBINATION
1 1/2	CUPS WATER
4	BLACK PEPPERCORNS
1	FRESH BAY LEAF, TORN IN HALF (IF NOT AVAILABLE, USE 1 DRIED BAY LEAF)
1	SPRIG OF FRESH THYME (OMIT IF FRESH IS NOT AVAILABLE)
1	MEDIUM WHITE MUSHROOM, QUARTERED, IF DESIRED
1	SMALL YELLOW ONION, SLICED
1	MEDIUM CLOVE GARLIC, PEELED

Combine clam juice, vermouth or white wine, and water in a saucepan. Add peppercorns, bay leaf, fresh thyme, mushroom, onion and garlic. Bring to just under a boil, reduce heat, cover and simmer for 20 to 30 minutes to allow flavors to develop. Stock will reduce to about 2 cups. Strain stock before using. Fish stock may be frozen.

MAKES 2 TO 3 CUPS.

JAMAICAN BOUILLABAISSE

2 TABLESPOONS UNSALTED BUTTER
2 TABLESPOONS VEGETABLE OIL
1 LARGE YELLOW ONION, CHOPPED
1 LARGE YELLOW BELL PEPPER, CHOPPED
2 CLOVES GARLIC, MINCED
2 JALAPEÑO PEPPERS, SEEDED AND MINCED
2 TEASPOONS INDIAN CURRY POWDER
1/3 CUP CANNED UNSWEETENED COCONUT MILK
1 CUP BOTTLED CLAM JUICE
ONE 16-OUNCE CAN ITALIAN PLUM TOMATOES, DRAINED AND COARSELY CHOPPED
1/4 CUP FRESHLY SQUEEZED LIME JUICE
1 POUND FIRM WHITE FISH FILLETS, SUCH AS SNAPPER OR MONKFISH, CUT INTO 3-INCH PIECES
1/2 POUND LARGE SHRIMP, SHELLED AND DEVEINED
1/2 POUND LUMP CRABMEAT
2 TABLESPOONS MINCED FRESH CILANTRO
1/2 TEASPOON SALT
1/4 TEASPOON FRESHLY GROUND BLACK PEPPER
4 TO 5 CUPS HOT COOKED RICE
fresh cilantro leaves, chopped, for garnish

Melt butter and oil over medium heat in a heavy saucepan or skillet. Add onion and yellow pepper and cook until the pepper is just softened, about 5 minutes. Add garlic, jalapeño peppers and curry powder and cook several minutes longer. Stir in coconut milk, clam juice and tomatoes and bring to a boil. Reduce heat to medium and simmer, partially covered, for 10 minutes. The recipe can be prepared to this point up to one day ahead. Cool, cover and refrigerate. Reheat before proceeding.

Stir in the lime juice. Add fish and shrimp and simmer over low heat until just cooked through, about 5 minutes. Stir in crabmeat and cilantro and cook a minute or two longer. Season with salt and black pepper.

Divide hot rice into 6 wide, shallow soup bowls or plates, and ladle the hot stew over the rice. Garnish with chopped cilantro.

For a "soupier" stew, do not drain the tomatoes; increase coconut milk to 2/3 cup, and add 1/2 cup water or wine to the clam juice.

This spicy stew is an easy-to-prepare main dish appropriate for a casual dinner. Serve with roasted seasonal vegetables and Iced Lemon Soufflé (page 227) for dessert.

6 SERVINGS

Dageneau Pouilly Fumé Late Harvest Maudit 1 9 9 0 (Loire)

SPICY GRILLED SWORDFISH OR TUNA

Begin 3 hours before serving.

4	TABLESPOONS SOY SAUCE
2	TABLESPOONS DRY SHERRY
4	TABLESPOONS RICE VINEGAR
4	TABLESPOONS SESAME OIL
2	TABLESPOONS OLIVE OIL
1	TABLESPOON HOT CHILI OIL
1/2	TABLESPOON MINCED GARLIC
4 TO 6	SWORDFISH OR TUNA STEAKS

lime slices and fresh mint, for garnish

Combine soy sauce, sherry, vinegar, sesame oil, olive oil, hot chili oil, and garlic. Marinate the fish steaks in this mixture for 2 to 3 hours. Grill fish over hot coals, 10 minutes per inch of thickness, turning once.

Garnish with lime slices and fresh mint.

Three excellent accompaniments to the grilled fish are Poblano Salsa (page 200), Peach Jalapeño Chutney (page 201), or Ginger-Mango Sauce (page 201). The salsa or chutney may be used to top the grilled fish; when using Ginger-Mango Sauce, ladle sauce on plate, top with fish, and garnish with lime slices and fresh mint.

4 TO 6 SERVINGS

Wirsching Würzberger Stein Sylvaner Kabinett 1 9 9 0 (Franken - Germany)

TARRAGON SHRIMP WITH GARLIC BUTTER SAUCE

GARLIC BUTTER SAUCE

1	TABLESPOON CHOPPED GARLIC
1/2	CUP HEAVY CREAM
1 1/2	POUNDS CHILLED UNSALTED BUTTER, CUT INTO SMALL PIECES

In a medium saucepan, cook the cream and garlic over high heat until reduced to half, stirring occasionally. Reduce heat and whisk in butter, one piece at a time, until all the butter has been added. Do not boil. Remove from heat and keep sauce warm until ready to use. The sauce should be creamy enough to coat a metal spoon.

SHRIMP

32	LARGE SHRIMP, PEELED AND DEVEINED
8	ARTICHOKE HEARTS, QUARTERED
1/2	CUP WHITE WINE
1	CUP SLICED GREEN ONIONS, TOPS ONLY
2	CUPS SLICED MUSHROOMS
2	TABLESPOONS CHOPPED FRESH TARRAGON
	SALT, TO TASTE
	FRESHLY GROUND BLACK PEPPER, TO TASTE
8	SLICES FRENCH BREAD, CUT WHEN READY TO SERVE

In a large sauté pan, poach the shrimp and artichoke hearts in wine over high heat for 5 to 8 minutes, or until the shrimp turn pink. Pour off all but 1 tablespoon wine. Add Garlic Butter Sauce, green onions, mushrooms and tarragon and cook over high heat for 3 to 5 minutes. Bring to a fast boil and add salt and pepper to taste.

Serve immediately in flat bowls. Place sliced French bread on top for dipping.

4 SERVINGS

Mastroberardino Avellino di Fiano 1 9 8 8 (Campania)

MEDITERRANEAN SPICED SHRIMP

Begin 3 hours before serving.

2	POUNDS LARGE SHRIMP, SHELLED AND DEVEINED
1	CUP OLIVE OIL
1/4	CUP CHILI SAUCE
1	TEASPOON SALT
1	TEASPOON DRIED OREGANO
1/2	TEASPOON HOT PEPPER SAUCE
2	CLOVES GARLIC, MASHED
3	TABLESPOONS FRESHLY SQUEEZED LEMON JUICE

Combine oil, chili sauce, salt, oregano, hot pepper sauce, garlic and lemon juice in a container with a tight-fitting lid. Add shrimp and marinate, covered, in refrigerator for 1 to 3 hours. Remove shrimp from marinade and thread on wooden skewers. Grill over hot coals 2 to 3 minutes per side. Remove shrimp from skewers and serve.

This is an unusual, spicy, but light summer dish that is delicious served with steamed white rice and a sauté of fresh vegetables.

4 TO 6 SERVINGS

J. J. Prum Wehlener Sonnenuhr Spätlese 1 9 8 9 (Mosel - Saar - Ruwer)

SALMON EN PAPILLOTE

4	12-INCH SQUARES PARCHMENT PAPER
1	TABLESPOON BUTTER, SOFTENED
3	TABLESPOONS MINCED SHALLOTS
1/2	CUP DRY WHITE WINE
1	CUP HEAVY CREAM
1 1/2	TABLESPOONS DIJON-STYLE MUSTARD
2	TABLESPOONS CHOPPED FRESH TARRAGON OR CHIVES
FOUR	6-OUNCE BONELESS, SKINLESS SALMON FILLETS FRESHLY GROUND BLACK PEPPER, TO TASTE

Fold each sheet of parchment in half and cut into a heart shape. Open flat, lightly butter one side of each piece and set aside.

In a small saucepan, cook shallots in wine over medium heat until softened, about 5 minutes. Drain and reserve shallots. In a separate pan, heat cream over medium heat until reduced to 1/2 cup. Stir in shallots, mustard and tarragon. Place a salmon fillet on a piece of buttered parchment, about 1 inch from center fold. Spoon 2 tablespoons of the cream mixture over the top of the fillet and sprinkle with pepper. Fold the other half of the parchment over the fillet and seal tightly by folding both edges over at 1/4-inch intervals. Repeat with remaining fillets and sauce.

Place packets on a baking sheet. The fillets may be prepared to this point and refrigerated for several hours. Bake in a preheated 450 degree oven until parchment is puffed and browned, about 8 to 10 minutes. Remove from oven and cut slits in parchment to release steam. With a spatula, remove fillets to warmed plates and serve immediately.

4 SERVINGS

Firestone Gewurztraminer 1 9 9 1 (Santa Ynez)

CATFISH
WITH MUSTARD CREAM AND PECANS

8	TABLESPOONS UNSALTED BUTTER
1/3	CUP DIJON-STYLE MUSTARD
2	POUNDS CATFISH FILLETS
1/2	CUP FRESHLY SQUEEZED LEMON JUICE
1	POUND GROUND PECANS
1	CUP ALL-PURPOSE FLOUR
3/4	CUP VEGETABLE OIL
1	CUP HEAVY CREAM

1/2 cup pecan pieces, for garnish, if desired

Melt butter and whisk in mustard. Set aside. Fifteen minutes before cooking, marinate catfish fillets in lemon juice. Pat fillets dry and dip in butter and mustard. Combine pecans and flour, then heavily coat fillets with the mixture. Heat oil in a large skillet over medium-high heat. Add fillets and sauté 2 minutes on each side. Remove fish to a covered dish and keep warm. After fish is cooked, pour off oil and discard any burnt pecans. Deglaze pan with cream and whisk in remaining mustard. Sauté pecan pieces in a small amount of butter and sprinkle over fillets.

6 SERVINGS

Pewsey Vale Rhine Riesling 1 9 9 1
(Barossa Valley - Australia)

CHESAPEAKE OYSTER STEW

2 1/2	POUNDS SHUCKED FRESH OYSTERS, LIQUOR RESERVED
1	CUP BUTTER
3	CUPS FINELY CHOPPED ONION
3	CUPS FINELY CHOPPED CELERY, INCLUDING LEAVES
3	FIRM MEDIUM APPLES, FINELY CHOPPED
3	CUPS HEAVY CREAM
1/2	CUP MILK, IF DESIRED, FOR THINNING

Strain the liquor from opened fresh oysters. Melt butter in a large pot and add oyster liquor, heating slowly. When the liquid begins to bubble, add onion, celery and apples. Cook slowly, stirring constantly, until onion and celery are soft, but not browned. Stir in cream and heat well. Add the oysters. Continue to cook slowly, without allowing liquid to boil, until oysters are hot. If the stew needs thinning, add milk.

Prepare one day ahead and reheat for enhanced flavor.

The addition of finely chopped apples is the secret to this fabulous oyster stew. Serve with a fresh green salad and Herbed Peppercorn Bread (page 90).

8 TO 10 SERVINGS

Jordan "J" Sparkling Wine 1 9 8 8 (Sonoma)

ORANGE ROUGHY, THAI STYLE

Begin 4 hours to 1 day before serving.

5   ORANGE ROUGHY FILLETS
6   LARGE TOMATOES, COARSELY CHOPPED
10   LARGE LEAVES FRESH BASIL, SHREDDED, OR 2 TABLESPOONS DRIED
2   TABLESPOONS CHOPPED FRESH CILANTRO, OR MORE IF DESIRED
1/2   CUP SHREDDED FRESH COCONUT OR 1/2 CUP SHREDDED UNSWEETENED COCONUT
1   TABLESPOON GRATED FRESH GINGER
1   TEASPOON CURRY POWDER
1   TEASPOON SALT
1/2   TEASPOON CINNAMON
1/2   TEASPOON DRIED RED PEPPER FLAKES
FRESHLY SQUEEZED JUICE OF 3 LARGE OR 4 MEDIUM LIMES
1/3   CUP TERIYAKI MARINADE
1/4   CUP RICE VINEGAR
1   TABLESPOON OLIVE OIL
1/3   CUP FRESH COCONUT MILK, IF FRESH COCONUT IS USED
FRESHLY SQUEEZED JUICE OF 1 LEMON
FRESHLY GROUND BLACK PEPPER, TO TASTE
ZEST OF 1 LARGE ORANGE
GREEN ONION TOPS, THINLY SLICED LENGTHWISE TO CURL

Combine tomatoes, basil, cilantro and coconut in a large mixing bowl. Add ginger, curry powder, salt, cinnamon and red pepper flakes to the tomato mixture. Stir in lime juice, teriyaki marinade, vinegar, oil and coconut milk (if used). Cover and let stand for several hours at room temperature or overnight in the refrigerator.

Strain tomato mixture and reserve liquid to use in sauce. Spread tomato mixture evenly in a large, shallow glass baking dish and arrange fillets on top. Squeeze lemon juice over fish and sprinkle lightly with pepper and orange zest. Top with green onion curls. Cover with aluminum foil and seal tightly. The dish may be prepared to this point several hours ahead and refrigerated. Bring to room temperature before baking.

Bake in a preheated 300 degree oven for 35 minutes. Do not open during baking. The dish can remain in the oven for 30 minutes or more after oven is turned off if foil remains closed.

Pour off liquid produced during baking into a saucepan. Add reserved tomato liquid. Cook sauce over high heat to reduce and thicken to desired consistency.

Using a long flat spatula, place a fillet and some of the tomato mixture on individual plates. Spoon sauce over fish or serve separately.

The flavor of this dish is not in the least diminished by using pre-frozen orange roughy.

5 SERVINGS

Domaine Trevallon Blanc - Marsanne 1 9 9 0 (White Provence)

GRILLED FISH STEAKS
WITH OLIVE-ROSEMARY BUTTER

4   FISH STEAKS—SALMON OR HALIBUT

OLIVE-ROSEMARY BUTTER

1/4   CUP UNSALTED BUTTER, SOFTENED
1   TABLESPOON PITTED, CHOPPED
     BRINE-CURED BLACK OLIVES
1   TEASPOON FRESHLY SQUEEZED
     LEMON JUICE
2   TEASPOONS CHOPPED FRESH
     ROSEMARY
1/4   TEASPOON PROVENÇAL- OR DIJON-
     STYLE MUSTARD

Blend butter, olives, lemon juice, rosemary and mustard in a small bowl. The butter may be prepared up to 2 days ahead and refrigerated, tightly covered. Bring to room temperature before serving.

MAKES 1/3 CUP.

MARINADE

4   TABLESPOONS OLIVE OIL
2   TABLESPOONS FRESHLY SQUEEZED
     LEMON JUICE
1   TEASPOON CRUSHED FENNEL SEED
1   TEASPOON CHOPPED FRESH
     ROSEMARY
1/8   TEASPOON FRESHLY GROUND BLACK
     PEPPER
1/2   TEASPOON PROVENÇAL- OR DIJON-
     STYLE MUSTARD
     sprigs of fresh rosemary, for garnish

In a glass dish large enough to hold the fish steaks in one layer, whisk together olive oil, lemon juice, fennel seed, rosemary, pepper and mustard. Add fish steaks, turning to coat both sides, and marinate for 20 to 30 minutes at room temperature, or for several hours, covered, in the refrigerator. Turn once or twice while marinating.

If fish has been refrigerated, return to room temperature before grilling. Grill fish steaks over hot coals, turning once, 5 minutes per inch of thickness.

Transfer to a serving platter or individual plates and top each steak with 1 teaspoon of the Olive-Rosemary Butter. Garnish with rosemary sprigs.

The amount of Olive-Rosemary Butter may be doubled and passed at the table. This is a simple recipe which allows the full flavor of the fish to come through. Serve with a variety of colorful summer vegetables— zucchini (both green and yellow), peppers, tomatoes, eggplant—whatever looks freshest at the market. Sauté the vegetables with garlic and fresh herbs, and serve a simple buttered orzo. Start with Cold Dilled Tomato Soup (page 67), and finish with Blackberry Tarts (page 220) for a memorable summer meal.

4 SERVINGS

For salmon:
Bandol Rosé Domaine Tempier 1 9 8 9 (Rosé Provence)

For halibut:
Clos Ste. Magdelaine 1 9 8 9 Cassis Blanc (White Provence)

SALMON FILLET
WITH GREEN PEPPERCORN CRUST

Begin at least 2 hours before serving.

PEPPER-HERB SAUCE

1/2	CUCUMBER, PEELED, SEEDED AND FINELY CHOPPED
1/2	RED BELL PEPPER, FINELY CHOPPED
1/2	YELLOW BELL PEPPER, FINELY CHOPPED
1/2	CUP FINELY CHOPPED FRESH PARSLEY
1	MEDIUM SHALLOT, FINELY CHOPPED
1	CLOVE GARLIC, FINELY CHOPPED
1	TABLESPOON FINELY GRATED FRESH GINGER
1/2	HOT RED CHILI PEPPER, IF DESIRED SEVERAL LEAVES OF FRESH CORIANDER, MINCED, OR 1 TEASPOON DRIED CORIANDER
2	FINELY CHOPPED FRESH BASIL LEAVES
1/2	CUP RICE VINEGAR
1/2	CUP CHICKEN STOCK, PREFERABLY HOMEMADE
1	TABLESPOON SESAME, PEANUT OR OLIVE OIL
1	TABLESPOON SOY OR TERIYAKI SAUCE FRESHLY SQUEEZED JUICE OF 1/2 LIME SALT, TO TASTE, IF DESIRED

lemon wedges, cucumber slices, or palm leaves, for garnish

Toss together cucumber, red and yellow peppers, parsley, shallot and garlic. Add ginger, chili pepper, coriander and basil leaves. Stir vinegar, chicken stock, oil, soy or teriyaki sauce, lime juice and salt into the vegetables and seasonings. Let stand at room temperature for at least 2 hours. Serve as a sauce or relish with salmon, depending on the amount of liquids used.

SALMON AND PEPPERCORN CRUST

1	LARGE FRESH SALMON FILLET, ABOUT 3 POUNDS, BONES REMOVED
2	TEASPOONS GREEN PEPPERCORNS
2	TEASPOONS BLACK PEPPERCORNS
2	TEASPOONS CHOPPED FRESH DILL OR 2 TEASPOONS DRIED DILLWEED
4	TABLESPOONS BUTTER
2	TEASPOONS OLIVE OIL FRESHLY SQUEEZED JUICE OF 3 LARGE LIMES

Lightly oil skin side of the salmon to prevent sticking. Place fish, skin side down, in a large, flat baking dish, preferably one with curved sides. Grind green and black peppercorns together. Combine with dill, butter, olive oil and lime juice. Adjust the liquid in the mixture so it can be spread over the salmon like mustard. Brush thickly over top of fish. Cover with foil and bake for 30 minutes in a preheated 350 degree oven, about 10 minutes per pound. Remove foil. Broil for the last 2 to 3 minutes, to brown.

Serve salmon on a large, oval platter, garnished with lemon wedges and fresh cucumber slices. For a dramatic presentation, serve on a bed of palm leaves. Slice salmon at the table and serve immediately.

6 SERVINGS

Adelsheim Pinot Noir 1 9 9 0 (Oregon)

FISH FILLETS IN PHYLLO

LEMON SAUCE

4	EGG YOLKS
1 1/2	TABLESPOONS ALL-PURPOSE FLOUR
1/2	TEASPOON SALT
1/8	TEASPOON FRESHLY GROUND WHITE PEPPER
1 1/2	CUPS CHICKEN BROTH, PREFERABLY HOMEMADE
	FRESHLY SQUEEZED JUICE OF 3 LEMONS, ABOUT 1/2 TO 2/3 CUP JUICE
	ZEST OF 2 LEMONS

Combine egg yolks, flour, salt and pepper and whisk, adding broth, until smooth. Place over medium-high heat and whisk 10 to 15 minutes until foamy and thick. Add lemon juice and zest. Keep warm over hot water or let stand at room temperature until ready to use. Reheat over hot water.

MAKES 2 CUPS.

FISH

4	SKINLESS HALIBUT OR SALMON FILLETS, ABOUT 4 OUNCES EACH, CUT 1-INCH THICK
1	BAY LEAF
1	TABLESPOON PEPPERCORNS
1	SPRIG FRESH PARSLEY
1	CUP CHOPPED ONION
4	TABLESPOONS BUTTER
1/2	CUP CRÈME FRAÎCHE (PAGE 198)
4 TO 6	TABLESPOONS CAPERS, DRAINED
2/3	CUP LONG-GRAIN WHITE RICE, COOKED AND COOLED
1/4	TEASPOON SALT
1/4	TEASPOON FRESHLY GROUND BLACK PEPPER
1/4	TEASPOON PAPRIKA
8	SHEETS PHYLLO PASTRY
1/2	CUP MELTED BUTTER
	SALT, TO TASTE
	FRESHLY GROUND BLACK PEPPER, TO TASTE

In a fish poacher or oblong pan, bring 1 inch of water to boil and add bay leaf, peppercorns and parsley. Poach fish for 10 minutes, then cover and set aside to cool in liquid. In a small skillet, sauté onion in butter over low heat until tender, about 7 to 10 minutes. Combine onion, crème fraîche, and capers with rice and mix thoroughly. Season carefully with salt, pepper and paprika.

Unroll one sheet of phyllo on a smooth surface. Brush lightly with melted butter. Top with a second sheet and brush again with butter. Fold the sheets in half crosswise and brush with butter once again. Place one-eighth of the rice mixture in the middle of the pastry. Top the stuffing with one of the fish fillets, cooled and patted dry. Season fish with salt and pepper and top with another eighth of the rice mixture. Fold two opposing edges of the pastry over the fish and rice, then fold over the two remaining edges to form a square package. Brush with butter once more and set the package seam side down in a buttered baking dish. Brush the top of the pastry with butter, and cut slits for steam holes. Repeat the process for the remaining fillets. The dish may be prepared in advance to this point and refrigerated for up to 2 hours. Bake in a preheated 375 degree oven for 30 minutes or until brown.

Arrange on a warmed platter and serve topped with Lemon Sauce.

4 SERVINGS

Jordan Chardonnay 1 9 8 9 (Sonoma)

SALMON
WITH SPICY ONION MARINADE

SPICY ONION MARINADE

- 1/4 CUP PLUS 2 TEASPOONS OLIVE OIL, DIVIDED
- 2 LARGE YELLOW ONIONS, HALVED LENGTHWISE AND THINLY SLICED CROSSWISE
- 1/4 CUP GOLDEN RAISINS, PLUMPED IN 1/2 CUP HOT WATER
- 1/4 CUP RED-WINE VINEGAR
- 2 TABLESPOONS WORCESTERSHIRE SAUCE
- 1 TABLESPOON FINELY GRATED ORANGE ZEST
- 2 TEASPOONS FINELY GRATED LEMON ZEST
- 1 TEASPOON ALLSPICE
- 1 TEASPOON DRIED CHIVES
- 1 TEASPOON DRIED CORIANDER
  SALT, TO TASTE
  FRESHLY GROUND BLACK PEPPER, TO TASTE

In a large nonreactive skillet, heat 1/4 cup oil over medium heat until hot, about 1 minute. Add onions, cover partially and cook, stirring until tender and translucent, about 20 minutes. Drain raisins and add to onions. Stir in vinegar, Worcestershire sauce, orange and lemon zest, allspice, chives and coriander. Reduce the vinegar mixture slightly to intensify flavors, cooking about 3 minutes. Season with salt and pepper. The recipe may be prepared to this point up to one day ahead. Cover and refrigerate. Reheat before proceeding.

SALMON

- FOUR 6-OUNCE SALMON STEAKS, 3/4-INCH THICK
- 1 TEASPOON SALT
- 1/2 TEASPOON FRESHLY GROUND BLACK PEPPER

1/4 cup toasted pine nuts, for garnish

Season salmon steaks on both sides with salt and pepper. In a large heavy skillet, heat the remaining 2 teaspoons olive oil over high heat. Add salmon steaks to the pan and cook until well-browned on one side, about 3 minutes. Turn and cook about 3 minutes longer. The salmon is done when the flesh separates easily with a fork and the thickest part is no longer translucent.

Transfer the salmon steaks to warm plates and spoon hot onion mixture on top. Garnish with toasted pine nuts.

Variation: Substitute fresh tuna for the salmon.

Serve with Braised Celery Hearts au Gratin (page 166).

4 SERVINGS

Josmeyer Pinot Gris 1 9 8 9 (Alsace)

SAGE-SEASONED TROUT

1/4 CUP ALL-PURPOSE FLOUR
1/3 CUP SLICED ALMONDS, TOASTED
3 TABLESPOONS DRIED SAGE
1 TEASPOON SALT
    FRESHLY GROUND BLACK PEPPER,
    TO TASTE
4 TROUT (ABOUT 1 POUND EACH),
    CLEANED, HEADS AND TAILS INTACT
6 TABLESPOONS OLIVE OIL, DIVIDED
    fresh whole sage leaves, for garnish

Place flour, almonds, sage, salt and pepper in a food processor and blend until mixture is finely ground. Thoroughly coat each trout with the mixture and lightly sprinkle the insides with additional salt and pepper.

Place a large skillet over medium-high heat and add 3 tablespoons of olive oil. Sauté the trout, two at a time, 5 minutes per side. Add oil as necessary. The trout should be crisp and golden in color.

Garnish with fresh whole sage leaves and serve immediately.

Serve with Tomatoes, Zucchini and Feta Cheese
(page 165).

4 SERVINGS

Schloss Groenesteyn Kiedricher Sandgrub Kabinett 1 9 8 3
(Rheingau)

SHRIMP VINDALOO

1 TABLESPOON CUMIN
1 TABLESPOON MUSTARD SEED
1 TABLESPOON GROUND TURMERIC
1 TABLESPOON CAYENNE PEPPER
1 TABLESPOON MINCED FRESH GINGER
1 CUP WHITE VINEGAR
3 LARGE CLOVES GARLIC, MINCED
2 CUPS CHOPPED ONION, DIVIDED
1 TO 1 1/2 POUNDS SHRIMP (30 TO 40),
    SHELLED AND DEVEINED
1 TABLESPOON VEGETABLE OIL
1 TEASPOON SALT
1/4 CUP WATER
2 CUPS TOMATOES, PEELED, SEEDED
    AND CHOPPED
3 LARGE POTATOES, DICED AND
    COOKED, IF DESIRED

Combine cumin, mustard seed, turmeric, cayenne, ginger, vinegar, garlic and 1 cup onion in a food processor. Process until pulverized. Pour mixture over shrimp and let stand at least 1 hour at room temperature. In a large skillet, brown remaining onions in oil. Add shrimp mixture and sauté for 2 to 3 minutes. Add salt, water, tomatoes and potatoes, if desired. Simmer 10 minutes or until liquid is absorbed.

This unusual and delicious dish may also be served with white or brown rice. For a less spicy dish, reduce the amount of cayenne and turmeric.

6 SERVINGS

Gunderloch Hasselbach Nackenheimer Rothenberg Auslese
1 9 9 0 (Rheinhessen)

GRILLED WHOLE SALMON
WITH FRESH HERB SAUCE

FISH

1   WHOLE SALMON, 5 TO 7 POUNDS
4   TABLESPOONS CHOPPED FRESH
    HERBS, SUCH AS BASIL, THYME AND
    OREGANO
    LEMON SLICES
    VEGETABLE OIL

Sprinkle chopped herbs inside and outside fish and insert lemon slices. Let stand for 30 to 60 minutes. To prepare fish for grilling, first wrap the head and tail with pieces of oiled wax paper. Then secure the wax paper by wrapping with foil. Brush oil on a wire grill and drizzle oil on fish before placing it on grill. Grill over medium-hot coals 7 to 15 minutes per side, or 10 minutes per inch of thickness.

FRESH HERB SAUCE

1   BUNCH FRESH WATERCRESS LEAVES,
    WELL RINSED AND STEMMED
2   EGGS
1 1/2   TEASPOONS TARRAGON VINEGAR
1   TEASPOON DIJON-STYLE MUSTARD
    SALT, TO TASTE
    FRESHLY GROUND BLACK PEPPER,
    TO TASTE
3/4 TO 1   CUP VEGETABLE OIL
2   TABLESPOONS FINELY MINCED FRESH
    PARSLEY
2   TABLESPOONS FINELY MINCED FRESH
    CHIVES
1   TABLESPOON FINELY MINCED FRESH
    TARRAGON OR DILL
1   TABLESPOON FINELY MINCED FRESH
    CHERVIL
lemon slices and sprigs of fresh basil or thyme, for garnish

Blanch watercress leaves in boiling salted water for 2 minutes. Drain and place on paper towels. Combine eggs, vinegar and mustard in a blender or food processor and season with salt and pepper. Blend at high speed until smooth, then add the oil very gradually, blending until thick and smooth. Add watercress and blend the mixture at high speed. Transfer sauce to a serving bowl. Add the parsley, chives, tarragon or dill and chervil. Taste and correct seasonings.

MAKES 1 1/2 CUPS.

Using two broad spatulas, carefully remove fish from grill and place on a large cutting board. Remove foil and wax paper. Transfer fish to a serving platter and garnish with lemon slices and sprigs of basil or thyme. Serve Fresh Herb Sauce separately.

6 TO 8 SERVINGS

Zind Humbrecht Sylvaner 1 9 9 0 (Alsace)

SALMON CAKES
WITH CILANTRO BUTTER SAUCE

Begin at least 2 hours before serving.

3	TABLESPOONS MAYONNAISE
1	TABLESPOON FRESHLY SQUEEZED LEMON JUICE
1	TEASPOON DRY MUSTARD
	A DASH OF HOT PEPPER SAUCE
1/2 TO 1	TEASPOON SALT, OR TO TASTE
1	TEASPOON FRESHLY GROUND BLACK PEPPER
1/4	CUP MINCED GREEN ONION
1	POUND SALMON FILLET, MINCED
1 1/2	CUPS FRESH BREADCRUMBS, DIVIDED
8	TABLESPOONS UNSALTED BUTTER, DIVIDED
1	CUP DRY WHITE WINE
1	TABLESPOON FRESHLY SQUEEZED LIME JUICE
1/2	CUP MINCED FRESH CILANTRO

Combine mayonnaise, lemon juice, mustard, hot pepper sauce, salt, pepper and green onion in a large bowl. Add the salmon and mix lightly. Add 1 cup of the breadcrumbs and mix again briefly. Divide the salmon mixture into 4 equal parts. Shape each portion into a cake 3 1/2 inches in diameter and 1 inch thick. Coat the cakes with remaining breadcrumbs and place on a rack. Cover and chill at least one hour. The recipe may be prepared up to this point one day ahead.

Over medium heat, melt 4 tablespoons butter in a non-stick skillet large enough to hold the salmon cakes in one layer without crowding. Add salmon cakes and cook until browned and resistant to the touch, about 5 minutes per side. Transfer to a warm plate and cover with foil to keep warm.

Discard the butter in the skillet and wipe skillet clean. Add wine and lime juice and bring to a boil over medium heat. Boil until liquid is reduced by half, about 5 minutes. Reduce heat to low and whisk in remaining 4 tablespoons of butter, 1/2 tablespoon at a time, beating thoroughly after each addition. Remove from heat and add cilantro.

Serve one salmon cake per person, with sauce spooned over each cake.

4 SERVINGS

Pascal Jolivet Pouilly Fumé 1 9 9 0 (Loire)

VEGETABLES

WINE WITH VEGETABLES

When vegetables are used as accompaniments to entrées, they require little consideration when matching food and wine. If the dish is assertive, however, it can be considered as nearly another sauce. For example, in ratatouille, which combines tomatoes, eggplant and herbs, the presence of the earthy vegetables and tomato will require a wine high in fruit and acidity. If white, that suggests a French Sauvignon Blanc (such as Sancerre), and if red, a classic Italian red wine.

However, for those who will use vegetables as entrées, the following recommendations may help. Vegetables vary a great deal from earthy to sweet, but are always light- to medium-bodied in weight, so rarely are appropriate with heavy-bodied wines. Most red wines, such as Cabernet, Syrah and many Merlots, are too heavy; try instead Pinot Noir from the lighter vintages. Côtes du Languedoc, southern French wines which are usually composed of Carignan, Syrah, Mourvèdre and Grenache are, on occasion, adequate to handle vegetarian dishes, especially if the vegetables are grilled.

Light Dolcettos from Italy and Cabernet Franc from the Loire in France (Chinon or Bourgueil) go well with many of these dishes if herbs such as basil, tarragon and dill are a factor. White wine, however, is a better course of action. Wines from the Loire (Sancerre, Pouilly Fumé, Vouvray, Muscadet) all have plenty of fruit (excepting Muscadet) and great acidity to cut through any vegetable dish. Condrieu from the northern Rhône (made of the rare Viognier grape) is a wonderful foil for lighter dishes. Côtes du Rhône Blanc can also work, although it is generally a heavier, almost oily wine.

Sauvignon Blanc from America, Australia and New Zealand always has an intensity that can overwhelm many vegetable flavors. At their best, however, these wines have great acidity, making each taste of a dish seem like the first. These wines can be served with almost any vegetable dish.

Preceding page: Asparagus in Lemon Vinaigrette, page 172

TOMATOES, ZUCCHINI AND FETA CHEESE

6 SMALL ZUCCHINI, THINLY SLICED
1 TABLESPOON OLIVE OIL
    SALT, TO TASTE
    FRESHLY GROUND WHITE PEPPER,
    TO TASTE
3 LARGE RIPE TOMATOES, PEELED,
    SEEDED AND CUT INTO EIGHTHS, OR
    ONE 14-OUNCE CAN ITALIAN PLUM
    TOMATOES, CUT UP
8 OUNCES FETA CHEESE, CUBED AND
    DIVIDED
3 TABLESPOONS CHOPPED FRESH
    PARSLEY

In a large skillet, sauté zucchini in oil until almost tender, about 4 to 6 minutes, seasoning with salt and pepper. Remove from pan and set aside. Add tomatoes, salt and pepper to skillet and sauté until liquid has been reduced, about 3 minutes. Return zucchini to pan with tomatoes and add 2/3 of the feta cheese to the mixture. Stir in parsley. Pour the mixture into a generously buttered 2-quart baking dish and top with remaining feta. Bake in a preheated 350 degree oven for 15 minutes.

Serve as an accompaniment to Sage-Seasoned Trout (page 159).

6 SERVINGS

SNOW PEAS
WITH CARROTS AND RED PEPPER

1   TABLESPOON UNSALTED BUTTER
2   MEDIUM CARROTS, PEELED AND CUT
      INTO 3-INCH JULIENNE
1   MEDIUM RED BELL PEPPER, CUT INTO
      3-INCH JULIENNE
3/4 POUND SNOW PEAS OR SUGAR SNAP
      PEAS, TRIMMED, STRINGS REMOVED
1/4 TEASPOON LEMON ZEST
1   TEASPOON FRESHLY SQUEEZED
      LEMON JUICE
1/8 TEASPOON FRESHLY GROUND BLACK
      PEPPER

In a heavy 10-inch skillet, melt butter over medium heat. Add carrots and red pepper, cover and cook for 3 minutes. Add peas, cover and cook 3 minutes longer, or until vegetables are tender. Stir in lemon zest, lemon juice and black pepper.

This is a good, quick, hot-summer-day vegetable—fresh, crisp, pretty and very easy. Try it with Salmon Sorrel (page 148).

4 SERVINGS

GOLDEN VEGETABLE PURÉE

1   SWEET POTATO, PEELED AND
    THINLY SLICED
1   PARSNIP, PEELED AND THINLY SLICED
2   CARROTS, PEELED AND THINLY
    SLICED
1   YELLOW TURNIP,
    PEELED AND THINLY SLICED
1/3 CUP CHOPPED FRESH DILL
2   TABLESPOONS CHOPPED FRESH
    PARSLEY
1/2 CUP HEAVY CREAM
4   TABLESPOONS BUTTER
    SALT, TO TASTE
    FRESHLY GROUND BLACK PEPPER,
    TO TASTE

In a large pot, cook sweet potato, parsnip, carrots and turnip in boiling, salted water until tender. Drain. Purée the vegetables in a blender or food processor. Add dill, parsley, cream, butter, and salt and pepper to taste. Transfer the purée to an ovenproof dish and bake, uncovered, in a preheated 350 degree oven until vegetables are heated through, about 15 minutes.

Serve with Chicken in Pear-Brandy Cream (page 139).

8 SERVINGS

BRAISED CELERY HEARTS AU GRATIN

1/2 CUP CHICKEN STOCK, PREFERABLY
    HOMEMADE
1/2 CUP DRY VERMOUTH
2   TABLESPOONS FRESHLY SQUEEZED
    LEMON JUICE
3/4 TEASPOON FENNEL SEED
10 BLACK PEPPERCORNS
4   CELERY HEARTS, SLICED IN
    QUARTERS LENGTHWISE (SEE
    BELOW)
4   TEASPOONS BUTTER
1/3 CUP FRESHLY GRATED PARMESAN
    CHEESE
1/3 CUP FRESH BREADCRUMBS

In a large skillet, combine chicken stock, vermouth, lemon juice, fennel seed and peppercorns over medium-high heat. Add celery hearts and simmer 15 to 20 minutes, until they are just tender when pierced. Remove celery and set aside. Reserve 1/3 cup of liquid. Arrange celery in a small buttered baking dish and pour reserved liquid over top. Sprinkle with Parmesan cheese and breadcrumbs and dot with butter. Bake in a preheated 350 degree oven until golden brown, about 15 minutes. Serve immediately.

To prepare celery: Keeping the form of the hearts intact, remove all tough outer stalks, leaving only those that will be tender when cooked. Cut off tops, making stalks about 8 inches long. Trim root ends, being careful not to detach stalks.

Serve as an accompaniment to Salmon with Spicy Onion Marinade (page 158).

6 TO 8 SERVINGS

SPINACH
WITH RAISINS AND PINE NUTS

1/4   CUP RAISINS

2   TABLESPOONS OLIVE OIL

3   TABLESPOONS PINE NUTS

1   MEDIUM VIDALIA ONION, FINELY
     CHOPPED

1   CLOVE GARLIC, FINELY MINCED

2   POUNDS FRESH SPINACH, WASHED
     AND STEMMED
     SALT, TO TASTE
     FRESHLY GROUND BLACK PEPPER,
     TO TASTE

Soak raisins in boiling water to plump, about 5 minutes. Drain and set aside. In a skillet, heat oil and add pine nuts. Sauté, stirring constantly, until golden brown. Remove pine nuts and set aside. Add chopped onion to skillet and sauté until golden; then add garlic. Remove skillet from heat.

In a covered pan, cook spinach for a few minutes in the water clinging to its leaves, turning leaves several times from top to bottom. Drain, pressing out liquid, and chop. Stir chopped spinach into sautéed onion, and add raisins and pine nuts. Season with salt and pepper and heat through.

Serve as an accompaniment to Rosemary Pork Medallions with Mushrooms (page 113).

6 SERVINGS

TURNIP POTATO GRATINÉE

4   SMALL WHITE TURNIPS, PEELED AND
     COARSELY GRATED

2   LARGE RED POTATOES, PEELED AND
     COARSELY GRATED

4   TABLESPOONS UNSALTED BUTTER

2   TEASPOONS SNIPPED FRESH DILL

1/8   TEASPOON FRESHLY GRATED
     NUTMEG
     FRESHLY GROUND WHITE PEPPER,
     TO TASTE
     SALT, TO TASTE

1/2   CUP HEAVY CREAM

1/2   CUP CHICKEN BROTH, PREFERABLY
     HOMEMADE

1/2   CUP FRESH BREADCRUMBS

1/2   CUP FRESHLY GRATED GRUYÈRE OR
     SWISS CHEESE

In a heavy skillet, cook turnips and potatoes in butter over low heat for 20 minutes, stirring occasionally. Stir in dill, nutmeg, white pepper and salt. Divide the mixture among 8 buttered 1-cup gratin dishes or pour into a 2-quart gratin dish.

In a small bowl, whisk together cream and broth. Pour some of the liquid into each dish and sprinkle the gratins with breadcrumbs and cheese. Bake on a baking sheet in a preheated 425 degree oven for 20 minutes, or until mixture bubbles around the edges and the top is browned.

Serve with Tenderloin with Roasted Shallots (page 122).

8 SERVINGS

SHERRIED SWEET POTATOES AND APPLES

3	LARGE SWEET POTATOES
3	GRANNY SMITH APPLES, PEELED AND CHOPPED
4	TABLESPOONS UNSALTED BUTTER
1/4	CUP FRESHLY SQUEEZED LEMON JUICE
1/4	CUP FIRMLY PACKED BROWN SUGAR
1/4	TEASPOON CINNAMON
1/3	CUP DRY SHERRY
	apple-peel rosette, for garnish

In a saucepan, combine sweet potatoes with enough cold water to cover and boil until just tender, about 30 minutes. Drain and cool. Peel and cut potatoes into 1/2-inch pieces. In a large skillet, cook apples in butter over moderate heat, stirring, for 3 minutes, or until soft. Stir in lemon juice, brown sugar, cinnamon and sherry. Bring to a boil and simmer for 3 minutes. Add the sweet potatoes and cook, stirring gently, for 2 minutes. Serve in a heated dish, garnished with an apple-peel rosette.

Try this with Mediterranean Pork Roast (page 114).

8 SERVINGS

GERMAN RED CABBAGE

4	TABLESPOONS UNSALTED BUTTER
1	LARGE YELLOW ONION, THINLY SLICED
1/2	CUP BALSAMIC VINEGAR
2	TABLESPOONS LIGHT BROWN SUGAR
9	WHOLE CLOVES
9	JUNIPER BERRIES
1	TEASPOON DRIED THYME
1	BAY LEAF
1	HEAD RED CABBAGE (ABOUT 2 POUNDS), FINELY SHREDDED
1	GRANNY SMITH APPLE, PEELED AND COARSELY GRATED
2	TABLESPOONS DARK UNSULPHURED MOLASSES
	SALT, TO TASTE
	FRESHLY GROUND BLACK PEPPER, TO TASTE

Melt butter in a large, heavy skillet over medium heat. Add onion and sauté until translucent, about 3 minutes. Add vinegar, brown sugar, cloves, juniper berries, thyme and bay leaf. Bring to a boil, stirring constantly. Stir in cabbage and apple and reduce heat to low. Cover and cook about 40 minutes, stirring occasionally, until cabbage is very tender and almost no liquid remains. Blend in molasses and season with salt and pepper. Remove bay leaf. If made ahead, cover and refrigerate. Reheat on low.

6 SERVINGS

RED ONION COMPOTE

1 1/2	POUNDS SMALL RED ONIONS
3	TABLESPOONS OLIVE OIL, DIVIDED
2	TABLESPOONS CHOPPED FRESH THYME
1	TABLESPOON CHOPPED FRESH ROSEMARY
1	RED BELL PEPPER, CHOPPED
1	YELLOW BELL PEPPER, CHOPPED
2	LARGE RIPE TOMATOES, CUT IN EIGHTHS
6	SMALL CLOVES GARLIC, PEELED
3	SHALLOTS, PEELED AND QUARTERED
	SALT, TO TASTE
	FRESHLY GROUND BLACK PEPPER, TO TASTE
2	TEASPOONS BALSAMIC VINEGAR, OR TO TASTE

Cut the onions in quarters, leaving root ends intact, and peel. Lightly oil a gratin dish and sprinkle thyme and rosemary over the bottom. Arrange onions, red and yellow peppers, tomatoes, garlic and shallots in the dish. Brush remaining oil over the vegetables, being certain to coat onions and peppers. Season with salt and pepper, cover, and bake for 1 1/2 hours in a preheated 350 degree oven.

Remove dish from oven and carefully transfer any remaining liquid to a small saucepan. Add vinegar, bring to a boil, and reduce until sauce is syrupy and thick. Add additional vinegar, to taste, and pour over vegetables.

This versatile vegetable blend may be served as a spread for Bruschetta (page 92) or as a sweet and sour accompaniment to salads. Or try it with Butterflied Leg of Lamb with Grilled Polenta (page 117) or Cold Summer Pork (page 113).

4 SERVINGS

KALAMATA BROCCOLI WITH FETA CHEESE

1	HEAD BROCCOLI, CUT IN 1-INCH FLOWERETS
2	TABLESPOONS OLIVE OIL
2	CLOVES GARLIC, THINLY SLICED
12	KALAMATA OLIVES, PITTED AND COARSELY CHOPPED
4	TABLESPOONS ROASTED RED PEPPERS, DICED (PAGE 177)
3	TEASPOONS FINELY CHOPPED FRESH MARJORAM OR 1/2 TEASPOON DRIED
2	TABLESPOONS FINELY CHOPPED FRESH PARSLEY
3	OUNCES FETA CHEESE
	SALT, TO TASTE
	FRESHLY GROUND BLACK PEPPER, TO TASTE
	lemon wedges, for garnish

Steam broccoli until just tender. Heat the oil in a large heavy skillet. Sauté garlic until lightly browned and remove. Add steamed broccoli, olives, peppers, marjoram and parsley to the skillet and sauté over medium-high heat until heated through. Sprinkle cheese over the broccoli and season with salt and pepper. Serve immediately, garnished with lemon wedges.

This dish may be served as a warm salad, over a combination of fresh greens. Or serve as a vegetable with Chicken Breasts with Capers, Pine Nuts and Raisins (page 137).

4 SERVINGS

BAKED VIDALIA ONIONS

6   MEDIUM VIDALIA ONIONS
2   TABLESPOONS OLIVE OIL, DIVIDED
2   TABLESPOONS BALSAMIC VINEGAR
1/4   CUP CHOPPED FRESH PARSLEY
1/4   CUP ITALIAN-STYLE BREADCRUMBS
1/4   CUP FRESHLY GRATED PARMESAN CHEESE
1/4   TEASPOON SALT
1/4   TEASPOON FRESHLY GROUND BLACK PEPPER
2   TABLESPOONS WHITE WINE

Trim root ends of onions so they will stand flat. Scoop out centers with a melon ball scoop and a knife, leaving 1/4-inch sides. Reserve cut-out onion. Pour one tablespoon of olive oil into a 9- by 13-inch glass baking dish. Roll each onion in oil until well-coated. Sprinkle with vinegar and arrange in dish, flat side down. Mince the reserved onion and mix with parsley, breadcrumbs, Parmesan cheese, salt, pepper and wine. Fill onions with the mixture. Cover with foil and bake in a preheated 350 degree oven for 1 hour, basting with remaining oil every 15 minutes. Remove foil for the last 15 minutes, baste again and cook until tender.

Serve these sweet onions with grilled meats during the summer when Vidalia onions are in season. Try them with Braised Pork with Orange Mustard Sauce (page 111).

6 SERVINGS

VEGETABLE STRATA

1/4   CUP OLIVE OIL, DIVIDED
1   POUND RED POTATOES, UNPEELED AND THINLY SLICED
1   RED BELL PEPPER, SLICED LENGTHWISE INTO 1/2-INCH STRIPS
1   YELLOW BELL PEPPER, SLICED LENGTHWISE INTO 1/2-INCH STRIPS
3   LARGE RIPE TOMATOES, SEEDED AND SLICED 1/4-INCH THICK, RESERVING JUICE
   SALT, TO TASTE
   FRESHLY GROUND BLACK PEPPER, TO TASTE
3   CLOVES GARLIC, COARSELY CHOPPED
12   COARSELY CHOPPED FRESH BASIL LEAVES
3   TEASPOONS DRIED OREGANO

Lightly grease an 8- by 12-inch baking dish with some of the olive oil. Layer potatoes, red pepper, yellow pepper and tomatoes. Season with salt and pepper and sprinkle garlic, basil and oregano over top. Continue layering until all ingredients have been used. Pour the reserved tomato juice and remaining olive oil over top. Bake in a preheated 400 degree oven for 45 minutes or until potatoes are tender. If vegetables become too dry, add a few tablespoons of water.

Serve with Grilled Herb Garden Chicken (page 136).

4 SERVINGS

BAKED SWISS CAULIFLOWER

1   LARGE HEAD CAULIFLOWER, CUT
    INTO 1-INCH FLOWERETS
2   CUPS SHREDDED GRUYÈRE CHEESE
2   EGG YOLKS, BEATEN
1   CUP HEAVY CREAM
1/4 TEASPOON NUTMEG
1/2 TEASPOON SALT
1/8 TEASPOON CAYENNE PEPPER
1/2 CUP CRUSHED GARLIC CROUTONS
1/4 CUP MELTED BUTTER

Steam cauliflower until crisp but tender. Remove from steamer and place in an 8- by 12-inch baking dish. Sprinkle with cheese. Combine egg yolks, cream, nutmeg, salt and cayenne pepper, and pour over cauliflower. Cover with crushed garlic croutons and drizzle melted butter over top. Bake 15 to 20 minutes in a preheated 350 degree oven.

Emmentaler or Jarlsberg cheese may be used in place of Gruyère to give a sharper edge to this rich and creamy dish. Try it as an accompaniment to Herb-Crusted Rack of Lamb (page 116).

6 SERVINGS

LAYERED SUMMER VEGETABLES

2   MEDIUM ZUCCHINI, THINLY SLICED
2   MEDIUM YELLOW SQUASH, THINLY
    SLICED
2   MEDIUM BAKING POTATOES,
    UNPEELED, THINLY SLICED
3   MEDIUM TOMATOES, THINLY SLICED
2   THINLY SLICED WHITE OR RED
    ONIONS
1/4 CUP OLIVE OIL
    FRESHLY GROUND BLACK PEPPER,
    TO TASTE
    SALT, TO TASTE
    CHOPPED FRESH BASIL, TO TASTE

Arrange zucchini, yellow squash, potatoes, tomatoes and onions in a lightly oiled 9- by 13-inch baking dish, alternating slices of vegetables for color. Drizzle olive oil over vegetables and bake in a preheated 400 degree oven for 40 to 50 minutes or until potatoes are done. Sprinkle with pepper, salt and basil.

This dish makes a colorful accompaniment to Splendid Beef Tenderloin (page 120). The amount of vegetables used may vary. Whole plum tomatoes may be substituted for slicing tomatoes and dried mixed herbs may be substituted for basil. The dish may be prepared a day ahead, tightly covered and refrigerated. Reheat in oven.

8 SERVINGS

ASPARAGUS IN LEMON VINAIGRETTE

1	POUND FRESH ASPARAGUS
1/4	CUP OLIVE OIL
1	TABLESPOON FRESHLY SQUEEZED LEMON JUICE
1	CLOVE GARLIC, CRUSHED
1/2	TEASPOON DRIED OREGANO
1/2	TEASPOON DRIED BASIL
1/2	TEASPOON SALT
	FRESHLY GROUND BLACK PEPPER, TO TASTE
3	TABLESPOONS PINE NUTS, TOASTED

Break off tough ends of asparagus stalks. Rinse well under cold running water; remove scales if sandy. Place asparagus in a steamer over boiling water and steam, covered, until tender but crisp, about 7 minutes. Drain well.

Whisk together olive oil, lemon juice, garlic, oregano, basil, salt and pepper until well blended. Pour into a large nonreactive skillet and cook over medium heat until hot, about 3 minutes. Add asparagus and toss well. Arrange asparagus on a serving platter and sprinkle with pine nuts. Let stand at room temperature until serving time.

Fresh asparagus is a wonderful addition to almost any meal. Try this version with Mushroom Stuffed Beef Tenderloin (page 121) or Savory Mahogany Chicken (page 138).

4 SERVINGS

POTATOES GRUYÈRE

6	MEDIUM BAKING POTATOES
6	TABLESPOONS BUTTER
	SALT, TO TASTE
	FRESHLY GROUND BLACK PEPPER, TO TASTE
	FRESHLY GROUND NUTMEG, TO TASTE
8	OUNCES FINELY GRATED GRUYÈRE CHEESE
1/2 TO 3/4	CUP BEEF BROTH, PREFERABLY HOMEMADE

Up to 1 hour ahead of preparation time, peel and thinly slice potatoes. Place in a bowl of cold water until ready to use. Butter a shallow 2-quart baking dish. Remove potatoes from water and pat dry. Place a single layer of potatoes in dish, overlapping slices until bottom of dish is covered. Dot with butter and sprinkle with salt, pepper and nutmeg. Cover lightly with grated Gruyère cheese. Repeat twice more. Gradually pour beef broth over potatoes; use enough broth to ensure that all layers are moistened, but not covered. Cover tightly. Place in a preheated 400 degree oven and bake 30 minutes. Remove cover and cook 15 minutes more, or until potatoes are brown on top. Serve immediately, or cover and keep warm up to 20 minutes.

Try these elegant potatoes with Dill Roasted Leg of Lamb (page 116).

6 SERVINGS

CURRY OF POTATOES AND CAULIFLOWER

2	POUNDS POTATOES, THINLY SLICED
2	POUNDS CAULIFLOWER, CUT IN FLOWERETS
1/2	CUP VEGETABLE OIL, DIVIDED
1	TABLESPOON WHOLE CUMIN
1/2	POUND FINELY CHOPPED ONION
1/4	TEASPOON CURRY POWDER
1/4	TEASPOON CINNAMON
1/4	TEASPOON CHILI POWDER
1/4	TEASPOON FRESHLY GROUND BLACK PEPPER
1/8	TEASPOON TURMERIC
1	CUP TOMATO SAUCE
1	TEASPOON FRESHLY SQUEEZED LEMON JUICE
	SALT, TO TASTE

cilantro leaves or slivers of fresh ginger, for garnish

Sauté potatoes and cauliflower separately in 2 tablespoons of oil, about 3 minutes each. Set aside. In a large skillet, heat 1/4 cup oil and sauté cumin until brown. Add onion and brown, stirring frequently. Stir in curry powder, cinnamon, chili powder, black pepper and turmeric and cook 4 minutes, stirring. Add tomato sauce and heat thoroughly. Stir in potatoes and cauliflower, lemon juice and salt. Cover and simmer until vegetables are tender. Garnish with cilantro leaves or slivers of ginger.

This spicy and unusual northern Indian dish goes well with Tandoori Lamb (page 118).

8 SERVINGS

SCALLOPED POTATOES BAKED IN CREAM

6	LARGE RED POTATOES, PEELED AND THINLY SLICED
1	MEDIUM WHITE ONION, THINLY SLICED
2	CLOVES GARLIC, CRUSHED
1/2	TEASPOON DRIED OREGANO
1	TABLESPOON LEMON PEPPER
8	TABLESPOONS BUTTER
6	OUNCES GRATED SWISS CHEESE
1	CUP HEAVY CREAM

Parboil potatoes in 3 cups salted water until just tender. Drain and set aside. Sauté onion, garlic, oregano and lemon pepper in butter until onion is translucent. In a 9- by 13-inch glass baking dish, layer potatoes, onion mixture, cheese and cream, ending with potatoes and cheese. Bake in a preheated 350 degree oven for 30 minutes.

Serve as an accompaniment to Hibachi Beef (page 122). Substitute Gruyère or cheddar cheese for a different flavor.

8 SERVINGS

BALSAMIC CARROTS

2 POUNDS CARROTS, CUT
   DIAGONALLY INTO 1-INCH SLICES
2 TABLESPOONS BUTTER
1 TEASPOON SALT

Place carrots in a medium saucepan and add butter, salt and 1/2 cup water. Cover tightly and cook over medium-high heat for about 15 minutes, or until carrots are crunchy, not soft. Be careful that carrots do not boil dry; add a small amount of water if necessary.

SAUCE

4 TABLESPOONS BUTTER
4 TABLESPOONS BROWN SUGAR
4 TABLESPOONS BALSAMIC VINEGAR

Melt butter in a small saucepan. Add brown sugar and balsamic vinegar and heat, mixing well. To serve, drain carrots, add sauce and stir. Serve immediately.

The pungent sweetness of the balsamic vinegar makes these carrots a perfect accompaniment to Crown Pork Roast with Cornbread Stuffing (page 114).

4 SERVINGS

ENGLISH PEAS WITH SHERRY

2   CUPS SHELLED FRESH GREEN PEAS
1 1/2 CUPS SLICED FRESH MUSHROOMS
1/4 CUP MINCED ONION
2   TABLESPOONS BUTTER
1/4 TEASPOON SALT
     A DASH OF FRESHLY GROUND BLACK
     PEPPER
1/4 TEASPOON NUTMEG
1/4 CUP DRY SHERRY

Cook peas in 1/2 cup boiling salted water until tender but crisp. Set aside and keep warm. In a large skillet, sauté mushrooms and onion in butter until barely tender, about 5 minutes. Add salt, pepper, nutmeg and sherry. Simmer about 5 minutes, then add hot peas. Cook about 1 minute more and serve.

Try these fresh peas with Dill Roasted Leg of Lamb (page 116) or with Sage-Seasoned Trout (page 159).

6 SERVINGS

ONION SOUFFLÉ

3 TABLESPOONS BUTTER
4 TABLESPOONS BACON FAT (FROM 4 SLICES COOKED BACON)
3 ONIONS, PREFERABLY VIDALIA OR WALLA WALLA, THINLY SLICED, HALVED AND SEPARATED INTO RINGS
4 EGGS, SEPARATED
1/4 CUP MAYONNAISE
1/4 CUP ALL-PURPOSE FLOUR
1 TEASPOON SALT
1/2 TEASPOON FRESHLY GROUND WHITE PEPPER
1/2 TEASPOON PAPRIKA
1/4 CUP GRATED PARMESAN CHEESE
additional Parmesan cheese, for garnish

Add butter to bacon fat in skillet over medium heat. Reserve bacon for another use. Add onions and sauté, stirring until softened. Remove from heat. In a bowl, mix egg yolks with mayonnaise, flour, salt, pepper and paprika. Whisk this mixture into lukewarm onions, blending well. Beat egg whites until stiff peaks form. Gently fold egg whites and Parmesan cheese into onion mixture. Turn mixture into a greased 6-cup soufflé dish or casserole and top with additional grated Parmesan cheese. Bake 40 to 45 minutes in a preheated 350 degree oven.

This soufflé is simple to prepare and goes with all but the mildest entrée.

8 TO 10 SERVINGS

ROZZELLE COURT SPICY GREEN BEANS

1 POUND FRESH GREEN BEANS OR CHINESE LONG BEANS, CLEANED, TRIMMED, STRINGS REMOVED AND CUT IN THIRDS
2 TABLESPOONS SESAME OIL
2 TO 4 TABLESPOONS CHINESE CHILI SAUCE, TO TASTE
4 TABLESPOONS WATER
4 TABLESPOONS RICE WINE, WHITE WINE OR DRY SHERRY
1 TABLESPOON OYSTER SAUCE
1 TABLESPOON FRESHLY SQUEEZED LEMON JUICE
1 TABLESPOON PEANUT BUTTER
2 TEASPOONS FINELY CHOPPED FRESH GINGER
FRESHLY SQUEEZED JUICE OF 1 LEMON
finely chopped green onions or cilantro, for garnish

In a wok, heat sesame oil over high heat. Reduce heat to low and add beans. Cover and cook 5 minutes, stirring occasionally. In a small bowl, combine chili sauce, water, wine, oyster sauce, lemon juice, peanut butter and ginger. Add sauce to beans, stir, and cook, covered, over low heat for 8 to 12 minutes. The length of cooking time will depend on age and tenderness of the beans. Beans should remain crisp. Squeeze lemon juice over beans before serving and garnish with green onions or cilantro.

This distinctive dish is a favorite of Museum visitors who frequent the Rozzelle Court Restaurant.

4 SERVINGS

ZUCCHINI FLAN

Prepare at least 3 hours before serving.
 FRESH, FLAT SPINACH LEAVES,
 ENOUGH TO COVER BOTTOMS AND
 SIDES OF EIGHT 3 1/2-INCH
 RAMEKINS
2 POUNDS FRESH SMALL ZUCCHINI,
 CUT IN 2- BY 4-INCH STRIPS
1 1/2 CUPS HEAVY CREAM
3 EGGS, LIGHTLY BEATEN
3/4 CUP PARMESAN CHEESE
 FRESHLY GROUND BLACK PEPPER,
 TO TASTE

Blanch spinach for 2 minutes. Drain and remove stems. Use leaves to cover the bottoms and sides of 8 individual ramekins, allowing enough spinach to fold over filling. Add zucchini to a large pan of boiling salted water, and return to boil. Cook 30 seconds, drain, and spread in single layer on towels until very dry, 2 to 3 hours or more.

Mix zucchini with cream, eggs, Parmesan cheese and pepper. Pour into ramekins, folding extra spinach over top. Place on a baking sheet and bake in a preheated 450 degree oven for 15 to 20 minutes, or until set. The flan may also be baked in a 10-inch pie pan for 40 minutes, or until set. Serve at once.

This custard-like side dish can be made without the spinach leaves. Sprinkle tops of ramekins with freshly ground nutmeg or paprika. Serve as an accompaniment to Crown Pork Roast with Cornbread Stuffing (page 114).

8 SERVINGS

CURRIED TOMATOES

6 RIPE TOMATOES
1 CUP TOMATO SAUCE
2 TABLESPOONS CURRANT JELLY
2 TEASPOONS CURRY POWDER
3 TABLESPOONS FRESH BREADCRUMBS
6 TABLESPOONS GRATED SHARP
 CHEESE
1 TABLESPOON DRIED BASIL
6 SLICES BACON, CRISPLY COOKED
 AND CRUMBLED

Peel tomatoes by plunging them into boiling water for 2 minutes, then slipping off the skins. Remove stem ends and cut into 1/2-inch slices. Place tomatoes in a shallow baking dish. In a saucepan, combine tomato sauce, currant jelly and curry powder, and cook for 5 minutes. Pour over the tomatoes. Sprinkle with breadcrumbs, cheese and basil and bake 15 minutes in a preheated 425 degree oven.

Garnish with crumbled bacon and serve very hot.

This unusual dish is full-flavored and tangy. Serve with Curry Grilled Flank Steak (page 123).

6 SERVINGS

VEGETABLE SAUTÉ

ROASTED PEPPERS

2 TABLESPOONS OLIVE OIL
4 GREEN ONIONS, CHOPPED
2 MEDIUM ZUCCHINI, CUT INTO
   JULIENNE
4 SMALL CARROTS, CUT INTO
   JULIENNE
1 SMALL JICAMA, CUT INTO JULIENNE
2 TABLESPOONS CHOPPED FRESH
   BASIL, OR MORE IF DESIRED
   fresh basil leaves, for garnish

Heat oil in skillet over medium-high heat. Add green onions and stir-fry 1 minute. Add zucchini, carrots and jicama and stir-fry 3 to 5 minutes, adding more oil if necessary. Do not allow vegetables to wilt, as they should be crunchy. Toss with basil immediately before serving. Garnish with basil leaves or any other fresh, leafy green herb.

Serve as an accompaniment to Sautéed Sunflower Lamb Chops (page 118) or Poulet en Persillade (page 137).

4 SERVINGS

To char peppers, pierce one end with a long fork or skewer. Roast, turning over a flame until blackened, blistered and charred, 3 to 5 minutes. This may be done over the flame of a gas burner or by broiling 2 inches from the broiler, turning frequently for about 20 minutes. Place the charred peppers in a plastic bag and let them steam in their own heat until cool. Cut off tops of peppers and peel or scrape skin with a sharp knife. Seed peppers, and use according to recipe.

SALADS

WINE WITH SALADS

*Salads dressed in the usual
fashion are death for wine.
Vinegar is essentially wine gone
sour, and when used in salads
will have a deleterious effect on
any wine. One solution is to
dispense with vinegar and dress
salads in oil (nut oils or olive
oil) and tart young wine—and
serve the same wine. Try a
Sauvignon Blanc for this. Still,
salad is usually a brief course
and generally does not require a
wine of its own.*

Preceding page: Caesar Salad, page 181

CAESAR SALAD

CROUTONS

4	CLOVES GARLIC
1/2	CUP BUTTER, SOFTENED
1/2	CUP OLIVE OIL
1	TEASPOON PAPRIKA
1/4	TEASPOON CAYENNE PEPPER
1/2	TEASPOON SALT
1/4	TEASPOON FRESHLY GROUND BLACK PEPPER
4	CUPS DAY-OLD FRENCH BREAD, CUT INTO 1/2-INCH CUBES

In a food processor, purée garlic with butter and olive oil. Place in a saucepan and simmer. Add paprika, cayenne pepper, salt and black pepper. Place bread cubes in a baking dish and toss with garlic mixture. Bake in a preheated 350 degree oven until lightly browned. Cool and set aside.

DRESSING

1	CUP OLIVE OIL
3	CLOVES GARLIC, PRESSED
2	OUNCES ANCHOVIES, RINSED AND FINELY CHOPPED
2	TEASPOONS DIJON-STYLE MUSTARD
1	TABLESPOON FRESHLY SQUEEZED LEMON JUICE
1	TABLESPOON SHERRY VINEGAR COARSELY GROUND BLACK PEPPER, TO TASTE
1	TABLESPOON STEAK SAUCE
3	EGG YOLKS, CODDLED
3	HEADS ROMAINE LETTUCE, INNER LEAVES ONLY
3/4	CUP SHREDDED PARMESAN CHEESE,

Blend olive oil and garlic. Add the anchovies, mustard, lemon juice, vinegar, pepper and steak sauce, mixing well. Stir in the egg yolks.

Toss the lettuce with the dressing, half of the Parmesan and half of the croutons, making sure all leaves are coated. Arrange on chilled plates or a serving platter. Sprinkle with the remaining cheese and croutons.

6 TO 8 SERVINGS

MEDITERRANEAN PEPPER SALAD

Begin 3 hours before serving.

2	CLOVES GARLIC, MINCED
1/2	TEASPOON DRIED RED PEPPER FLAKES
1	TABLESPOON CHOPPED FRESH BASIL
1	TEASPOON SALT
1/4	CUP WHITE-WINE VINEGAR
1/2	CUP OLIVE OIL
4	RED BELL PEPPERS, ROASTED AND SLICED (PAGE 177)
1 1/2	CUPS PITTED, BRINE-CURED BLACK OLIVES
1/2	POUND FRESH GREEN BEANS, TRIMMED AND BLANCHED
6	OUNCES FETA CHEESE, SLICED OR CHUNKED

Combine garlic, red pepper flakes, basil, salt and vinegar in a bowl and whisk in oil. Pour over peppers, olives and beans and marinate for at least two hours. Drain vegetables, reserving marinade.

On a decorative platter, arrange cheese and vegetables and pour marinade over all.

This salad makes an excellent side dish for pizza or pasta. Yellow, green, and orange bell peppers may also be used.

6 SERVINGS

GREEN BEAN AND RASPBERRY SALAD

1   POUND FRESH GREEN BEANS
5   TABLESPOONS SNIPPED FRESH
     CHIVES
     ZEST OF 1 ORANGE
1/3   CUP RASPBERRY VINEGAR
1   TEASPOON DIJON-STYLE MUSTARD
1/2   CUP OLIVE OIL
     SALT, TO TASTE
     FRESHLY GROUND BLACK PEPPER,
     TO TASTE
1   CUP FRESH RASPBERRIES

Blanch green beans in boiling water until crisp and tender, about 1 minute. Cool in cold water and drain. Toss green beans with chives and orange zest. In a small bowl, whisk together raspberry vinegar, mustard, olive oil, salt and pepper. Pour over green beans, add raspberries and toss gently.

4 TO 6 SERVINGS

MASHED POTATO SALAD

1 1/2   POUNDS POTATOES, PEELED AND
     CUBED
5   TABLESPOONS OLIVE OIL, DIVIDED
3/4   CUP WHOLE MILK, WARMED
     A DASH OF NUTMEG
     SALT, TO TASTE
     FRESHLY GROUND BLACK PEPPER,
     TO TASTE
1/2   POUND SLAB BACON, CUT INTO 1/4-
     INCH CUBES
2   CUPS SHREDDED ROMAINE LETTUCE
4   TEASPOONS CHOPPED PARSLEY
1 TO 2   MEDIUM TOMATOES, CHOPPED
2   GREEN ONIONS, CHOPPED

Cover potatoes with water and bring to a boil, cooking until tender. Drain and mash the potatoes, or put through ricer. Mix in 2 tablespoons olive oil, warmed milk, nutmeg, salt and pepper. Keep potatoes warm in the top of a double boiler until ready to use. Sauté bacon cubes in a heavy skillet until browned on all sides. Remove with a slotted spoon onto a paper towel. Pour off all but 2 tablespoons bacon fat and set aside.

VINAIGRETTE
1   TABLESPOON FINELY CHOPPED
     SHALLOTS
1   TABLESPOON DIJON-STYLE MUSTARD
1 1/2   TABLESPOONS RED-WINE VINEGAR

Combine shallots, mustard and vinegar and whisk in remaining 3 tablespoons olive oil. Add vinaigrette to bacon fat in skillet and heat through for 1 minute, stirring well.

Divide potatoes among four plates. Spread shredded lettuce evenly on top of potatoes and sprinkle with bacon. Spoon warm vinaigrette evenly over potatoes, lettuce and bacon. Sprinkle with parsley, chopped tomatoes and green onions. Serve immediately.

4 SERVINGS

Henschke Semillon 1 9 8 9 (Hunter Valley - Australia)

SPINACH, CABBAGE AND CARROT SLAW

DRESSING
1/2   CUP VEGETABLE OIL
1/4   CUP WHITE WINE VINEGAR
1/3   CUP KETCHUP
1/3   CUP SUGAR
1   TEASPOON GARLIC SALT
1   TEASPOON PAPRIKA

At least one hour before serving, combine oil, vinegar and ketchup. Add sugar, garlic salt and paprika, blending well. Pour into a shaker or jar and set aside.

SALAD
1/2   HEAD GREEN CABBAGE, SHREDDED
2   LARGE CARROTS, GRATED
1   POUND SPINACH, WASHED AND THINLY SLICED
1/4   POUND SALTED MIXED NUTS

In a large bowl, combine cabbage, carrots and spinach. Toss with nuts and dressing just before serving.

6 TO 8 SERVINGS

CHICKEN CURRY SALAD

DRESSING
1/2   CUP MAYONNAISE
1/2   CUP PLAIN YOGURT
2   TABLESPOONS CURRY POWDER
   SALT, TO TASTE
   FRESHLY GROUND BLACK PEPPER, TO TASTE

In a small mixing bowl, whisk together mayonnaise, yogurt, curry powder, salt and pepper. Chill until ready to use.

SALAD
3   WHOLE CHICKEN BREASTS, SPLIT
4   CUPS CHICKEN STOCK OR BROTH, PREFERABLY HOMEMADE
1   ONION, HALVED
1   STALK CELERY, CUT INTO CHUNKS
1   CARROT, CUT INTO CHUNKS
3   SPRIGS OF FRESH PARSLEY
1   BAY LEAF
6   BLACK PEPPERCORNS
1   MEDIUM CUCUMBER, PEELED, SEEDED AND DICED
1   CUP ROASTED PEANUTS
1/2   CUP RAISINS
fresh watercress and 1/4 cup roasted peanuts, for garnish

Poach chicken for 20 minutes in chicken stock seasoned with the onion, celery, carrot, parsley, bay leaf and peppercorns. Cool chicken in the liquid. When cool, remove chicken breasts and discard the skin and bones. Cut meat into 3/4-inch chunks. In a large bowl, combine chicken, cucumber, peanuts, raisins and dressing. Chill.

Serve salad on a platter surrounded with watercress and garnished with additional peanuts.

6 SERVINGS

*Rosemont Traminer/ Riesling 1 9 9 1
(Hunter Valley - Australia)*

GINGERED CHICKEN AND MELON SALAD

3   LARGE WHOLE CHICKEN BREASTS,
    SPLIT
1   CARROT, SLICED
1   BUNCH GREEN ONIONS, WHITE PART
    ONLY, SLICED
1   STALK CELERY, CHOPPED

Place chicken breasts in a large, deep pan with enough salted water to cover. Add carrot, green onions and celery and bring to a boil. Reduce heat and poach chicken over low heat for 20 minutes. Remove chicken, reserving broth. When chicken is cool enough to handle, remove skin and bones and place chicken in a large bowl. Return chicken skin and bones to cooking broth and boil until broth is reduced to about 2 cups. Strain and pour broth over the chicken breasts. Cover and let cool.

DRESSING

1   JUMBO EGG
2   TABLESPOONS FRESHLY SQUEEZED
     LEMON JUICE
1/2 TEASPOON SALT
1/4 TEASPOON FRESHLY GROUND BLACK
     PEPPER
1   CUP VEGETABLE OIL
1   TABLESPOON FINELY CHOPPED
     FRESH TARRAGON
2   TABLESPOONS FINELY GRATED FRESH
     GINGER
1/2 CUP HEAVY CREAM, WHIPPED
1   SMALL CANTALOUPE CUT INTO
     NARROW, SHORT SLICES
1   SMALL HONEYDEW CUT INTO
     NARROW, SHORT SLICES
1   BUNCH SEEDLESS RED GRAPES,
     SLICED LENGTHWISE
     leaf lettuce, for garnish

Combine egg, lemon juice, salt and pepper in a blender or food processor and blend until the egg is foamy. With the machine running, slowly add oil in a thin stream until mixture thickens. Pour dressing into a bowl and fold in tarragon, ginger and whipped cream, until well blended. Cover and chill.

Remove chicken from broth and slice into narrow strips. Place in a large bowl with cantaloupe, honeydew, grapes and dressing, and toss until salad is well coated. Line a platter with lettuce leaves and mound salad in the center.

6 TO 8 SERVINGS

Joseph Panel 1 9 9 0 Condrieu (Northern Rhône)

CURRIED SHRIMP AND CASHEW SALAD

1	MEDIUM APPLE, PEELED AND SLICED
1/2	GREEN BELL PEPPER, CHOPPED
4	LARGE GREEN ONIONS, SLICED
1	POUND MEDIUM SHRIMP, SHELLED AND COOKED
2	OUNCES SALTED CASHEWS
1	CUP COOKED RICE
1/2	TEASPOON SALT, OR TO TASTE

Combine apple, pepper and onions with shrimp, cashews, rice and salt. Set aside.

DRESSING

1	TABLESPOON WHITE-WINE VINEGAR
1/2	TEASPOON SALT
1/2	TEASPOON DIJON-STYLE MUSTARD
1	EGG YOLK
1	EGG
1	CUP VEGETABLE OIL
1/2	CUP SOUR CREAM
1	SMALL AVOCADO, PITTED, PEELED AND SLICED
1	TEASPOON CURRY POWDER

lettuce leaves and avocado strips, for garnish

Blend vinegar, salt, mustard, egg yolk and egg in food processor. Add oil slowly, blending until mixture is the consistency of mayonnaise. Add sour cream, avocado and curry powder. Process, using pulse action, until well blended. Pour dressing over salad and toss. Arrange individual servings in lettuce leaves and garnish with strips of avocado.

4 SERVINGS

Kuentz Bas 1 9 9 0 Pinot d'Alsace (Alsace)

ROQUEFORT CHEESE DRESSING

1/2	POUND ROQUEFORT CHEESE, CRUMBLED
6	TABLESPOONS HEAVY CREAM
1	CUP SOUR CREAM
1 3/4	TEASPOONS SALT
3/4	TEASPOON ONION POWDER
1 1/4	TEASPOONS COARSELY GROUND BLACK PEPPER
2 1/3	TEASPOONS ENGLISH-STYLE DRY MUSTARD
1	CLOVE GARLIC, MINCED A DASH OF WORCESTERSHIRE SAUCE
1/2	CUP WHITE-WINE VINEGAR
3/4	CUP VEGETABLE OIL
3	CUPS MAYONNAISE
1/3	TEASPOON FRESHLY SQUEEZED LEMON JUICE

Combine Roquefort cheese, heavy cream and sour cream by mashing with a fork. Add salt, onion powder, pepper, mustard, garlic and Worcestershire sauce. Stir in the vinegar, oil, mayonnaise and lemon juice, mixing well. Refrigerate.

This dressing keeps well. The quality of cheese is important—buy the best and strongest available. The dressing may also be used as a dip.

MAKES 1 QUART.

BACON AND POTATO SALAD

Prepare several hours before serving.

10 TO 12   MEDIUM RUSSET POTATOES, PEELED, COOKED AND CUBED
1   MEDIUM ONION, CHOPPED
1/2   CUP CRUMBLED COOKED BACON
1 1/2   CUPS MAYONNAISE
1 1/2   CUPS SOUR CREAM
  SALT, TO TASTE, IF DESIRED
  FRESHLY GROUND BLACK PEPPER, TO TASTE

Place potatoes, onion and bacon in a large bowl. In a separate bowl, combine mayonnnaise, sour cream, salt and pepper. Pour over potato mixture and combine well. Chill for several hours to allow flavors to blend.

This do-ahead salad is perfect for buffets and is even better served the second day.

10 TO 12 SERVINGS

HONG KONG SALAD

1   POUND BEAN SPROUTS, RINSED AND DRAINED
8   OUNCES WATER CHESTNUTS, SLICED
1   GREEN BELL PEPPER, CHOPPED
1/2   CUP TOASTED SLIVERED ALMONDS
8   CUPS SALAD GREENS, TORN INTO SMALL PIECES

In a large bowl, toss bean sprouts, water chestnuts, green pepper and almonds with salad greens. Set aside.

HERB DRESSING

1 1/2   CUPS MAYONNAISE
1/3   CUP VEGETABLE OIL
1 1/2   TEASPOONS PREPARED MUSTARD
1/2   TEASPOON HOT PEPPER SAUCE
2   TEASPOONS CHILI POWDER
1   TEASPOON ONION JUICE
2   TABLESPOONS VINEGAR
3/4   TEASPOON DRIED THYME
1 1/2   TEASPOONS MINCED GARLIC
1 1/2   TEASPOONS DRIED MARJORAM

In a separate bowl, combine mayonnaise, oil and mustard. Whisk in hot pepper sauce, chili powder, onion juice, vinegar, thyme, garlic and marjoram. To serve, pour dressing over salad and toss.

6 TO 8 SERVINGS

Morgadio Albarino 1 9 9 1 (Spain)

SPICY POTATO SALAD

Prepare at least 3 hours before serving.

GREEN ONION DRESSING

1	EGG
1	EGG YOLK
1 1/8	CUPS VEGETABLE OIL
1/2	CUP FINELY CHOPPED GREEN ONION
1 1/2	TABLESPOONS SPICY BROWN MUSTARD
1	TABLESPOON WHITE VINEGAR
1/4	TEASPOON SALT
1/8	TEASPOON FRESHLY GROUND WHITE PEPPER

In a blender, combine egg and egg yolk until frothy. With blender running, add oil very slowly in a thin stream until mixture is thick and creamy. Add green onions, mustard, vinegar, salt and pepper and blend thoroughly. Set aside.

SALAD

4	MEDIUM POTATOES, COOKED, PEELED AND COARSELY CHOPPED
3	HARD-COOKED EGGS, CHOPPED
1/4	CUP FINELY CHOPPED GREEN ONION
1/2	CUP CHOPPED CELERY
2	TEASPOONS CAYENNE PEPPER
2	TEASPOONS SPICY BROWN MUSTARD
1 1/4	TEASPOONS SALT
1/4	TEASPOON FRESHLY GROUND WHITE PEPPER

In a large bowl, combine potatoes, eggs, green onion and celery. Add cayenne pepper, mustard, salt and white pepper, mixing well. Pour Green Onion Dressing over potatoes and toss gently. Refrigerate several hours before serving.

6 TO 8 SERVINGS

GORGONZOLA AND WATERCRESS SALAD

DRESSING

2	CUPS VEGETABLE OIL
1/2	CUP BALSAMIC VINEGAR
1	TEASPOON SALT
	FRESHLY GROUND BLACK PEPPER, TO TASTE
2	TEASPOONS FINELY MINCED ONION

In a small bowl, combine oil, vinegar, salt, pepper and onion. Mix well and set aside.

SALAD

3	BUNCHES WATERCRESS (ABOUT 6 CUPS)
1	HEAD ROMAINE LETTUCE, SHREDDED AND CHILLED
1 1/2	CUPS GORGONZOLA OR BLUE CHEESE, CRUMBLED
1	CUP CHOPPED WALNUTS, SAUTÉED IN 1 TABLESPOON BUTTER

Gently wash and dry watercress and separate into small pieces. Combine with romaine lettuce in a large bowl and pour dressing over salad. Toss gently and arrange on individual salad plates or on a large platter. Sprinkle with cheese and top with walnuts.

6 SERVINGS

Dr. Taurino 1 9 8 5 Salice Salentino Riserva (Apulia)

TOMATOES WITH FETA CHEESE

FRESH BASIL LEAVES—ENOUGH TO
LINE A 9- BY 13-INCH OVENPROOF
SERVING DISH
4 TO 5 RIPE TOMATOES, PEELED AND
THICKLY SLICED
1 TABLESPOON BALSAMIC VINEGAR
2 TABLESPOONS OLIVE OIL
1/2 CLOVE GARLIC, CRUSHED
SALT, TO TASTE
FRESHLY CRACKED BLACK PEPPER,
TO TASTE
2 CUPS FETA CHEESE, CRUMBLED

Arrange the basil leaves in a single layer on the
bottom of a 9-by-13-inch serving dish. Arrange
tomato slices on top of basil. Whisk together
vinegar, olive oil, garlic, salt and pepper and
drizzle over the tomatoes. Sprinkle generously
with feta cheese. Broil about 5 inches from heat
until the cheese is golden. Remove from oven
and cool to room temperature or chill and serve
cold.

*This salad is especially attractive made with yellow or
orange tomatoes. It is good for entertaining as it can be
prepared in advance.*

6 TO 8 SERVINGS

*Vaselli Orvieto Classico Torre Sant'Andrea 1 9 9 0
(Umbria - Italy)*

MARINATED VEGETABLES JULIENNE

Prepare at least 2 hours before serving.
DRESSING
2 CUPS VEGETABLE OIL
1/2 CUP CIDER OR WHITE VINEGAR
1 TEASPOON SALT
1 TEASPOON DRIED TARRAGON
1 TEASPOON DRIED DILLWEED
1 TEASPOON DRIED BASIL
1 CLOVE GARLIC, CRUSHED

Whisk together the oil, vinegar, salt, tarragon,
dillweed, basil and garlic. Set aside.

SALAD
2 CUPS CARROTS, CUT INTO JULIENNE
AND COOKED UNTIL TENDER
2 CUPS POTATOES, PEELED, CUT INTO
JULIENNE AND COOKED UNTIL
TENDER
2 CUPS FRESH GREEN BEANS, TRIMMED
AND BLANCHED
2 CUPS ASPARAGUS TIPS, BLANCHED

Toss dressing with the carrots, potatoes, green
beans and asparagus tips in a large bowl. Chill
at least 2 hours. To serve, lift vegetables out of
the dressing with a slotted spoon and place in a
clear glass serving bowl.

10 TO 12 SERVINGS

*Bert Simon Serriger Würtzberg Kabinett 1 9 9 0
(Mosel - Saar - Ruwer)*

GREEK POTATO PLATTER SALAD

DRESSING

1/4	CUP CIDER VINEGAR
1/2	CUP OLIVE OIL
1/2	CUP VEGETABLE OIL
1	TEASPOON SALT
1	CLOVE GARLIC, PRESSED
1	TEASPOON DRIED OREGANO
	COARSELY GROUND BLACK PEPPER,
	TO TASTE

Place vinegar in a food processor and, using pulse action, slowly add olive oil and vegetable oil in a thin stream. Add salt, garlic, oregano and pepper and blend. Set aside.

POTATO SALAD

4	LARGE POTATOES, PEELED, COOKED
	AND CUBED
2	TABLESPOONS CIDER VINEGAR
2	TEASPOONS WHOLE MUSTARD SEED
1	TEASPOON SALT
3	STALKS CELERY, CHOPPED
2	HARD-COOKED EGGS, CHOPPED
1/2	CUP CHOPPED ONION
2	SWEET PICKLES, CHOPPED
1	CUP MAYONNAISE

Sprinkle warm potatoes with vinegar, mustard seed and salt. When cool, add the celery, eggs, onion, pickles and mayonnaise and toss gently to blend.

GREEN SALAD

6	OUNCES MIXED GREENS—ROMAINE,
	BUTTER AND LEAF LETTUCE
1	CUP COOKED WHOLE BABY BEETS
1	CUP GARBANZO BEANS
1	CUP PITTED KALAMATA OLIVES
1	CUP CRUMBLED FETA CHEESE
1/2	LARGE RED ONION, SLICED
1	RED BELL PEPPER, SLICED INTO RINGS
1	GREEN BELL PEPPER, SLICED INTO RINGS
1	CUP SHREDDED RED CABBAGE

Select a large serving platter with a wide edge. Spread potato salad on the platter. Arrange the mixed greens, beets, beans, olives, cheese, onion, red and green pepper and cabbage over the potato salad. Drizzle liberally with dressing.

This is a beautiful buffet salad, but make sure that guests reach the potato salad at the bottom. The salad may also be served in individual bowls at a seated dinner.

8 SERVINGS

La Vieille Ferme 1 9 9 0 Blanc Reserve (Côtes du Rhône)

SMOKED SAUSAGE, TURKEY AND MOZZARELLA SALAD

DRESSING

2	CUPS VEGETABLE OIL
1/2	CUP CIDER VINEGAR
1/3	CUP SUGAR
2	TEASPOONS SALT
2	TEASPOONS CELERY SEED
2	TEASPOONS PAPRIKA
2	TEASPOONS DRY MUSTARD

Place oil, vinegar, sugar, salt, celery seed, paprika and mustard in a quart jar and shake vigorously. Set aside.

SALAD

8	CUPS CRISP ROMAINE LETTUCE, TORN INTO SMALL PIECES
2	CUPS COOKED TURKEY, CUT INTO JULIENNE
1 1/2	CUPS SMOKED SAUSAGE, CUT INTO JULIENNE
1 1/2	CUPS SLIVERED MOZZARELLA CHEESE
1/2	CUP CRUMBLED BLUE CHEESE

ripe tomato wedges and crumbled blue cheese, for garnish

Place romaine in a large bowl and sprinkle turkey, sausage, mozzarella and blue cheese evenly over the top. If preparing ahead, chill at this point. To serve, toss 1 to 1 1/2 cups of dressing with salad mixture.

Garnish with tomatoes and more blue cheese if desired.

4 MAIN DISH SERVINGS

Audebert 1 9 8 9 Bourgueil (Loire - non-tannic red)

ARTICHOKE SALAD DRESSING

Prepare several hours before serving.

6	TABLESPOONS FRESHLY GRATED PARMESAN CHEESE
4	TABLESPOONS RED-WINE VINEGAR
4	TABLESPOONS FRESHLY SQUEEZED LEMON JUICE
1	CUP VEGETABLE OIL
1 1/2	TEASPOONS SALT
1/2	TEASPOON FRESHLY GROUND BLACK PEPPER
1 1/2	TABLESPOONS SUGAR
1	TEASPOON DRY MUSTARD
1/2	TEASPOON GARLIC POWDER
1	MEDIUM RED ONION, THINLY SLICED
4	TABLESPOONS PIMIENTO, CHOPPED
4	MARINATED ARTICHOKE HEARTS, CHOPPED

Blend together Parmesan cheese, vinegar, lemon juice, oil, salt, pepper, sugar, mustard and garlic powder. Add the onion, pimiento, and artichoke hearts and mix well. Refrigerate several hours before serving.

MAKES 2 CUPS.

CRUNCHY ORIENTAL SHRIMP SALAD

DRESSING

3	TABLESPOONS BROWN SUGAR
1/2	CUP RICE VINEGAR
1/2	CUP VEGETABLE OIL
1	TABLESPOON SOY SAUCE
1/2	TEASPOON FRESHLY GROUND BLACK PEPPER
1/2 TO 1	TEASPOON SESAME OIL

Combine sugar, vinegar, oil, soy sauce, pepper and sesame oil. Mix well and set aside.

SALAD

1	TABLESPOON BUTTER
3	OUNCES RAMEN NOODLES, BROKEN INTO SMALL PIECES
1/2	CUP SLIVERED ALMONDS
1/3	CUP SESAME SEEDS
10 TO 12	CUPS BUTTER LETTUCE, RINSED, CRISPED AND TORN INTO SMALL PIECES
1	CUP CHOPPED GREEN ONION
1	POUND MINIATURE SHRIMP, SHELLED AND COOKED

Heat butter in a skillet until it sizzles. Stir in noodles and almonds and cook over medium-high heat, stirring often, until golden. Add sesame seeds and stir until mixture is toasted. Spoon onto a paper towel and cool.

In a large bowl, combine lettuce, onion, shrimp and noodle mixture. Stir dressing to blend and pour over lettuce mixture. Toss gently and serve immediately.

6 TO 8 MAIN DISH SERVINGS

Zilliken Saarburger Rausch Auslese 1 9 9 0 (Mosel - Saar - Ruwer)

FRESH CORN AND PINE NUT SALAD

DRESSING

1	CUP VEGETABLE OIL
1/4	CUP CIDER VINEGAR
1	TEASPOON SALT
1	SMALL GARLIC CLOVE, PRESSED FRESHLY GROUND BLACK PEPPER, TO TASTE

Whisk together oil, vinegar, salt, garlic and pepper. Set aside.

SALAD

4	LARGE EARS FRESH YELLOW CORN, KERNELS REMOVED AND BLANCHED (ABOUT 4 CUPS CORN)
1	LARGE RED BELL PEPPER, CHOPPED
1/2	CUP CHOPPED GREEN ONION
1/2	CUP CHOPPED FRESH CILANTRO
1/2	CUP TOASTED PINE NUTS

In a large mixing bowl, combine corn, red pepper, onion and cilantro. Pour dressing over the salad and toss well. Chill for at least one hour.

To serve, place salad in an attractive serving dish and sprinkle with pine nuts.

6 SERVINGS

Sanford Chardonnay 1 9 9 0 (Santa Barbara)

CHEESE AND TOMATO SALAD PIZZA

TOPPING

4   LARGE SHALLOTS, THINLY SLICED
4   LARGE GARLIC CLOVES, THINLY
     SLICED
3   TABLESPOONS OLIVE OIL
2   TABLESPOONS CHOPPED FRESH
     PARSLEY

Sauté the shallots and garlic in olive oil until tender. Remove from heat and add parsley. Set aside.

PIZZA

2/3   CUP CRUMBLED FETA CHEESE
2/3   CUP FRESHLY GRATED ROMANO
      CHEESE
1   MEDIUM OR LARGE PIZZA CRUST,
     READY TO BAKE

Sprinkle crumbled feta and Romano cheeses over top of pizza dough, leaving a 3/4-inch border. Dot with the shallot and garlic mixture and bake in a preheated 425 degree oven until the crust is golden brown and cheeses are melted, about 20 minutes.

SALAD

4   LARGE PLUM TOMATOES, SEEDED
     AND CHOPPED
1/4   CUP FRESHLY GRATED ROMANO
      CHEESE
1/2   CUP CHOPPED FRESH PARSLEY
1/4   CUP OLIVE OIL
1   TABLESPOON BALSAMIC OR RED-
     WINE VINEGAR
1/4   CUP CHOPPED FRESH BASIL
1   RED BELL PEPPER, GRILLED AND
     SLICED INTO STRIPS, IF DESIRED
1   WHOLE BONELESS CHICKEN BREAST,
     COOKED AND SLICED INTO STRIPS,
     IF DESIRED
     SALT, TO TASTE
     FRESHLY GROUND BLACK PEPPER,
     TO TASTE

Combine tomatoes, Romano cheese, parsley, olive oil, vinegar, basil, bell pepper and chicken. Season to taste with salt and pepper. When the pizza has finished baking, top with the salad and serve immediately.

MAKES 6 TO 8 SLICES.

Cline Cellars Zinfandel 1 9 9 0 (California)

GRILLED MARINATED BEEF SALAD

Begin at least 3 hours before serving.

MARINATED BEEF

1/2	CUP DRY SHERRY
1/2	CUP SOY SAUCE
1	TEASPOON DRY MUSTARD
1	CLOVE GARLIC, MINCED
1	TABLESPOON FRESH GINGER, PEELED AND MINCED
	SALT, TO TASTE
	FRESHLY GROUND BLACK PEPPER, TO TASTE
3/4	POUND BEEF TENDERLOIN OR FLANK STEAK

In a bowl, combine sherry, soy sauce, mustard, garlic, ginger, salt and pepper and whisk until well blended. Place beef in a large, shallow baking dish and pour on the marinade. Cover and marinate 2 to 3 hours. Grill beef 4 inches above hot coals until medium rare. Remove meat from grill and slice into 2-inch strips.

SALAD

1/2	HEAD BROCCOLI, CUT INTO SMALL FLOWERETS AND BLANCHED
1	CUP TOASTED PINE NUTS
2	TABLESPOONS CHOPPED FRESH TARRAGON
1/2	CUP MAYONNAISE
1/2	CUP SOUR CREAM
2	TEASPOONS DIJON-STYLE MUSTARD
1	TABLESPOON FRESHLY SQUEEZED LIME JUICE
	SALT, TO TASTE
	FRESHLY GROUND BLACK PEPPER, TO TASTE

Belgian endive leaves, for garnish

In a large bowl, toss together broccoli, pine nuts and tarragon. Add the beef. In a small bowl, combine mayonnaise, sour cream, mustard, lime juice, salt and pepper, stirring until well blended. Pour dressing over the beef mixture and toss gently until coated. Line a serving platter with endive leaves and mound salad in the center.

6 TO 8 SERVINGS

Bonny Doon Vin Gris 1 9 9 0 (California)

SAUCES

&

ACCOMPANIMENTS

WINE WITH SAUCES

According to the dictum of traditional food and wine, the sauce determines the wine. The ingredients of béarnaise sauce (lemon juice, eggs, butter, tarragon) seem to be a good combination with Tavel Rosé. However, on a prime fillet, béarnaise becomes simply a condiment—much as the Tavel would seem if it were paired with fillet and béarnaise. The focus of the dish is what determines the wine; but the sauce usually gives direction—mostly because a good recipe pairs sauces and dishes appropriately.

Common components of sauces beg for illumination. Tomatoes are pure acid and, when vine-ripe, are also sweet and delicious. They need high-acid wines with lots of fruit— Zinfandel, Dolcetto, great Beaujolais and many Australian blends. Cream sauce, which is all fat; needs rich wines with good acid, such as French Chardonnay (Chablis Grand Cru or Meursault), some very lush Australian Chardonnay (Rosemount, Rothbury), and southern California Chardonnay (Calera, Sanford, Morgan). The only danger with the American and Australian wines is that their alcohol levels may, on occasion, be too strong for cream sauces. Experience can be a guide.

A reduction sauce becomes more and more intense in the flavor of its origin, often gaining in sweetness as well as richness, until, if overdone, it becomes bitter. Consider using a wine with more fruit. If the sauce becomes too reduced, add some of the wine to it.

 Preceding page: Roasted Red Pepper Sauce, page 135

DANISH MUSTARD

2 OUNCES DRY ENGLISH-STYLE
MUSTARD
1/2 CUP FIRMLY PACKED DARK BROWN
SUGAR
A PINCH OF SALT
1/4 CUP CIDER VINEGAR
1/4 CUP VEGETABLE OIL
1 TEASPOON WORCESTERSHIRE SAUCE
1 TEASPOON FRESHLY SQUEEZED
LEMON JUICE

In a food processor, combine dry mustard, brown sugar, salt, vinegar and oil. Add Worcestershire sauce and lemon juice. Blend until smooth.

English-style mustard, made from a blend of white and brown mustard seeds, is quite a bit more pungent than American-style mustard, which is made from the less spicy white mustard seed. This very hot sauce is excellent served with grilled sausage, ham or other smoked meats, or with Summer Sausage (page 237).

MAKES ABOUT 1 CUP.

AÏOLI

5 TO 6 CLOVES GARLIC
1/2 TEASPOON COARSE SALT
2 EGG YOLKS
FRESHLY GROUND WHITE PEPPER,
TO TASTE
2 TABLESPOONS WHITE VINEGAR OR
1 TABLESPOON FRESHLY SQUEEZED
LEMON JUICE
1 CUP OLIVE OR PEANUT OIL

Crush garlic and salt with mortar and pestle. Beat egg yolks until thick, and add pepper and vinegar or lemon juice. Add garlic paste to mixture and blend well. Gradually add oil, whisking until smooth and thick. Refrigerate until ready to serve.

Alternate Method: Place egg yolks in a food processor with steel blade, add vinegar or lemon juice, salt and pepper. Process. While machine is running, slowly add oil in a steady stream until blended. Add garlic and process until smooth.

Try Aïoli as a sauce with cold roast chicken or grilled fish. It makes an excellent dip for raw vegetables. The sauce will keep about 1 week in the refrigerator.

MAKES 1 CUP.

CRÈME FRAÎCHE

Prepare at least 8 hours before serving.

2   CUPS HEAVY CREAM (DO NOT USE
    ULTRA-PASTEURIZED)
1   CUP BUTTERMILK OR SOUR CREAM

Combine cream and buttermilk or sour cream and whisk until well blended. Pour into a small saucepan and warm over low heat until temperature of mixture registers 85 to 90 degrees on a candy thermometer. Remove from heat, pour into a container and cover. Set in a warm place for 8 hours until cream thickens. Crème Fraîche will keep about 2 weeks in the refrigerator.

One cup of crème fraîche can be used in place of buttermilk or sour cream as the starter for another batch.

MAKES 1 1/2 CUPS.

TAPENADE PROVENCE

2   OUNCES ANCHOVY FILLETS
3/4 CUP PITTED, OIL-CURED BLACK
    OLIVES
2   TABLESPOONS CAPERS, RINSED AND
    DRAINED

Soak anchovies in water for 5 minutes. Drain and pat dry. Place olives, anchovies and capers in a food processor and purée for about 45 seconds.

This salty spread is extremely versatile—it is an excellent accompaniment to Layered Omelet Terrine (page 53). Or try it served with icy melon balls, chilled raw vegetables, or spread on toast rounds.

8 SERVINGS

CAPER SAUCE

1/2	CUP FINELY CHOPPED FRESH PARSLEY
3/4	CUP FINELY CHOPPED FRESH BASIL
1/2	POUND FINELY CHOPPED FRESH SPINACH, RINSED AND PATTED DRY
1	CUP OLIVE OIL
1	CUP VEGETABLE OIL
1/2	CUP TARRAGON VINEGAR
1/2	CUP DIJON-STYLE MUSTARD
1	TABLESPOON FRESHLY SQUEEZED LEMON JUICE
ONE	2-OUNCE JAR CAPERS, DRAINED
2	CLOVES GARLIC, MINCED SALT, TO TASTE FRESHLY GROUND BLACK PEPPER, TO TASTE

Combine parsley, basil and spinach in a small bowl and set aside. In another bowl, whisk together olive oil, vegetable oil, vinegar, mustard and lemon juice until smooth and thick. Add capers and garlic. Blend in spinach mixture and season to taste with salt and pepper. Refrigerate until ready to serve.

This is an excellent sauce to serve with fish, shrimp and cold vegetables such as zucchini and broccoli.

MAKES 4 CUPS.

SWEET RED PEPPER SAUCE

1	SMALL YELLOW ONION, CHOPPED
2	TABLESPOONS OLIVE OIL
1 1/2	TABLESPOONS RED-WINE OR BALSAMIC VINEGAR
1 1/2	TABLESPOONS TOMATO PASTE
1	RED BELL PEPPER, CHOPPED
1/2	CUP CHICKEN BROTH, PREFERABLY HOMEMADE
1/4	TEASPOON SALT FRESHLY GROUND BLACK PEPPER, TO TASTE

Sauté onion in olive oil over medium heat until soft. Add vinegar and tomato paste and simmer 5 minutes, stirring occasionally. Add red pepper, cover and cook 4 minutes. Transfer mixture to the bowl of a food processor. Add broth and process until smooth. Season to taste with salt and pepper. Serve hot or at room temperature.

This sauce makes a colorful background for the Layered Omelet Terrine (page 53).

MAKES 1 1/2 CUPS.

PROVENÇAL SAUCE

1   LARGE RIPE TOMATO, PEELED,
    SEEDED AND CUT INTO 1/4-INCH
    CUBES (APPROXIMATELY 1/2 CUP)
2   TABLESPOONS RED WINE VINEGAR
1/4 CUP FINELY CHOPPED SHALLOTS
3/4 TEASPOON FINELY MINCED GARLIC
1/4 CUP OLIVE OIL
1/4 CUP FINELY CHOPPED FRESH BASIL
    OR PARSLEY
3/4 TEASPOON LEMON ZEST
    SALT, TO TASTE
    FRESHLY GROUND WHITE PEPPER,
    TO TASTE

Combine tomato, vinegar, shallots, garlic, oil and basil or parsley. Add lemon zest, salt and pepper, stirring well. Serve at room temperature.

This sauce is a wonderful accompaniment to grilled tuna. Use only the freshest tomatoes. For a different flavor, substitute Roasted Red Peppers (page 177) for the tomato.

MAKES 1 CUP.

POBLANO SALSA

4   MEDIUM POBLANO OR ANAHEIM
    CHILIES (4 TO 7 INCHES LONG)
1/3 CUP FRESH TOMATILLO, STEM
    REMOVED, DICED
1   SMALL SERRANO OR JALAPEÑO CHILI,
    SEEDED AND DICED (WEAR GLOVES)
1/2 CUP CHOPPED TOMATO, SEEDED
    AND DICED
1/4 CUP DICED ONION
2   TABLESPOONS CHOPPED FRESH
    CILANTRO
2   TABLESPOONS FRESHLY SQUEEZED
    LIME JUICE
1/2 TEASPOON CUMIN
1/2 TEASPOON SALT

Place the poblano or Anaheim chilies on a baking sheet. Broil in a preheated oven, 6 inches from the heat, turning often with tongs until peppers are charred on all sides. Immediately place in a plastic storage bag, fasten securely, and let steam for 10 to 15 minutes. Remove skin from chilies, then seed and dice. Combine the chilies, tomatillo, serrano or jalapeño chili, tomato and onion. Add cilantro, lime juice, cumin and salt and mix well. Cover and chill.

This cool and fresh-tasting salsa goes well with Spicy Grilled Swordfish or Tuna (page 151).

MAKES 2 CUPS.

GINGER MANGO SAUCE

2   TABLESPOONS UNSALTED BUTTER
6   TABLESPOONS CHOPPED SHALLOTS
    OR YELLOW ONION
2   TABLESPOONS MINCED FRESH
    GINGER
1   TEASPOON MINCED GARLIC
1   CUP DRY WHITE WINE
2   RIPE MANGOES, PITTED AND PEELED
1   CUP FISH OR CHICKEN STOCK,
    PREFERABLY HOMEMADE
1/2   CUP LIGHT CREAM
1/4   CUP FRESHLY SQUEEZED LIME JUICE
    SALT, TO TASTE
    FRESHLY GROUND BLACK PEPPER,
    TO TASTE
1/4   CUP CHOPPED FRESH MINT
    sprigs of fresh mint, for garnish

Melt butter in a saucepan over medium-high heat. Add shallots or onion and ginger and sauté until soft but not brown, about 5 minutes. Add garlic and sauté 1 minute longer. Add wine and simmer until the liquid is reduced to about 1/4 cup. Transfer the mixture to a food processor or blender. Add mango pulp and stock and purée until smooth. Return mixture to saucepan over medium heat. Add cream, lime juice, and salt and pepper to taste. Simmer until sauce is reduced by half. Stir in mint just before serving.

Serve this rich yellow sauce with Spicy Grilled Swordfish or Tuna (page 151).

MAKES ABOUT 2 CUPS.

PEACH JALAPEÑO CHUTNEY

2   POUNDS FRESH PEACHES OR FRESH-
    FROZEN PEACHES WITHOUT SYRUP
2   MEDIUM CLOVES GARLIC, MINCED
1   SMALL ONION, FINELY CHOPPED
3/4   CUP APPLE CIDER VINEGAR
1   CUP DARK BROWN SUGAR
2   JALAPEÑO CHILIES, SEEDED AND
    FINELY CHOPPED (WEAR GLOVES)
1   TABLESPOON MINCED FRESH GINGER
1   TEASPOON MUSTARD SEED
1/2   CUP GOLDEN RAISINS
1   TEASPOON CINNAMON
1   TEASPOON ALLSPICE

Immerse fresh peaches in boiling water for 60 seconds. Remove, immediately peel, pit and coarsely chop. Place peaches, garlic, onion, vinegar, brown sugar and chilies in a heavy nonreactive saucepan. Add ginger, mustard seed, raisins, cinnamon and allspice. Mix well and bring to a boil over medium heat. Lower heat to simmer, partially cover, and cook 30 minutes, stirring frequently. Remove from heat and cool.

The chutney is wonderful served with Spicy Grilled Swordfish or Tuna (page 151) or with chicken. It can be stored in the refrigerator for up to 2 months.

MAKES ABOUT 4 CUPS.

PAPAYA-MANGO RELISH

1	SMALL PAPAYA, PEELED, SEEDED AND DICED (ABOUT 1 CUP)
1	SMALL MANGO, PITTED, PEELED AND DICED (ABOUT 1 CUP)
1	MEDIUM GREEN BELL PEPPER, DICED
1	MEDIUM YELLOW BELL PEPPER, DICED
1	JALAPEÑO OR SERRANO CHILI, SEEDED AND DICED (WEAR GLOVES)
4	TABLESPOONS OLIVE OIL
1	TABLESPOON FRESHLY SQUEEZED LIME JUICE
2	TABLESPOONS BALSAMIC VINEGAR SALT, TO TASTE FRESHLY GROUND BLACK PEPPER, TO TASTE
1	SMALL AVOCADO, PITTED, PEELED AND DICED

In a nonreactive bowl, combine papaya, mango, and green and yellow peppers. Add jalapeño or serrano chili, olive oil, lime juice and vinegar. Season to taste with salt and pepper. Add avocado.

Serve with Curry Glazed Chicken (page 138).

MAKES 3 CUPS.

CRANBERRY CHUTNEY

3/4	CUP FIRMLY PACKED LIGHT BROWN SUGAR
1/4	CUP GRANULATED SUGAR
1	CUP WATER
2	TABLESPOONS CIDER OR RASPBERRY VINEGAR
1/2	CUP GOLDEN RAISINS
1/4	CUP TOASTED SLIVERED ALMONDS, CHOPPED IF DESIRED
3/4	TEASPOON GRATED FRESH GINGER
1/4	TEASPOON MINCED GARLIC
2	CUPS FRESH CRANBERRIES, RINSED AND PICKED OVER

Dissolve sugars in water over medium-high heat, stirring constantly. Bring to a boil but do not stir. Add vinegar, raisins, almonds, ginger, garlic and cranberries. Return to a boil slowly and cook until somewhat thick, stirring occasionally, about 5 to 7 minutes. Remove from heat, cool and refrigerate. The chutney will keep 1 week in the refrigerator, or it may be stored in sterilized jars. Seal and process according to manufacturer's instructions.

The brief cooking time and relatively few ingredients result in a beautiful, fresh red color. The chutney is delicious on turkey sandwiches, ladled over Brie as an appetizer, or served as an accompaniment to wild game or pork, or Duck with Black Pepper and Bourbon Sauce (page 142).

MAKES 2 CUPS.

HONEY MIDAS SAUCE

1	CUP HONEY
4	TABLESPOONS BUTTER
1/2	TEASPOON CINNAMON
1/2	TEASPOON CUMIN
8 TO 12	DROPS HOT PEPPER SAUCE, OR TO TASTE
	FRESHLY GROUND BLACK PEPPER, TO TASTE
	SALT, TO TASTE
	FINELY MINCED FRESH SAGE, CHERVIL OR MARJORAM, TO TASTE

Combine honey and butter in a saucepan and heat until butter melts. Stir in cinnamon, cumin and hot pepper sauce. Season with salt and pepper and heat until the mixture bubbles. Sprinkle with herbs. Serve hot or warm.

Use this spicy sweet sauce as a dipping sauce for egg rolls or grilled chicken wings, or as a glaze for grilled chicken or pork.

MAKES 1 1/4 CUPS.

PLUM SAUCE

ONE	10-OUNCE JAR PLUM JAM
1/2	CUP WHITE WINE
1/3	CUP ORANGE-FLAVORED LIQUEUR

Place jam in a medium saucepan and add wine and liqueur. Cook over medium-high heat 10 to 12 minutes, stirring constantly. Remove from heat and allow to cool for 1 hour. Transfer to a sterilized jar and store, covered, for later use, or place in a serving bowl and serve with pork, chicken, or egg rolls.

MAKES 2 CUPS.

HOT APPLE RELISH

1 TABLESPOON BUTTER
1/3 CUP SLIVERED ALMONDS OR 1/2 CUP
CHOPPED ENGLISH WALNUTS
4 LARGE OR 6 SMALL SLICED APPLES
(PEEL IF SKINS ARE THICK)
1/2 CUP RAISINS, DARK OR GOLDEN, OR
1/2 CUP CURRANTS
1/2 TEASPOON CINNAMON
1/4 TEASPOON SALT OR 1 TEASPOON
FRESHLY SQUEEZED LEMON JUICE
1/4 CUP SUGAR, IF APPLES ARE TART
1/2 CUP ALMOND-FLAVORED LIQUEUR,
IF DESIRED

Coat skillet with nonstick cooking spray. Add butter and nuts and brown lightly over medium-high heat. Add apples and raisins and cook, stirring, for 2 to 3 minutes. Reduce heat and add cinnamon, salt or lemon juice, sugar and liqueur, if used. Simmer 15 to 20 minutes, or until apples are tender.

This recipe is easily altered to reflect individual tastes. For example, substitute two large fresh pears for the two apples, or add a sliced Vidalia onion. Serve with pork, ham, sausage, wild fowl or venison.

4 SERVINGS

CHAMBORD SAUCE

20 OUNCES FROZEN RASPBERRIES IN
SYRUP, THAWED
1/3 CUP SUGAR
1/4 CUP CHAMBORD LIQUEUR
2 TEASPOONS FRESHLY SQUEEZED
LEMON JUICE

Purée raspberries and sugar in a food processor. Pour into a mesh strainer over a small bowl to catch liquid, and press raspberry mixture through the strainer to separate juice and pulp from the seeds. Stir Chambord and lemon juice into raspberries. Refrigerate until ready to serve. The sauce will keep about 1 week in the refrigerator.

MAKES 1 1/2 CUPS.

CRÈME ANGLAISE

2   CUPS WHOLE MILK
1   VANILLA BEAN, SPLIT, OR
    2 TEASPOONS VANILLA EXTRACT
5   EGG YOLKS
1/4   CUP SUGAR

Scald milk (180 degrees). Add split vanilla bean, remove from heat and let stand for 10 minutes. In a small, heavy saucepan, whisk egg yolks and sugar until well blended and light, about 3 to 4 minutes. Stir several tablespoons of the hot milk into the egg yolk mixture. Gradually add remaining milk and vanilla bean. Heat the mixture slowly, stirring constantly with a wooden spoon until custard thickens only slightly. At this point, a clearly defined trail will be left when a finger is drawn across the back of the spoon. Do not overcook or allow temperature to exceed 180 degrees.

Remove custard from heat immediately and strain into a small cold mixing bowl. Scrape seeds from vanilla bean into sauce. (If using vanilla extract, add it now.) Stir with whisk until vanilla seeds are evenly distributed. Cover tightly and refrigerate. The sauce will keep in the refrigerator 5 days, or it may be frozen.

For a variation that is especially good with fruit, add 2 to 3 tablespoons of Grand Marnier or Kirsch and blend. Crème Anglaise may also be served with fruit compote, hot soufflé, Chocolate Pâté (page 209), Holiday Plum Pudding (page 226), or Baked Apples in Phyllo (page 229).

MAKES 2 CUPS.

CARAMEL PECAN TOPPING

4   TABLESPOONS UNSALTED BUTTER
1   CUP PECAN HALVES
1   CUP DARK BROWN SUGAR
1   CUP HEAVY CREAM

In a heavy 1-quart saucepan, melt butter over medium heat. Add pecans and sauté, stirring constantly until pecans are lightly toasted. Add sugar and cream. Cook, stirring constantly until sugar is dissolved and sauce begins to boil. Serve at room temperature.

This delicious dessert sauce may be stored in the refrigerator for several weeks. Return to room temperature before serving. If sauce separates, stir vigorously until thoroughly blended.

MAKES 2 CUPS.

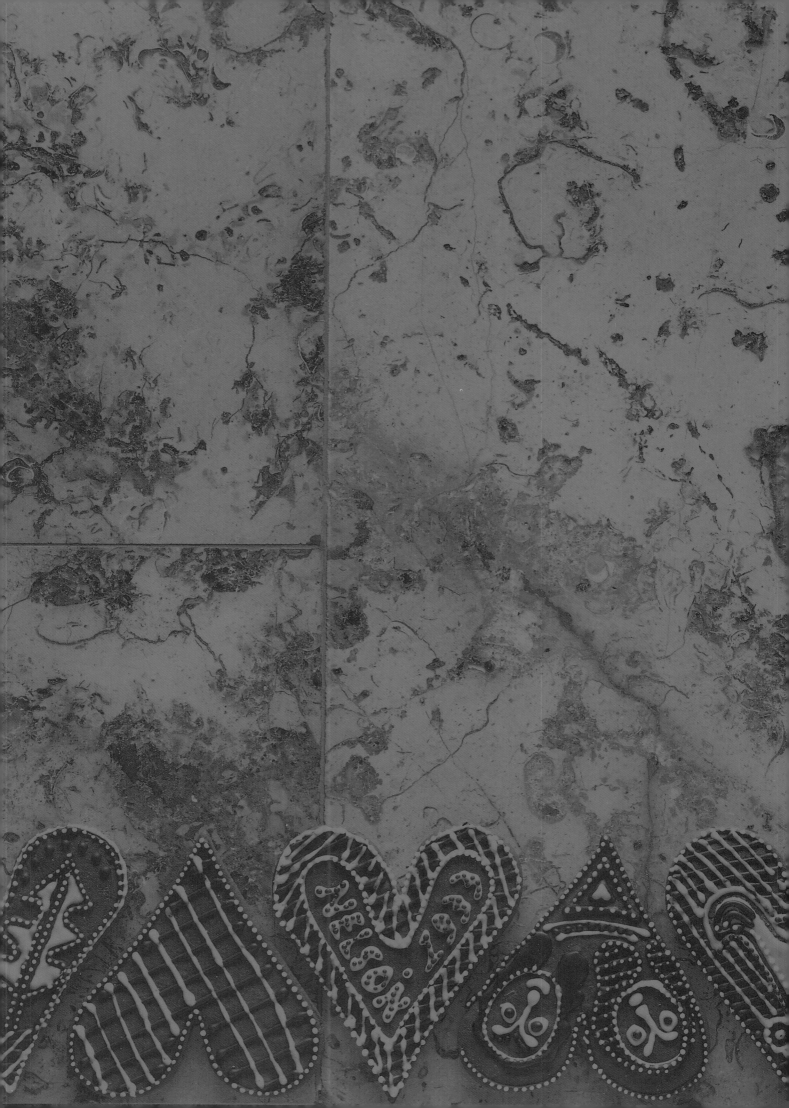

DESSERTS

WINE WITH DESSERTS

The dessert course is the hardest to match with wine, because people forget that the wine must be slightly sweeter than the dessert. Forgo a wine if the match is not reasonable. If the dessert is not overwhelmingly sweet, a suitable wine can usually be found. Below is a list of dessert wines and their characteristics, as well as some suggestions for their use.

(White Bordeaux) *Sauternes*— not as sweet as one would expect; rich and acidic enough to be combined with foie gras as an appetizer. Combine with low sugar fruit tarts and fruit with sabayon sauce.

(Rhône) *Muscat Beaumes de Venise*—tawny, sweet and clean; a wine that is marvelous with poached fruit and many pastries.

(Southern France) *Banyuls*—bizarre late harvest red wine (made from Grenache) that turns grey after barrel aging and tastes like liquid chocolate. Serve with chocolate desserts.

(Eastern France) *Vin Jaune*—serve after dinner, like port; or consider using at the beginning of a meal like a rich, very dry sherry.

(Alsace) *Selection des Grains Nobles (SGN)*—the Alsatian equivalent of Trockenbeerenauslese. The Alsace, home of the greatest dry white wines, also makes intensely sweet and alcoholic white wines. The Gewurztraminers can be so intense as to seem bitter. SGNs can handle just about any sweet dessert, short of chocolate.

(Champagne) *Champagne*—all styles from Doux to Demi-Sec; the best choice to match with the texture of most cakes.

(Loire) *Quarts de Chaume or Coteaux de Layon*— incredibly rich wines, dry and sweet. Serve with oranges, apricots, peaches and strawberries.

(Germany) *Eiswein, Beerenauslese and Trockenbeerenauslese*—the world's greatest region for sweet wine produces wine which almost asks to be drunk alone, so compelling are its flavors. Serve with citrus or other fruits.

(Hungary) *Tokaji Aszu*—very sweet; serve with any dessert but ice cream or chocolate.

(Italy – Soave) *Recioto della Soave*—somewhat like Sauternes; serve with fruit desserts, lemon custard, poached pears.

(Italy – Piedmont) *Moscato d'Asti or Asti Spumante*—sweet, rich, and a marvelous dessert wine.

(Italy – Tuscany) *Vin Santo*—a strange, bitter, powerful dessert wine from central Italy. Serve with a plate of fruit and nuts rather than with desserts.

(Italy – Sicily) *Moscato di Pantelleria*—serve with candied cakes.

(Italy – Sicily) *Malvasia di Lipari*—a perfect companion to custard, flan or crème brulée.

(Italy – Veneto) *Torcalato*—similar to Sauternes; serve with fruit topped with custard or whipped cream.

(Spain – Sherry) *Oloroso*—a rich, sweet fortified wine; as rich in itself as any dessert.

(Portugal – Madeira) *Malmsey 15-year-old*—fig bars and rich sweet flavors with a certain dryness perfectly describe this great wine.

(Portugal – Lisbon) *Moscato di Setúbal*—serve with oranges and lemon custard desserts.

(America – West Coast) *Select Late Harvest Riesling*—sweet and rich, not dry or clean; serve with sweet fleshy fruits such as peaches or apricots.

(America – West Coast) *Select Late Harvest Gewurztraminer*—serve with fruit tarts.

(America – West Coast) *Select Late Harvest Sauvignon Blanc or Semillon*—delicious and rather herbal; good with pastry.

(Australia – Victoria) *Tokay*—intensely sweet, caramelly wines; good accompaniments to licorice, fennel and ginger, especially in custard form.

(Australia – Victoria) *Muscat*—perfect with marmalade or treacle, the sweeter, the better.

(Australia – Barossa Valley) *Tawny Port*—perfect with fruit and nuts.

(Portugal – Douro Valley) *Tawny Port*—the real tawny port; serve with fruit and/or nuts.

(Portugal – Douro Valley) *Vintage, LBV or Vintage Character Port*— a good wine for many desserts, but especially for chocolate.

 Preceding page: Gingerbread Heart Cookies, page 231

BOURBON FUDGE BUNDT CAKE

Prepare 1 to 2 days before serving.

- 2 TEASPOONS UNSWEETENED POWDERED COCOA
- 1 3/4 CUPS WATER
- 2 TEASPOONS INSTANT COFFEE
- 1/2 CUP BOURBON
- 5 OUNCES UNSWEETENED CHOCOLATE, CHOPPED
- 1/2 POUND UNSALTED BUTTER, CUT INTO SMALL PIECES, SOFTENED
- 2 CUPS GRANULATED SUGAR
- 2 CUPS ALL-PURPOSE FLOUR
- 1 TEASPOON BAKING SODA A DASH OF SALT
- 2 EGGS, AT ROOM TEMPERATURE
- 1 TEASPOON VANILLA EXTRACT
- 12 OUNCES RASPBERRY JELLY, MELTED OVER HOT WATER

fresh raspberries, for garnish, if desired

Grease a 12-cup bundt pan and dust with unsweetened cocoa powder, tapping pan sharply to remove excess cocoa. In a heavy saucepan, combine water, instant coffee and bourbon and simmer for 3 minutes. Add chocolate and butter and cook over medium heat, stirring until mixture is melted and smooth. Remove from heat and stir in sugar until well blended. Let cool 3 minutes. Transfer chocolate mixture to large bowl of electric mixer. Combine flour, baking soda and salt in a small bowl. Beating at medium speed, add flour mixture to chocolate, 1/2 cup at a time. When all flour has been added, continue to beat for one minute. Beat in eggs, one at a time, then add vanilla and mix until smooth. The batter will be thin.

Pour into prepared pan and bake in a preheated 275 degree oven for 1 hour and 20 to 30 minutes, or until cake tester comes out clean and cake pulls away from sides of pan. Cool in pan. Invert cake onto a serving dish, tapping sharply to loosen. Spoon melted jelly over the top. Serve plain or garnished with fresh raspberries. Do not refrigerate. The cake may be stored, unsliced and covered, for up to 3 days at room temperature, or frozen, wrapped tightly in foil.

12 TO 16 SERVINGS

Cline Cellars Late Harvest Zinfandel 1 9 8 8 (Sonoma)

CHOCOLATE PÂTÉ

Begin 1 day before serving.

- 8 OUNCES BITTERSWEET CHOCOLATE
- 2/3 CUP CONFECTIONERS' SUGAR
- 3/4 CUP UNSALTED BUTTER, SOFTENED, CUT INTO SMALL PIECES
- 5 EGGS, SEPARATED A PINCH OF SALT

Crème Anglaise (page 205) or Chambord Sauce (page 204), as an accompaniment

In the top of a double boiler, melt chocolate over simmering water. Beat in sugar, and then butter, one piece at a time. Stir in egg yolks, one at a time, mixing well after each addition. Place egg whites in a mixing bowl, add salt and beat until very stiff. Remove chocolate mixture from heat and fold in egg whites, one third at a time. Blend well but do not overmix.

Rinse a 4 1/2- by 8 1/4-inch loaf pan with cold water. Without drying pan, fill with chocolate mixture. Refrigerate 12 to 24 hours before serving. To remove from pan, wrap pan in a towel that has been soaked in very hot water, then turn out pâté onto a serving platter.

To serve, place a thin slice of pâté on each plate and surround with several tablespoons of a favorite dessert sauce, such as Crème Anglaise or Chambord Sauce.

8 TO 10 SERVINGS

Dr. Parcé Banyuls 1 9 8 3 (Banyuls)

PINEAPPLE BOURBON CHEESECAKE

Prepare 1 day before serving.

CRUST

1 1/4	CUPS TOASTED SLIVERED ALMONDS
3	TABLESPOONS SUGAR
1/4	TEASPOON GROUND GINGER
6	FINELY CRUSHED GRAHAM CRACKERS (1- BY 3-INCH) FINELY GRATED ZEST OF 1 LEMON FINELY GRATED ZEST OF 1/2 ORANGE
6	TABLESPOONS MELTED BUTTER

Using a food processor, grind almonds with sugar and ginger until very fine. Add graham cracker crumbs, lemon and orange zest and butter, mixing well. Pat into bottom of a buttered 10-inch springform pan. Bake in a preheated 350 degree oven until golden, about 10 minutes. Cool completely.

FILLING

ONE	1-INCH PIECE OF FRESH GINGER, PEELED
ONE	20-OUNCE CAN PINEAPPLE CHUNKS, DRAINED
1/2	CUP BOURBON
2 1/2	POUNDS CREAM CHEESE, SOFTENED
1 3/4	CUPS SUGAR
3	TABLESPOONS ALL-PURPOSE FLOUR FINELY GRATED ZEST OF 1 LEMON FINELY GRATED ZEST OF 1 ORANGE
1/4	TEASPOON VANILLA EXTRACT
5	EGGS
2	EGG YOLKS
	toasted slivered almonds, for garnish

Preheat oven to 500 degrees, making certain oven temperature is accurate. With food processor running, drop in ginger to mince, scraping bowl once or twice if necessary. Stop the machine, add pineapple and process until very fine. Add the bourbon and blend until smooth. Place cream cheese, sugar, flour, lemon and orange zest and vanilla in the bowl of an electric mixer and beat until very smooth. Beat in eggs, one at time, followed by the egg yolks. Add pineapple mixture and mix until blended. Pour batter into crust. Bake for 10 minutes, cover with foil, then reduce oven temperature to 200 degrees and bake 1 hour longer, or until barely set. Remove cheesecake from oven and cool on a wire rack. Cover and refrigerate until serving time.

Slip a knife around edge of cake and remove springform sides. Bring cake to room temperature and garnish with toasted slivered almonds.

14 TO 16 SERVINGS

Sandeman Imperial Corregidor Oloroso (Sherry - Spain)

WHITE CHOCOLATE CHEESECAKE
WITH LIME CURD

Prepare 1 day before serving.

LIME CURD

1 CUP PLUS 2 TABLESPOONS SUGAR
2 TABLESPOONS CORNSTARCH
1/2 CUP PLUS 1 TABLESPOON FRESHLY SQUEEZED LIME JUICE, STRAINED
1/2 CUP HEAVY CREAM
5 EXTRA-LARGE EGG YOLKS
3 TABLESPOONS FINELY GRATED LIME ZEST
1 DROP GREEN FOOD COLORING
6 TABLESPOONS UNSALTED BUTTER, CUT INTO PIECES

Combine sugar and cornstarch in a small heavy saucepan. Gradually add lime juice, whisking until smooth. Stir in cream, egg yolks, lime zest and food coloring. Add butter. Bring to a a boil over medium heat, stirring constantly. Reduce heat to low and stir until thickened and butter is melted, about 1 minute. Immediately pour into a small bowl. Place plastic wrap directly on surface of curd to prevent skin from forming. Refrigerate until well chilled. The Lime Curd can be prepared up to 1 week ahead.

The Lime Curd also makes a delicious tart topping for fresh fruits and berries.

MAKES ABOUT 2 1/2 CUPS.

CRUST

3/4 CUP TOASTED, SLIVERED BLANCHED ALMONDS
7 WHOLE GRAHAM CRACKERS, BROKEN
2 1/2 TABLESPOONS SUGAR
5 TABLESPOONS CHILLED UNSALTED BUTTER, CUT INTO PIECES

Lightly butter a 9-inch springform pan. Finely chop almonds, graham crackers and sugar in food processor. Add butter and process until crumbs just hold together. Press crumb mixture into bottom and 2 inches up sides of prepared pan. Bake on center rack of a preheated 325 degree oven for 10 minutes. Cool on a wire rack. Keep oven temperature at 325 degrees.

FILLING

16 OUNCES CREAM CHEESE, SOFTENED
1/4 CUP SUGAR
9 OUNCES WHITE CHOCOLATE, MELTED AND COOLED TO LUKEWARM
3 EXTRA-LARGE EGGS, AT ROOM TEMPERATURE
1/4 CUP HEAVY CREAM
1 TEASPOON LIGHT RUM
1 TEASPOON VANILLA EXTRACT
A PINCH OF SALT
3 EXTRA-LARGE EGG WHITES, AT ROOM TEMPERATURE

grated white chocolate or paper-thin slices of lime, for garnish

Beat cream cheese in a large bowl with an electric mixer until light and fluffy. Gradually beat in sugar. Add white chocolate and beat just until blended. Beat in eggs, cream, rum, vanilla and salt. Spread half of filling evenly in crust, then bake until barely set, about 20 minutes. Cool 5 minutes on rack. Keep oven temperature at 325 degrees.

Mix 1 1/2 cups Lime Curd with the egg whites in a small bowl. (Refrigerate remaining curd for another use). Beginning at outer edge, carefully spoon Lime Curd over cheese filling, covering completely. Bake 20 minutes. Transfer to a rack and cool 5 minutes.

Starting at outer edge, carefully spoon remaining cheese filling over curd, covering completely. Bake cheesecake until edges are set and center moves only slightly when shaken, about 25 minutes. Cool completely on rack. Cover and refrigerate at least 24 hours.

Slide a sharp knife around sides of pan to loosen, then remove sides. Transfer cheesecake to a platter and garnish with grated white chocolate, Lime Curd rosettes or paper-thin slices of lime.

12 SERVINGS

Domaine Durban Muscat Beaumes de Venise (Southern Rhône)

CREAMY CHOCOLATE CHEESECAKE

Begin at least 6 hours before serving.

CRUST

2	CUPS CHOCOLATE WAFER CRUMBS
1/4	CUP PLUS 2 TABLESPOONS MELTED BUTTER

Combine wafer crumbs and butter and firmly press into bottom and 1 inch up sides of a 10-inch springform pan. Set aside until ready to use.

FILLING

12	OUNCES SEMISWEET CHOCOLATE BITS
2	POUNDS CREAM CHEESE, SOFTENED
2	CUPS SUGAR
4	EGGS
1	TABLESPOON COCOA
2	TEASPOONS VANILLA EXTRACT
1	PINT SOUR CREAM

Place chocolate bits in top of double boiler; bring water to boil. Reduce heat to low and cook until chocolate is melted. Beat cream cheese with an electric mixer until light and fluffy. Gradually add sugar, mixing well. Add eggs, one at a time, beating well after each addition. Stir in melted chocolate, cocoa, and vanilla and beat until blended. Add sour cream and blend well. Pour into prepared crust. Bake in a preheated 300 degree oven for 1 hour and 40 minutes (the center may be soft but will firm when chilled). Let cool to room temperature on a wire rack, then chill for at least 5 hours.

RASPBERRY SAUCE

10	OUNCES FROZEN RASPBERRIES, THAWED
1 1/2	TEASPOONS CORNSTARCH
1	TEASPOON SUGAR

Combine raspberries, cornstarch, and sugar in a saucepan. Cook over low heat, stirring constantly, until smooth and thickened. Cool. Spoon about a tablespoon of sauce over each slice of chocolate cheesecake and serve.

12 SERVINGS

Graham's Six Grape nv (Portugal)

CHOCOLATE BAKLAVA

1	POUND FROZEN PHYLLO DOUGH (ABOUT 24 SHEETS)
1	POUND FINELY CHOPPED WALNUTS
ONE	6-OUNCE PACKAGE SEMISWEET CHOCOLATE BITS, CHOPPED
3/4	CUP SUGAR
1 1/2	TEASPOONS CINNAMON
1 1/2	CUPS MELTED BUTTER
3/4	CUP ORANGE JUICE
1/2	CUP SUGAR
1/2	CUP WATER
1/2	CUP HONEY
2	TABLESPOONS FRESHLY SQUEEZED LEMON JUICE

Thaw phyllo dough according to package directions. Combine walnuts, chocolate, sugar and cinnamon, mix well and set aside.

Brush the bottom of a 15- by 11- by 2-inch baking pan with melted butter. Layer 8 phyllo sheets in the pan, brushing each sheet with butter. Sprinkle about 2 cups of the nut mixture over phyllo layers. Continue with another 8 sheets of phyllo pastry, brushing each sheet with butter. Top with remaining nut mixture and remaining phyllo sheets, brushing each sheet with butter. Drizzle remaining butter over top layer. Bake in a preheated 325 degree oven for one hour. Remove from oven and cut into diamond-shaped pieces.

While baklava is baking, combine orange juice, sugar, water, honey and lemon juice in a medium saucepan. Heat to boiling, then reduce heat and simmer for 20 minutes. Pour over warm baklava in pan. Cool completely and refrigerate.

Yalumba Brut Rosé (Australia)

CHOCOLATE MOUSSE TART WITH CHERRY CORDIALS

Prepare 1 day before serving.

CHOCOLATE CRUST

25 1/2	OUNCES DARK CHOCOLATE WAFERS
2	TABLESPOONS MELTED BUTTER

Place wafers in a food processor and process until crumbs are very fine. Mix with butter and pat evenly onto bottom and sides of a buttered 9-inch springform pan. Bake in a preheated 325 degree oven for 10 minutes. Remove from oven and cool completely.

CHERRY CORDIALS

13	MARASCHINO CHERRIES WITH STEMS, DRAINED
1/2	CUP BRANDY
6	OUNCES SEMISWEET CHOCOLATE

Soak cherries in brandy, place on a baking sheet and freeze. Melt chocolate slowly over simmering water. When cherries are frozen, dry on paper towels and dip quickly, one at a time, into chocolate. Swirl around by stem until completely covered. Chocolate will harden almost immediately. Place on a wax paper-lined rack in refrigerator until ready to use.

CHOCOLATE MOUSSE

8	EGG YOLKS
1 1/2	CUPS PLUS 3 TABLESPOONS SUGAR, DIVIDED
2	TEASPOONS VANILLA EXTRACT
1/4	TEASPOON SALT
1/2	CUP BRANDY
10	OUNCES UNSWEETENED CHOCOLATE
2	OUNCES SEMISWEET CHOCOLATE
3/4	CUP BUTTER, DIVIDED AND SOFTENED
1/2	CUP COFFEE
8	EGG WHITES, AT ROOM TEMPERATURE
1 1/2	CUPS HEAVY CREAM, STIFFLY WHIPPED

Combine egg yolks, 1 1/2 cups sugar, vanilla, salt and brandy in top of double boiler. Place over simmering water and whisk until mixture is thick and pale yellow, about 8 to 10 minutes. Remove from water and set aside. Slowly melt unsweetened and semisweet chocolate over hot water. Remove and beat in butter, a bit at a time. Gradually whisk chocolate into egg yolk mixture until smooth. The mixture will congeal and become very stiff. Beat in coffee. Beat egg whites into soft peaks, add 3 tablespoons sugar, and beat until stiff peaks form. Whisk 1 cup beaten egg white into chocolate mixture to thin, then carefully fold in remaining egg white until thoroughly blended. Gently fold whipped cream into chocolate mixture.

To assemble, pour mousse into chocolate crust and chill overnight in refrigerator. Garnish with cherry cordials.

8 TO 10 SERVINGS

Kirsch

COCONUT CHEESECAKE

Prepare at least 1 day before serving.

CRUST

2/3	CUP ALL-PURPOSE FLOUR
5	TABLESPOONS PLUS 1 TEASPOON COLD BUTTER, CUT INTO SMALL PIECES
4	TEASPOONS SUGAR

Butter the bottom of a 10-inch springform pan. With a pastry cutter, blend flour, butter and sugar until the mixture just begins to hold together. Press into bottom of prepared pan and bake in a preheated 325 degree oven for 25 minutes, or until golden brown. Remove from oven and set aside, keeping oven temperature at 325 degrees.

FILLING

2 1/2	CUPS FLAKED SWEETENED COCONUT
1	CUP HEAVY CREAM, SCALDED
20	OUNCES CREAM CHEESE, SOFTENED
1/2	CUP SUGAR
4	EGGS
2	EGG YOLKS
2 1/2	TABLESPOONS COCONUT-FLAVORED LIQUEUR
1	TEASPOON FRESHLY SQUEEZED LEMON JUICE
1/2	TEASPOON VANILLA EXTRACT
1/2	TEASPOON ALMOND EXTRACT

In a processor, purée coconut with scalded cream until finely shredded, about 4 minutes. Set aside to cool. In a large mixing bowl, beat cream cheese and sugar together until well blended. With mixer at low speed, add cooled coconut mixture. Blend in eggs and yolks, one at a time. Mix in liqueur, lemon juice, vanilla and almond extracts. Pour into prepared crust and bake about 1 hour, until sides of cake are dry and center is firm. Remove from oven and cool on wire rack about 35 minutes or until a depression forms in the center. Keep oven temperature at 325 degrees.

TOPPING

1	CUP SOUR CREAM
1/4	CUP CREAM OF COCONUT
1/2	TEASPOON COCONUT-FLAVORED LIQUEUR

coconut flakes, lightly toasted, for garnish

Combine sour cream, cream of coconut and coconut liqueur. Spread on top of cooled cake and bake 10 minutes to set topping. Remove and cool completely on a wire rack, then refrigerate, uncovered, 4 hours. Remove, cover tightly, and refrigerate 24 hours to allow flavors to blend. The cake may be made up to 3 days ahead.

Before serving, remove sides of pan and spread coconut flakes in a 1-inch border around the rim of cake.

12 SERVINGS

Yalumba Show Reserve Muscat nv (Victoria - Australia)

FRESH COCONUT MOUSSE WITH HOT CARAMEL SAUCE

Begin 6 hours to 1 day before serving.

MOUSSE

1	QUART WHOLE MILK
1 1/2	CUPS SUGAR
1/4	TEASPOON SALT
1	TEASPOON ALMOND EXTRACT
3	TABLESPOONS UNFLAVORED GELATIN
1/4	CUP COLD WATER
2	CUPS GRATED FRESH COCONUT (SEE BELOW)
5	EGG WHITES, STIFFLY BEATEN
2	CUPS HEAVY CREAM, WHIPPED

In a heavy saucepan, heat milk just to boiling. Stir in sugar, salt and almond extract and remove from heat. Soften gelatin in cold water, then stir coconut and gelatin into milk mixture. Pour into a large bowl and cool in refrigerator. When mixture thickens, fold in beaten egg whites and whipped cream. Pour into a wet 2-quart mold and chill, preferably overnight.

Fresh coconuts are plentiful in December. The meat is easily grated in a food processor. Fresh coconut is also available frozen in some grocery stores. Do not substitute dried or sweetened coconut.

CARAMEL SAUCE

1	TABLESPOON BUTTER
1	POUND DARK BROWN SUGAR
2	EGG YOLKS
1	CUP LIGHT CREAM
1/8	TEASPOON SALT
1	TEASPOON VANILLA EXTRACT

sprigs of fresh mint and fresh cherries, for garnish

In top of a double boiler, mix butter, sugar, egg yolks, cream, salt and vanilla. Stir constantly over simmering water until smooth and creamy. Cook over low to medium heat so that egg yolks do not curdle.

Unmold mousse onto a serving plate and garnish with mint sprigs and cherries. Serve Caramel Sauce separately.

10 SERVINGS

SPICED CRANBERRY WALNUT TART

TART SHELL

1 1/2	CUPS FLOUR
2	TABLESPOONS SUGAR
1/4	TEASPOON SALT
1/2	CUP CHILLED UNSALTED BUTTER
1	EGG, LIGHTLY BEATEN WITH 1 1/2 TABLESPOONS WATER

Combine flour, sugar and salt, then cut in butter until mixture resembles coarse crumbs. Stir in egg mixed with water. Mold dough into a ball, cover with plastic wrap and let stand for one hour. On a floured surface, roll dough into a 12-inch circle, 1/8-inch thick. Fit dough into a 10- or 11-inch round tart pan with removable rim and chill for 30 minutes. Line the shell with foil and fill with dried beans or pie weights. Bake in a preheated 425 degree oven for 15 minutes. Remove foil and weights and bake 5 to 10 minutes longer, or until tart is pale gold in color. Remove from oven and cool in pan on wire rack. Reduce oven temperature to 350 degrees.

FILLING

1/4	CUP UNSALTED BUTTER, MELTED
2/3	CUP BROWN SUGAR
2/3	CUP CORN SYRUP
3	EGGS
1/2	TEASPOON SALT
1	TEASPOON VANILLA EXTRACT
1	TEASPOON CINNAMON
1 1/2	CUPS CHOPPED FRESH CRANBERRIES, LIGHTLY RINSED AND PICKED OVER
1	CUP CHOPPED WALNUTS

Whisk together melted butter, brown sugar, corn syrup, eggs, salt, vanilla and cinnamon until smooth. Stir in cranberries and walnuts and pour into cooled tart shell. Bake on middle rack of oven for 40 to 45 minutes, or until golden brown. Cool completely in pan on a wire rack.

To serve, remove rim of tart pan and cut tart into wedges. The tart can be made up to one day ahead. Store covered at room temperature.

10 SERVINGS

Martin Brothers Aleatico (Paso Robles)

LEMON RASPBERRY TART

CRUST

1	CUP ALL-PURPOSE FLOUR
1/4	CUP CONFECTIONERS' SUGAR
1/4	TEASPOON SALT
1/3	CUP GROUND ALMONDS
8	TABLESPOONS MELTED BUTTER, SLIGHTLY COOLED
1/2	TEASPOON ALMOND EXTRACT
2	OUNCES SEMISWEET CHOCOLATE, MELTED

Lightly grease a 9 1/2-inch tart pan with nonstick cooking spray, coating the sides well. Sift together flour, confectioners' sugar and salt. Add almonds, melted butter and almond extract and beat until well blended and a thick dough is formed. Press dough into tart pan with fingers, distributing dough evenly. Bake in a preheated 350 degree oven for 15 to 18 minutes, or until lightly browned. While crust is still warm, brush melted chocolate evenly over the surface. Allow crust to cool. Keep oven temperature at 350 degrees.

FILLING

1	CUP GRANULATED SUGAR
2	TABLESPOONS ALL-PURPOSE FLOUR
1/2	TEASPOON BAKING POWDER
3	EGGS, LIGHTLY BEATEN
	FRESHLY SQUEEZED JUICE OF 1 1/2 MEDIUM OR LARGE LEMONS
	FINELY GRATED ZEST OF 2 SMALL LEMONS

Sift together sugar, flour and baking powder. Beat in eggs, lemon juice and lemon zest. Pour into cooled crust and bake for 20 to 25 minutes, or until filling is lightly browned. Cool completely on wire rack. When cool, remove outer ring of tart pan, leaving tart on pan bottom.

TOPPING

1 1/2	PINTS FRESH RASPBERRIES
12	OUNCES CURRANT JELLY

Arrange raspberries on top of the cooled tart, starting at the outside and working toward center. The raspberries should cover the tart completely. Melt currant jelly over low heat until liquid. Brush melted jelly over each raspberry with a pastry brush. The jelly must be very hot to glaze well. Let cool until glaze is set. Cut into wedges.

8 TO 10 SERVINGS

Schramsberg Demi-Sec 1 9 8 8 (Napa)

CARAMEL WALNUT TART

SUGAR DOUGH

1   CUP PLUS 2 TABLESPOONS BUTTER, SOFTENED

1/2 CUP PLUS 1 TABLESPOON SUGAR

2   EGGS

3   CUPS PLUS 2 TABLESPOONS ALL-PURPOSE FLOUR
A PINCH OF SALT

Cream butter and sugar. Add eggs one at a time, beating well. Stir in flour and salt and mix. The dough will be thick and soft. Wrap in plastic and chill at least 30 minutes.

CARAMEL FILLING

2 1/2 CUPS SUGAR

1   CUP PLUS 3 TABLESPOONS WATER

1/4 TEASPOON CREAM OF TARTAR

3/4 CUP HEAVY CREAM, AT ROOM TEMPERATURE

12   OUNCES COARSELY CHOPPED WALNUTS

14   TABLESPOONS BUTTER, CUT INTO SMALL PIECES

1   EGG, SLIGHTLY BEATEN

Combine sugar, water and cream of tartar in a medium saucepan, swirling the pan to mix. Bring to a boil over high heat and cook without stirring until syrup is a rich, medium brown (334 degrees on a candy thermometer). Wash down any crystals on sides of pan with a brush dipped in cold water. Remove from heat and let stand 15 seconds. Add heavy cream, swirling saucepan gently until foam subsides; do not stir. Mix in walnuts. Drop pieces of butter on top of mixture, let melt a minute and stir until combined. Transfer to a large bowl and let cool.

ICING

1   CUP HEAVY CREAM

1/2 POUND SEMISWEET CHOCOLATE, CUT INTO VERY SMALL PIECES

Bring cream to a boil over medium heat. Pour over chocolate slowly, stirring until blended. Refrigerate until chilled, but spreadable.

Divide dough—two thirds for the bottom and sides of tart, and one third for the top. Between two sheets of wax paper, roll larger portion of dough into a circle, 3/8-inch thick. Press into a 9-inch springform pan, leaving a slight overlap. Pour caramel filling into pan. Brush edges of pastry with beaten egg. Roll remaining dough between layers of wax paper into a circle 3/8-inch thick and carefully place over caramel. Roll across pastry top with a rolling pin to seal edges completely. Trim excess pastry and chill 5 minutes. Bake in the lower third of a preheated 400 degree oven for 40 to 45 minutes. Cool partially in pan, then remove and cool completely. Spread icing over top of tart. Refrigerate.

Let tart stand at room temperature for about 1 1/2 hours before serving. The tart can be baked and frozen up to one month ahead, and iced just before serving.

12 SERVINGS

Lustau East India Cream Solera (Sherry - Spain)

PEAR ALMOND TART

PASTRY

6   TABLESPOONS COLD BUTTER, DICED
1 1/4   CUPS WHOLE WHEAT PASTRY FLOUR, DIVIDED
1/4   CUP ICE WATER

In a mixing bowl, cut butter into flour until mixture is crumbly. Add ice water. If mixture is too wet, add a little more flour and knead lightly on a heavily floured board to blend. Roll the pastry into a circle large enough for a 10-inch fluted tart pan with a removable bottom. Fit pastry into the pan without stretching, and press into fluted sides. Cut off excess by rolling the pin over top of pan. Refrigerate while preparing the filling.

ALMOND FILLING

1 1/2   CUPS WHOLE ALMONDS
3/4   CUP SUGAR
1/4   CUP BUTTER
2   TABLESPOONS ALL-PURPOSE FLOUR
1/4   CUP ALMOND-FLAVORED LIQUEUR
2   EGGS, BEATEN

Grind almonds in a food processor or blender, then mix in sugar, butter and flour. Whisk together liqueur and eggs, then stir into almond mixture. Spread mixture evenly in unbaked pastry.

PEAR TOPPING

8   FIRM, RIPE ANJOU PEARS, PEELED, HALVED AND THINLY SLICED

Arrange pear slices in concentric circles over the filling, overlapping tightly. There should be about two layers. In the center arrange several slices into a half-pear shape with the rounded side up. Bake filled tart 1 to 1 1/4 hours in a preheated 400 degree oven, until pears are tender. Remove and cool. Remove outer ring from tart pan, leaving tart on bottom.

The three parts of the tart—crust, filling, and pears—may be prepared in advance and refrigerated. Bring the almond filling to room temperature, assemble and bake.

GLAZE

1   CUP APRICOT JAM OR PRESERVES, STRAINED
1/4   CUP ALMOND-FLAVORED LIQUEUR
3 tablespoons chopped pistachio nuts, for garnish

In a saucepan, combine apricot jam and liqueur and cook until jam is melted. Spoon or brush glaze over the cooked tart and sprinkle with pistachios. The tart is best served slightly chilled or at room temperature.

8 TO 10 SERVINGS

Dr. Richter Muhlheimer Helenkloster Eiswein 1 9 8 3
(Mosel - Saar - Ruwer)

BLUEBERRY RICOTTA TART

CRUST

3/4 CUP UNSALTED BUTTER
6 TABLESPOONS SUGAR
3 HARD-COOKED EGG YOLKS, MASHED
1 1/2 CUPS ALL-PURPOSE FLOUR
1 TEASPOON FINELY GRATED LEMON ZEST

Mix butter, sugar and egg yolks until creamy. Add flour and lemon zest. Knead dough on a lightly floured surface to blend ingredients. Form dough into ball, wrap in wax paper and refrigerate for 1 hour. Place dough between two sheets of lightly floured wax paper and roll out 1/8-inch thick. Fit dough into a lightly greased 9-inch tart pan with removable bottom. Pierce dough with tines of fork, line with foil and fill with pie weights or dried beans. Bake in a preheated 375 degree oven about 15 minutes, until crust is set and edges are brown. Reduce oven temperature to 350 degrees.

FILLING

10 OUNCES RICOTTA CHEESE
5 OUNCES PLAIN YOGURT
2/3 CUP SUGAR
3 EGGS, AT ROOM TEMPERATURE
2 TEASPOONS ALL-PURPOSE FLOUR
1 TABLESPOON FRESHLY SQUEEZED LEMON JUICE

Combine ricotta cheese, yogurt, sugar, eggs, flour and lemon juice and mix well. Turn into prepared crust and bake, 40 to 45 minutes, until filling is set and a light golden color. Place on a wire rack and cool completely. Chill thoroughly.

TOPPING

1/2 CUP APRICOT JAM
2 CUPS FRESH BLUEBERRIES, RINSED
CONFECTIONERS' SUGAR
curls of slivered lemon peel, for garnish

Melt jam over low heat. Strain and brush lightly over filling. Top with blueberries and dust lightly with sugar. Garnish with lemon peel curls.

8 SERVINGS

Quady Elysium (California)

BLACKBERRY TARTS

CRUST

2   CUPS ALL-PURPOSE FLOUR
1   CUP WHOLE WHEAT FLOUR
1   TEASPOON SALT
1   CUP VEGETABLE SHORTENING
6   TABLESPOONS COLD WATER
2   EGG WHITES, LIGHTLY BEATEN

In a large bowl, combine flours and salt. With a pastry cutter, cut in shortening until mixture resembles small peas. Stir in water and mix well. Divide dough in half. On a lightly floured surface, roll out one half of the dough 1/8-inch thick. Fit the dough into a 10-inch tart pan. (The tarts may also be baked in 3-inch tart pans.) Trim edge and reserve. Chill. Make a second tart with the remaining dough. Combine reserved scraps of dough and cut out leaf shapes. Reserve to place on top of tarts.

FILLING

6   CUPS FRESH BLACKBERRIES, RINSED
1/3   CUP CORNSTARCH
1 1/2   CUPS SUGAR
1/4   CUP FRESHLY SQUEEZED LEMON JUICE
1/8   TEASPOON CINNAMON
1/8   TEASPOON NUTMEG

In a large bowl, gently toss together blackberries, cornstarch, sugar, lemon juice, cinnamon and nutmeg. Fill tarts with blackberry mixture. Arrange leaf shapes on top and brush crusts with egg whites. Bake in a preheated 400 degree oven for 10 minutes. Reduce oven temperature to 350 degrees and bake until done, about 35 minutes longer.

MAKES 2 LARGE TARTS OR TWELVE 3-INCH TARTS.

Lucien Jacob Crème de Cassis nv (Provence)

RASPBERRY-WALNUT TORTE

CRUST

1 1/3   CUPS ALL-PURPOSE FLOUR
3   TABLESPOONS SUGAR
8   TABLESPOONS CHILLED BUTTER, CUT INTO SMALL PIECES
1   CUP GROUND ENGLISH WALNUTS
1   EXTRA-LARGE EGG YOLK
1/3   CUP SEEDLESS RASPBERRY JAM

Combine flour and sugar in food processor. Cut in butter using on/off switch until mixture resembles coarse crumbs. Blend in walnuts. With machine running, add egg yolk and mix just until dough comes together. Do not form a ball. Remove dough from processor and press into bottom and two thirds of the way up sides of a 9-inch springform pan. Spread bottom with jam and chill while preparing filling.

FILLING

1 1/2   CUPS LIGHT BROWN SUGAR
1   EXTRA-LARGE EGG
1 1/4   CUPS COARSELY CHOPPED ENGLISH WALNUTS
3/4   CUP SHREDDED COCONUT
1/4   CUP PLUS 1 TABLESPOON ALL-PURPOSE FLOUR
1/2   TEASPOON BAKING POWDER
1/3   CUP SEEDLESS RASPBERRY JAM

Using an electric mixer, beat brown sugar and egg in a medium bowl until very thick, about 10 minutes. Mix in walnuts, coconut, flour and baking powder. The batter will be very thick. Spread evenly over jam in prepared crust and bake in a preheated 350 degree oven for 30 minutes. Reduce oven temperature to 300 degrees and continue baking until filling is set and top has browned, about 25 minutes longer. Cool completely.

Spread top of torte with remaining jam. The torte keeps well in the refrigerator for several days, but is best served on the day it is prepared. If torte has been refrigerated, bring to room temperature before serving.

8 SERVINGS

Warres Warrior Port nv (Portugal)

FRESH APPLE CAKE WITH CALVADOS

Begin 1 day before serving.

APPLE TOPPING

2   GRANNY SMITH APPLES, PEELED, QUARTERED AND SLICED 1/3-INCH THICK
    FRESHLY SQUEEZED JUICE OF 1 LEMON
2   TABLESPOONS GRANULATED SUGAR
2   TEASPOONS CINNAMON

Toss apples with lemon juice. Mix sugar and cinnamon. Dry apples, then dip each slice in sugar mixture and set aside until ready to use.

CAKE

1/2   CUP BUTTER, SOFTENED
1   CUP GRANULATED SUGAR
1   CUP DARK BROWN SUGAR
5   EGGS
1   CUP VEGETABLE OIL
1   TEASPOON VANILLA EXTRACT
2 1/2 CUPS ALL-PURPOSE FLOUR
1   TEASPOON SALT
1   TEASPOON BAKING SODA
1   TEASPOON BAKING POWDER
1/2   TEASPOON MACE
1   TEASPOON GROUND CLOVES
1   TEASPOON CINNAMON
3 1/4 CUPS GRANNY SMITH APPLES (ABOUT 4), PEELED AND CHOPPED
1/2   CUP WHOLE WHEAT FLOUR
1 3/4 CUPS CHOPPED WALNUTS
1   CUP RAISINS
3/4   CUP CALVADOS (DRY APPLE BRANDY)

In a mixing bowl, cream butter and sugars. Beat in eggs, one at a time, then stir in oil and vanilla. Sift together flour, salt, baking soda, baking powder, mace, cloves and cinnamon and add gradually to egg mixture. Mix well and fold in apples. Combine whole wheat flour, walnuts and raisins and stir into batter.

Pour batter into a buttered and floured 11-inch springform pan. Arrange Apple Topping in an overlapping circle over batter. Bake in a preheated 350 degree oven for 45 minutes. Reduce oven temperature to 325 degrees and bake 45 minutes longer. Remove cake from oven and cool for 15 minutes in pan. Remove springform sides and finish cooling on rack. When cake is completely cool, drizzle Calvados over top, wrap in foil and store overnight at room temperature.

GLAZE

2   TABLESPOONS BUTTER
2   TABLESPOONS DARK BROWN SUGAR
2   TABLESPOONS GRANULATED SUGAR
6   TABLESPOONS HEAVY CREAM
4   TABLESPOONS CALVADOS

In a saucepan, combine butter, sugars, cream and Calvados. Boil until mixture becomes too thick to spread. Cool, then thin with more Calvados until glaze is of spreading consistency. Drizzle glaze decoratively on cake and serve.

14 TO 16 SERVINGS

Rollon Calvados (Calvados)

ROZZELLE COURT APPLE CRUMB PIE

Begin 1 day before serving.

PASTRY

2 1/2	CUPS UNBLEACHED WHITE FLOUR
8	TABLESPOONS VEGETABLE SHORTENING
1	TABLESPOON CHILLED UNSALTED BUTTER
1	TEASPOON SALT
1	TABLESPOON GRANULATED SUGAR
4 TO 6	TABLESPOONS ICE WATER

Place flour, shortening, butter, salt and sugar in the bowl of a food processor and pulse 4 or 5 times with the chopping blade, just until shortening and butter are broken up. Add 4 tablespoons of the ice water, and pulse 2 or 3 times. The mixture should resemble small peas, and will adhere to fingers to form a pliable dough. If pastry seems dry and crumbly, add remaining water, 1 tablespoon at a time, testing after each addition. Turn dough onto a piece of plastic wrap and shape into a flattened round, 6 to 8 inches in diameter. Wrap tightly and chill at least 2 hours. For best results, chill overnight. The dough may be frozen for several months.

Remove dough from refrigerator and let stand at room temperature for one hour. Place on a floured surface and roll into a 13- to 14-inch circle. Fit pastry into a 10- or 11-inch tart pan with removable bottom. Gently press pastry down into the pan, leaving a 1- to 1 1/2-inch overhang. Crimp pastry decoratively to extend about 3/4 to 1 inch above the top of the pan. Cover loosely with plastic wrap and chill 1 to 2 hours before filling and baking.

APPLE FILLING

6	CUPS GRANNY SMITH APPLES (ABOUT 1 1/2 POUNDS APPLES), PEELED AND THINLY SLICED
2/3	CUP GRANULATED SUGAR
1	TEASPOON CINNAMON
1	TEASPOON FRESHLY GRATED NUTMEG
2	TABLESPOONS CORNSTARCH
1 1/2	TABLESPOONS UNSALTED BUTTER, CUT INTO PIECES

In a large bowl, toss apples with sugar, cinnamon, nutmeg and cornstarch. Place in chilled unbaked pastry shell and dot with butter.

STREUSEL TOPPING

4	TABLESPOONS UNSALTED BUTTER, CUT INTO PIECES
3/4	CUP PLUS 2 TABLESPOONS BROWN SUGAR
1/4	CUP ALL-PURPOSE FLOUR
1	TEASPOON CINNAMON
1/2	CUP CHOPPED ALMONDS OR PECANS

Using a pastry cutter or fork, work butter, sugar, flour and cinnamon together until well blended. Stir in nuts and sprinkle over apples, covering them completely. Bake in a preheated 375 degree oven for 10 minutes, then reduce temperature to 350 degrees and bake 30 to 45 minutes longer, just until apples are tender. If streusel topping becomes too brown, cover loosely with foil until baking is done.

The pie is best served warm with vanilla ice cream, whipped cream or Crème Fraîche (page 198).

8 TO 10 SERVINGS

RHUBARB STREUSEL PIE

CRUST

1 1/3	CUPS ALL-PURPOSE FLOUR
1/2	TEASPOON SALT
1/2	CUP SHORTENING
3 TO 4	TABLESPOONS COLD WATER

Measure flour into a bowl and add salt. With a pastry cutter, cut shortening into flour until mixture resembles coarse crumbs. Stir in water with a fork until mixture sticks together. Form dough into a ball. Roll out on a floured surface and fit into a 10-inch pie pan. Line the crust with foil and fill with dried beans or pie weights. Bake in a preheated 425 degree oven for 10 minutes. Remove foil and weights and increase oven temperature to 450 degrees. Bake crust 2 minutes longer. Remove and let cool.

FILLING

1	CUP SUGAR
3	TABLESPOONS QUICK-COOKING TAPIOCA
1/2	TEASPOON VANILLA EXTRACT
5	CUPS FRESH RHUBARB (ABOUT 2 POUNDS), CUT INTO 1/2-INCH CHUNKS
2	TABLESPOONS BUTTER, CUT INTO SMALL PIECES

In a large bowl, combine sugar, tapioca, vanilla, rhubarb and butter. Let stand for 15 minutes, stirring occasionally.

STREUSEL TOPPING

1/2	CUP ALL-PURPOSE FLOUR
1/4	CUP LIGHT BROWN SUGAR
2	TABLESPOONS BUTTER, CUT INTO SMALL PIECES
1/2	TEASPOON CINNAMON
1/4	CUP CHOPPED ENGLISH WALNUTS
1	EGG, BEATEN WITH 1 TABLESPOON WATER
1/4	CUP RED CURRANT JELLY

Combine flour, sugar, butter and cinnamon and blend until mixture resembles coarse meal. Stir in walnuts.

Spoon filling into baked shell and sprinkle streusel topping in a 2-inch border around filling, leaving center uncovered. Brush egg mixture over edges of crust. Bake in a preheated 450 degree oven for 15 minutes. Reduce oven temperature to 350 degrees and bake 50 minutes longer, until rhubarb is bubbly. Do not allow streusel topping to become too brown. Remove from oven. Melt jelly over low heat and brush it over center circle of pie. Cool on a wire rack for 2 hours.

8 SERVINGS

Bonny Doon Strawberry Infusion (California)

ALMOND POUND CAKE

3/4 CUP BUTTER
1/2 CUP ALMOND PASTE
1 1/4 CUPS GRANULATED SUGAR, DIVIDED
1 TEASPOON VANILLA EXTRACT
6 EGGS, SEPARATED
1 1/2 CUPS ALL-PURPOSE FLOUR
3/4 CUP YELLOW CORNMEAL
1 TEASPOON BAKING POWDER
1 CUP HEAVY CREAM

confectioners' sugar and fresh berries, for garnish

Cream together butter, almond paste, 1 cup sugar and vanilla. Add egg yolks and beat well. Sift together flour, cornmeal and baking powder and add to butter mixture, alternating with cream. Mix until well blended. Beat egg whites with the remaining 1/4 cup sugar until soft peaks form. Gently fold into the batter and blend well. Pour into a greased and floured tube or bundt pan. Bake for about 60 minutes in a preheated 350 degree oven, or until the top of the cake is firm to the touch and cake tester comes out clean. Cool on a wire rack, then turn onto a serving plate. Dust with powdered sugar and garnish with fresh berries. This cake is best made one day ahead.

The combination of almond and cornmeal gives this pound cake a different texture. Try it toasted for breakfast.

12 SERVINGS

One of the Bonny Doon berry Infusions, depending on fresh berries used.

CITRUS TORTA

Prepare at least 1 day before serving.

2 ORANGES
2 LEMONS
4 EGGS
3/4 CUP SUGAR
1 CUP UNBLEACHED ALL-PURPOSE FLOUR
3 TEASPOONS BAKING POWDER
1/2 TEASPOON SALT
2/3 CUP OLIVE OIL
1/2 CUP FINELY CHOPPED TOASTED ALMONDS
1/2 CUP HEAVY CREAM
1 TABLESPOON GRAND MARNIER LIQUEUR

In a sauce pan, simmer whole oranges and lemons in water until very soft, about 30 minutes. Drain and cool fruit, reserving liquid. Scoop and discard pulp. Process the skins to a very fine purée in food processor, adding a small amount of the reserved cooking liquid if necessary. In a mixing bowl, beat eggs and sugar until fluffy and pale yellow. In another bowl, mix flour, baking powder and salt, and add to the eggs, alternating with the olive oil. Fold in almonds and puréed citrus skins. Pour batter into a 9-inch springform pan and bake in a preheated 350 degree oven for 50 minutes, or until cake tester comes out clean. Cool and store covered in a cool place.

Before serving, whip cream and Grand Marnier together. Slice cake and serve with flavored cream.

The unusual use of fruit in this simple-to-prepare cake results in a dark, dense texture with an intense citrus flavor.

8 TO 10 SERVINGS

Pfeffingnen Ungsteiner Herrenberg Beerenauslese 1 9 8 3 (Rheinpfalz)

SUN-DRIED FRUITCAKE

1 CUP DARK RAISINS
1 CUP GOLDEN RAISINS
1 CUP DRIED CHOPPED APRICOTS
1 CUP DRIED CHOPPED PEACHES
1 CUP DRIED CHOPPED PEARS
1 CUP DRIED CHOPPED PINEAPPLE
ZEST OF 2 LARGE ORANGES, FINELY GRATED
1 CUP CHOPPED WALNUTS
1 CUP CHOPPED PECANS
2 CUPS FLOUR (UNBLEACHED WHITE, WHOLE WHEAT OR A COMBINATION), DIVIDED
1 TEASPOON BAKING POWDER
1/2 TEASPOON SALT
1 TEASPOON CINNAMON
1 TEASPOON ALLSPICE
1 TEASPOON NUTMEG
1 TEASPOON GROUND CLOVES
1 CUP BUTTER, SOFTENED
1 CUP HONEY
5 EGGS, LIGHTLY BEATEN
1 TABLESPOON VANILLA EXTRACT
1/4 CUP ORANGE JUICE
1 1/2 CUPS BRANDY

Line three 8-inch loaf pans with wax paper. Toss raisins, apricots, peaches, pears, pineapple, orange zest, walnuts and pecans with 1/2 cup flour and set aside. In a mixing bowl, sift together the remaining 1 1/2 cups flour, baking powder, salt, cinnamon, allspice, nutmeg and cloves and set aside.

In a large bowl, cream butter and honey together until light and fluffy. Beat in eggs one at a time, and add vanilla. Beat flour mixture into butter mixture, alternating with the orange juice. Stir in fruits and nuts. Spread mixture in loaf pans and bake in a preheated 275 degree oven for 1 1/2 to 2 hours, or until a cake tester comes out clean. Remove fruitcakes from pans and cool slightly; then peel off wax paper and cool cakes completely on a wire rack.

Soak rectangular pieces of cheesecloth in brandy, wring to remove excess liquid, and wrap around cakes. Wrap cakes tightly with aluminum foil and store at room temperature. Resoak with brandy if fruitcakes are kept more than a week.

This fruitcake is unique in its use of dried instead of candied fruits. It can be made in double batches and in a variety of sizes.

MAKES 3 OR MORE LOAVES.

Graham Six Grape nv (Portugal)

HOLIDAY PLUM PUDDING
WITH FOAMY HARD SAUCE

Prepare at least 4 weeks before serving.

ONE	1-POUND LOAF WHITE BREAD, CRUSTS REMOVED
2 1/4	CUPS MILK
4	EGGS
1/2	POUND FINELY GROUND BEEF SUET
2 1/2	CUPS RAISINS
2	CUPS CURRANTS
1 3/4	CUPS UNBLEACHED FLOUR
1	CUP DARK BROWN SUGAR
4	OUNCES CHOPPED SLIVERED ALMONDS
3/4	CUP GRATED CARROT
1	TABLESPOON FINELY GRATED LEMON ZEST
2	TEASPOONS FRESHLY GRATED NUTMEG
1 1/4	TEASPOONS CINNAMON
1/2	TEASPOON GROUND CLOVES
1/2	TEASPOON GROUND GINGER
1/4	TEASPOON SALT
1 1/2	CUPS DARK BEER
1/4	CUP BRANDY
4 TO 6	TABLESPOONS BUTTER

Process bread to make crumbs. Whisk together milk and eggs and add the breadcrumbs. Chill, covered, for 24 hours. Combine beef suet, raisins, currants, flour, sugar, almonds, carrot, lemon zest, nutmeg, cinnamon, cloves, ginger, salt, beer and brandy. Stir in breadcrumb mixture. Pour into well-buttered steamed pudding molds—three 1-quart pudding molds (6 to 8 servings each), or one 2-quart mold (10 to 12 servings) and one 1-quart mold.

Steam the puddings in pans of water for 8 hours. (Cooking time is the same for both 1- and 2-quart puddings.) The water in each pan should be about 3 inches deep; stockpots and deep saucepans work well. Keep water simmering, not boiling, and the pans half-covered. Replenish water if necessary. Cool puddings in the molds, then remove and wrap in foil. Store in a cool place for at least 4 weeks, or up to 2 months. The puddings freeze very well if tightly wrapped in foil.

To serve, unwrap the pudding. Wrap in cheesecloth, then loosely in foil. Set a rack in a shallow pan of simmering water. Place a 4-inch square of folded foil on the rack beneath the pudding. Cover pan loosely with foil, or with a domed lid. Steam 2 to 3 hours, adding water as needed. Serve with Foamy Hard Sauce and/or Crème Anglaise (page 205).

FOAMY HARD SAUCE

1	EGG, SEPARATED
4	TABLESPOONS BUTTER
1	CUP CONFECTIONERS' SUGAR A PINCH OF SALT
1/2	PINT HEAVY CREAM, WHIPPED
1	TABLESPOON VANILLA EXTRACT, OR 2 TABLESPOONS BRANDY OR RUM

Beat egg white until stiff. Cream butter and sugar until smooth and pale yellow, then add egg yolk. Beat the mixture for 1 or 2 minutes and add salt. Fold in beaten egg white, then the whipped cream. Flavor with vanilla, rum or brandy. Chill.

MAKES 2 CUPS.

Warres 1979 Quinta da Cavadinha Port (Portugal)

CRANBERRY NUT PUDDING

2   CUPS FRESH CRANBERRIES, LIGHTLY
     RINSED AND PICKED OVER
1/2 CUP BROWN SUGAR
1/2 CUP CHOPPED PECANS
     FINELY GRATED ZEST OF 1 MEDIUM
     ORANGE
2   EGGS
1/2 CUP SUGAR
2/3 CUP ALL-PURPOSE FLOUR
1/2 TEASPOON CINNAMON
1/8 TEASPOON SALT
1/2 CUP MELTED BUTTER

heavy cream or vanilla ice cream, as an accompaniment

Layer cranberries, brown sugar, pecans and orange zest in a buttered 8-inch square baking dish. Beat together eggs and sugar. Add flour, cinnamon, salt and butter and beat until smooth. Pour mixture over cranberries in baking dish and bake in a preheated 350 degree oven until golden, about 40 to 45 minutes. Serve warm with cream or vanilla ice cream.

6 TO 8 SERVINGS

*Renaissance Sauvignon Blanc 1 9 8 4 Late Harvest
(North Yuba)*

ICED LEMON SOUFFLÉ

Begin at least 4 hours before serving.
2   TABLESPOONS GELATIN
2   TABLESPOONS WATER
     FINELY GRATED ZEST OF 4 MEDIUM
     LEMONS
1/2 CUP FRESHLY SQUEEZED LEMON
     JUICE, STRAINED
1   CUP SUGAR
1   CUP EGG WHITES (7 TO 8 EGGS),
     STIFFLY BEATEN
1   CUP HEAVY CREAM, WHIPPED

*lemon slices and sprigs of fresh mint, for garnish
Chambord Sauce (page 204), as an accompaniment*

In a small saucepan, soften gelatin in water. Add lemon zest, lemon juice and sugar. Stir constantly over low heat until sugar and gelatin are fully dissolved. Chill until mixture is of a syrup-like consistency. Watch carefully and stir from time to time. Beat lemon-gelatin mixture into egg whites. Gently fold in whipped cream until well mixed, but still buoyant. Pour into a 2-quart soufflé dish and chill at least 4 hours.

To serve, spoon Chambord Sauce onto chilled dessert plates and place three small scoops of soufflé on top. Garnish with mint and lemon slices.

6 TO 8 SERVINGS

Phelps Delice du Semillon 1 9 8 8 (Napa)

FROZEN RUM RAISIN CREAM

Begin several hours or 1 day before serving.

1/2	CUP FINELY CHOPPED RAISINS
1/2	CUP DARK RUM
1	CUP HEAVY CREAM
1/2	CUP MACAROON CRUMBS (SEE BELOW)
1/3	CUP CHOPPED WALNUTS
1 1/2	PINTS VANILLA ICE CREAM, SLIGHTLY SOFTENED

chocolate curls or chocolate leaves, for garnish

Soak raisins in rum for one hour. Whip the cream until it holds its shape, then fold into rum-raisin mixture. Fold in macaroon crumbs and walnuts. Gradually stir mixture into the ice cream (if ice cream is too soft, mixture will sink to bottom). Spoon into parfait glasses or a decorative 2-quart glass dish and freeze. Stir occasionally as mixture freezes so that raisins and nuts do not sink to the bottom. Decorate with chocolate curls or chocolate leaves.

Macaroon crumbs can be made quickly in a food processor.

6 SERVINGS

CHAMPAGNE POACHED PEARS DIPPED IN CHOCOLATE

Begin 1 day before serving.

ONE	750 ML BOTTLE CHAMPAGNE
1	CUP SUGAR
1/2	VANILLA BEAN, SPLIT LENGTHWISE
	ZEST OF 1 LEMON
6	BOSC PEARS WITH STEMS, PEELED
1/2	PINT FRESH RASPBERRIES
1/4	CUP GRAND MARNIER LIQUEUR
1	POUND DARK COUVERTURE CHOC-OLATE, BROKEN INTO PIECES
2	CUPS HEAVY CREAM, DIVIDED

12 fresh mint leaves, for garnish

In a large saucepan, combine champagne, sugar, vanilla bean and lemon zest. Bring to a boil and cook 10 minutes. Reduce heat, add pears and cook until pears are tender, about 30 to 45 minutes. Turn pears occasionally with tongs to ensure even cooking. Refrigerate overnight in liquid.

Early on day pears will be served, macerate raspberries in Grand Marnier. Remove pears from syrup. (The champagne syrup may be reduced to use as a dessert sauce or tart glaze.) Core pears from the bottom to about two thirds of the way up, removing seeds and some of pear, leaving stems intact. Fill cored pears with raspberries and refrigerate.

Melt chocolate in a double boiler, then pour into a 2-cup bowl. Hold pears by the stems and dip in chocolate, one at a time, covering about two thirds of each pear. Let chocolate drip slightly. Place on wax or parchment paper to set.

To serve, place one pear in each dessert bowl. Pour 1/3 cup cream around pear and garnish with two mint leaves.

6 SERVINGS

Ramos Pinto Bom Retiro Twenty-Year-Old Tawny Port (Portugal)

6	LARGE APPLES
1	TEASPOON CINNAMON
1/2	TEASPOON ALLSPICE
1/4	TEASPOON GROUND CLOVES
1	CUP HONEY
2	TABLESPOONS CHILLED UNSALTED BUTTER, CUT INTO SMALL PIECES
1	CUP CHOPPED WALNUTS
2/3	CUP RAISINS
18	SHEETS FROZEN PHYLLO DOUGH, THAWED
1	EGG
1/2	CUP HEAVY CREAM
	COTTON TWINE
	PARCHMENT PAPER

Crème Anglaise (page 205), as an accompaniment

Remove a 1-inch core from each apple. Combine cinnamon, allspice, cloves, honey, butter, walnuts and raisins. Fill cored apples with the honey mixture and place in a baking pan large enough that apples do not touch sides of pan or each other. Bake in a preheated 325 degree oven for 1 hour.

Unroll one sheet of phyllo dough and place it on a floured surface. Lightly beat egg with cream and brush the shorter edges of the phyllo dough with the mixture. Fold the pastry in half crosswise, so that the two short edges meet evenly. The dough will form a rectangle, with long edges now at the top and bottom, and shorter edges to the sides. Brush the shorter edges with the egg mixture and fold in half again so that the short edges meet evenly. The pastry will now be nearly square.

Place an apple in the center of the folded pastry, and wrap the phyllo around the apple snugly. The top of the apple will be uncovered. Unroll two more sheets of phyllo and lay them on the floured surface, one on top of the other. Cut them to form a square and brush the center of the top sheet with the egg mixture. Center the phyllo-wrapped apple on the phyllo square. Carefully pull one corner of both bottom sheets up and hold them over the center of the apple. Pull up the remaining corners to the center of the apple. All of the apple should now be covered with pastry. Gently pinch dough together above top of apple and tie with a 6-inch piece of cotton twine. Pick up apple at the base and place on parchment paper on a baking sheet. Repeat the process with the remaining apples.

Carefully brush apples with egg mixture. To prevent phyllo from burning on top, form a hollow ball from a sheet of aluminum foil and cover top lightly, leaving rest of apple exposed. Bake in a preheated 400 degree oven for 2 to 6 minutes until phyllo is a light golden color. When apples are cool enough to handle, remove twine.

Serve warm, accompanied by Crème Anglaise.

6 SERVINGS

Rosemount Late Harvest Botrytis Semillon 1985
(Hunter Valley - Australia)

GREEK ORANGES

12 GOOD-QUALITY EATING ORANGES
1 TABLESPOON BRANDY
6 OUNCES CURRANT JELLY OR TART
  MARMALADE
sprigs of fresh mint or chocolate leaves, for garnish

Juice 3 oranges and discard peel. Carefully remove zest from 3 oranges, taking care not to include bitter white membrane, and chop or cut into slivers. In a heavy saucepan, combine juice, zest, brandy and jelly. Cook over low heat, stirring occasionally, for 15 minutes or until jelly is melted.

Slice or section peeled oranges and peel, slice or section remaining oranges. Arrange all slices flat on a serving dish. Pour juice mixture over fruit and let stand 1 to 2 hours, basting frequently. Chill until ready to serve. Garnish with mint sprigs or chocolate leaves.

8 SERVINGS

Quady Essencia nv (California)

ITALIAN BISCOTTI

1/2 CUP BUTTER, SOFTENED
1/2 CUP SUGAR
  2 EGGS
1/2 TEASPOON VANILLA EXTRACT
  2 CUPS ALL-PURPOSE FLOUR
  2 TEASPOONS BAKING POWDER
1/2 TEASPOON SALT
1/2 CUP CHOPPED ALMONDS,
  PISTACHIOS, WALNUTS OR PINE
  NUTS

Cream together butter and sugar, then beat in eggs and vanilla. In another bowl, sift together flour, baking powder and salt. Mix in nuts. Gradually add flour mixture to egg mixture, beating well, forming a fairly stiff dough. Divide dough in half and shape each half into two rolls, each about 16 inches long. Place on a buttered baking sheet and bake in a preheated 350 degree oven for 30 minutes, or until lightly golden. Remove from oven and cut diagonally into 1/2-inch slices. Each roll should yield about 24 biscotti. Spread biscotti on a rack over a baking sheet and return to oven. Bake 15 minutes, or until firm and golden. Cool and store in a tightly covered tin.

48 BISCOTTI

Martin Brothers Vin Santo (Paso Robles)

GINGERBREAD HEART COOKIES

Begin at least 4 hours before serving.

1/2	CUP BROWN SUGAR
1/2	CUP VEGETABLE SHORTENING
3/4	CUP MOLASSES
1	EGG
2	TEASPOONS WHITE VINEGAR
1	TEASPOON BAKING SODA
1	TEASPOON CINNAMON
1	TEASPOON SALT
1	TEASPOON GROUND CLOVES
1	TEASPOON GROUND GINGER
3 TO 3 1/2	CUPS ALL-PURPOSE FLOUR

In a large mixing bowl, cream sugar and shortening. Add molasses, egg and vinegar. Sift together baking soda, cinnamon, salt, cloves, ginger and flour. Add to the sugar mixture in thirds, mixing well. The dough will be stiff. Refrigerate at least 3 hours or overnight.

Bring dough to room temperature. On a floured surface (sprinkle cinnamon into the flour to give cookies more color), roll out dough 1/4-inch thick. Cut with a heart-shaped cookie cutter and transfer to a well-greased baking sheet. Decorate if desired. Bake in a preheated 325 degree oven for 8 to 10 minutes.

MAKES ABOUT 20 COOKIES,
DEPENDING ON SIZE OF CUTTERS.

SPRINGERLE BIRD COOKIES

Begin 1 day before serving.

4	EGGS
2	CUPS SUGAR
4	CUPS SIFTED ALL-PURPOSE FLOUR
1	TEASPOON BAKING POWDER
1/2	TEASPOON SALT
2	TABLESPOONS MELTED BUTTER
1	TEASPOON LEMON ZEST
2 TO 3	TABLESPOONS ANISE SEED

In a mixing bowl, beat eggs and sugar for 10 minutes. Stir in flour, baking powder and salt. Add butter and lemon zest. On a lightly floured board, gently roll out dough 1/3-inch thick. Press in design from a springerle board or cookie cutter. Cover dough on board and refrigerate 12 to 24 hours to set the design.

Butter a cookie sheet and sprinkle with anise seed. Separate cookies and place on cookie sheet. Bake in a preheated 350 degree oven for 5 minutes, then reduce oven temperature to 300 degrees and bake 15 minutes longer. Watch carefully, as cookies should have only a hint of yellow on the bottom.

Remove and cool. Arrange cookies in a small grapevine basket woven with fresh herbs.

3 DOZEN COOKIES

We all treasure special recipes
that enhance our cooking
skills—the secret ingredient or
unusual method of preparation
that makes an otherwise
ordinary recipe unique. The
recipes we return to time and
again are those we trust—those
that make us look good with a
minimal amount of effort. Often,
when time is limited, we turn to
reliable recipes that please and
impress our guests, but which we
know are simple and
uncomplicated.

Each of these Best Kept Secrets
is unique, yet all share elements
that make them an important
part of a cook's repertoire. Some
contain a special ingredient that
one would never guess, as in the
Raspberry Barbecue Sauce.
Others have an unusual method
of preparation which may seem
peculiar, but which is the secret
to a delicious finish, as in the
Burgundy Mushrooms. Several
dishes, such as Baked
Asparagus or Hot Spiced
Blueberry Sauce, are easy and
require little preparation, leaving
time for more complicated
recipes. But all of these Best
Kept Secrets are elegant enough
to serve to guests.

We hope that these selections
will add to an existing collection
of your own Best Kept Secrets,
and that they will also inspire
you to experiment and to create
new ones.

 Preceding page: Boxes holding clues to a party game are attached to the cake shown on page 27.

SPICY CHILI CHEESE BREAD

1   LOAF FROZEN BREAD DOUGH,
     THAWED
1   CUP SHREDDED CHEDDAR CHEESE
2/3 CUP CHORIZO (MEXICAN SAUSAGE),
     COOKED AND DRAINED
4   OUNCES CHOPPED GREEN CHILIES,
     DRAINED
1   EGG, SLIGHTLY BEATEN
1/2 CUP MELTED BUTTER

Stretch thawed dough on a greased baking sheet into a 6- by 12- inch rectangle. Set aside. Combine cheese, sausage, chilies and egg. Spread mixture on top of dough and roll up from short end. Place rolled dough, seam side down, on a greased baking sheet. Allow dough to rise at room temperature until doubled in bulk. Brush top of loaf with melted butter and bake in a preheated 375 degree oven for 20 minutes.

To thaw frozen bread dough quickly, place loaf in microwave for 10 minutes on medium-low/defrost, turning several times.

8 SERVINGS

BUNDT PAN CORNBREAD

8   TABLESPOONS BUTTER
2   CUPS SELF-RISING CORNMEAL
1   CUP SELF-RISING FLOUR
2   TABLESPOONS SUGAR
1   EGG, SLIGHTLY BEATEN
2   CUPS BUTTERMILK

Place the butter in a bundt pan and melt in a preheated 425 degree oven until sizzling. In a large mixing bowl, combine cornmeal, flour, sugar, egg and buttermilk. Pour into the hot bundt pan with melted butter. Bake for 30 minutes.

Serve with Sausage Lentil Soup (page 69).

24 SERVINGS

GARLIC POPOVERS

2	CUPS MILK
4 TO 5	LARGE CLOVES GARLIC, PRESSED
2	EGGS
2	EGG YOLKS
3	TABLESPOONS MINCED FRESH PARSLEY
1/2	TEASPOON SALT
1/2	TEASPOON FRESHLY GROUND BLACK PEPPER
2 1/2	CUPS ITALIAN BREAD, CUBED

Scald milk with garlic in a saucepan and let cool for 15 minutes. In a mixing bowl, whisk together whole eggs and egg yolks. Add the milk in a stream, whisking, and stir in parsley, salt and pepper. Divide the bread cubes among 8 well-buttered muffin tins. Ladle egg mixture over bread cubes and let stand 10 minutes. The popovers may be prepared up to 8 hours ahead and refrigerated. Bake in a preheated 350 degree oven for 45 minutes. Let cool for 10 minutes and lift out carefully.

The popovers are an elegant, easy and flavorful accompaniment to roast beef, roast chicken or Red Pepper Soup with Fresh Dill (page 65).

8 SERVINGS

FOCACCIA

1	POUND FROZEN WHITE BREAD DOUGH, THAWED
1/4	CUP OLIVE OIL
3	CLOVES GARLIC, CRUSHED
2	TABLESPOONS DRIED HERBS— ROSEMARY, BASIL, THYME OR OREGANO, OR A COMBINATION COARSELY GROUND SALT, TO TASTE FRESHLY GROUND BLACK PEPPER, TO TASTE

Mix olive oil and garlic. Coat a jelly-roll pan with half of the seasoned oil. Using fingertips, stretch thawed dough into a rectangle, approximately 10 by 12 inches; the shape is more attractive when irregular. Spread with remaining oil, dried herbs, salt and pepper, and allow dough to rise 15 to 20 minutes or bake flat (the bread will have a chewier texture). Bake in the bottom third of a preheated 375 degree oven for 10 to 15 minutes until golden brown. Break or tear in pieces and serve in a basket.

This versatile bread lends itself to a variety of seasonings and toppings. Try one or more of the following: sliced green onions, fresh tomatoes, brine-cured black olives, oil-packed sun-dried tomatoes, roasted peppers, grated or shredded Parmesan or Romano cheese.

6 TO 8 SERVINGS

SUMMER SAUSAGE

Prepare at least 2 days before serving.

2	POUNDS GROUND BEEF ROUND
3/4	CUP WATER
1/2	TEASPOON FRESHLY GROUND BLACK PEPPER
1/4	TEASPOON GARLIC POWDER
1/2	TEASPOON GARLIC SALT
1/2	TEASPOON ONION POWDER
2	TABLESPOONS TENDERIZING SALT
2	TABLESPOONS LIQUID SMOKE FLAVORING, IF DESIRED
1	TABLESPOON MUSTARD SEED
1/2	TEASPOON CAYENNE PEPPER, IF DESIRED
1 1/2	TABLESPOONS WHOLE BLACK PEPPERCORNS, OR MORE IF DESIRED

In a small bowl, combine water, pepper, garlic powder, garlic salt, onion powder, tenderizing salt, liquid smoke flavoring, mustard seed, cayenne pepper and peppercorns. Pour over ground beef and mix well. Form into two rolls and wrap each with foil. Refrigerate at least 48 hours. The longer the mixture is refrigerated, the better the seasonings will blend.

Perforate bottom of each sausage roll with a toothpick. Bake rolls on a wire rack over a pan of water in a preheated 350 degree oven for 1 hour. Allow to cool, then refrigerate. Slice and serve on small rye bread rounds with Danish Mustard (page 197).

This appetizer has wide appeal and disappears quickly.

8 SERVINGS

Pedroncelli Zinfandel 1 9 8 9 (Dry Creek)

BACHELOR'S SOUP

2	POUNDS GROUND BEEF ROUND
2	MEDIUM ONIONS, THINLY SLICED
ONE	28-OUNCE CAN TOMATOES, BROKEN UP WITH SPOON
ONE	16-OUNCE CAN STEWED TOMATOES
1	CAN TOMATO SOUP
1	CAN CONSOMMÉ
3	CUPS WATER
1	BEEF BOUILLON CUBE
ONE	8-OUNCE PACKAGE FROZEN MIXED VEGETABLES
1/2	CUP YELLOW CORN
1/2	CUP GREEN BEANS, CUT IN 1-INCH PIECES
1	TABLESPOON BROWN SUGAR
1	TABLESPOON PREPARED MUSTARD SALT, TO TASTE FRESHLY GROUND BLACK PEPPER, TO TASTE

In a skillet, sauté ground beef until browned, stirring with a wooden spoon. Add onion and sauté until onion is translucent. In a large stockpot, combine tomatoes, stewed tomatoes, tomato soup, consommé, water, bouillon cube and vegetables. Stir in ground beef and onions and bring to a boil over medium-high heat. Reduce heat to low and simmer, partially covered, for 1 1/2 to 2 hours. Stir in brown sugar and mustard and season to taste.

Mustard and brown sugar give this easy-to-make soup an unusual spark. Canned or frozen vegetables are used for convenience—fresh vegetables can easily take their place.

8 TO 10 SERVINGS

Samuel Smith Nut Brown Ale (England)

RASPBERRY BARBECUE SAUCE

4	CUPS BARBECUE SAUCE (PREFERABLY SMOKE-FLAVORED)
6	OUNCES FROZEN UNSWEETENED RASPBERRIES
4	TABLESPOONS RASPBERRY VINEGAR, OR MORE TO TASTE

Place barbecue sauce, raspberries and vinegar in a food processor and process until smooth. Refrigerate. The sauce will keep up to 4 weeks.

Serve with wild duck, grilled chicken or egg rolls.

MAKES 2 1/2 CUPS.

LEMON MUSTARD SAUCE

2	TABLESPOONS BUTTER
2	TABLESPOONS ALL-PURPOSE FLOUR
1/4	TEASPOON SALT
1/8	TEASPOON FRESHLY GROUND BLACK PEPPER
1	CUP HOT WATER
1	TEASPOON DIJON-STYLE MUSTARD GRATED ZEST AND JUICE OF 1/2 LEMON
1/2	CUP MAYONNAISE

Melt butter in a small saucepan. Remove from heat and stir in flour, salt and pepper. Gradually stir in water and mustard. Cook over medium heat, stirring until thickened. Add lemon zest and lemon juice. Remove from heat and blend in mayonnaise. Refrigerate until serving time.

This easily prepared sauce is similar to hollandaise. It can be served with hot or cold fresh asparagus or broccoli, or with almost any simply prepared fish. To serve hot, reheat carefully over hot water or in microwave.

MAKES ABOUT 1 1/3 CUPS.

GARLIC TOMATO SAUCE

Prepare 1 day before serving.

12	TABLESPOONS BUTTER
2	LARGE BULBS GARLIC, CLOVES SEPARATED AND PEELED
TWO	28-OUNCE CANS ITALIAN PLUM TOMATOES
ONE	28-OUNCE CAN TOMATO PURÉE
ONE	28-OUNCE CAN CRUSHED TOMATOES
1	TABLESPOON DRIED BASIL
1	TABLESPOON DRIED OREGANO
1	BAY LEAF
1 1/2	TEASPOONS SALT, OR TO TASTE
1 1/2	TEASPOONS FRESHLY GROUND BLACK PEPPER, OR TO TASTE

In a large stockpot, melt butter over low heat. Add peeled garlic cloves and simmer until garlic is soft. Do not sauté. Add the tomatoes and stir, breaking up tomatoes and garlic with a wooden spoon. Increase heat to medium and cook, partially covered, 10 to 15 minutes. Add tomato purée, crushed tomatoes, basil, oregano, bay leaf, salt and pepper, and stir to blend. Simmer, partially covered, over low heat until sauce thickens, about 3 hours. Stir sauce occasionally, and taste for seasoning. Remove bay leaf.

Serve over hot pasta or let cool and refrigerate.

This is a wonderful, garlicky sauce to serve with any type of pasta. It is even better after it has been refrigerated for a day or two, and freezes very well. Because of the labor involved in peeling garlic cloves, it makes sense to make a large amount all at one time. The sauce is also a perfect base for additions such as shrimp, scallops, or garden vegetables.

8 SERVINGS

CHARCOALED LEMON CHICKEN

Begin 1 day before serving.

1/2	CUP MELTED BUTTER
2	CUPS FRESHLY SQUEEZED LEMON JUICE
1/2	CUP PLUS 2 TABLESPOONS WORCESTERSHIRE SAUCE
3	TEASPOONS HOT PEPPER SAUCE, OR MORE IF DESIRED
2	TABLESPOONS CELERY SALT
1	TABLESPOON FRESHLY GROUND BLACK PEPPER
1	TABLESPOON GRATED ONION
8	CHICKEN BROILER HALVES

grilled vegetables, as an accompaniment

Combine butter, lemon juice, Worcestershire sauce and hot pepper sauce. Add celery salt, pepper and onion. Blend well. Pour over chicken halves, cover and refrigerate overnight. Remove chicken from marinade and grill skin side up, about 3 inches from hot coals. Cook approximately 50 minutes, turning once. Serve with grilled vegetables.

This dish is surprisingly flavorful for such a simple recipe. Try it with Vegetable Pasta Salad (page 97).

8 SERVINGS

Kreydenweiss 1 9 8 9 Pinot Gris (Alsace)

CORNISH HENS TARRAGON

Begin 1 day before serving.

- 4 CORNISH GAME HENS, 20 TO 22 OUNCES EACH, SPLIT
- 1/4 CUP OLIVE OIL
- 1/4 CUP FRESHLY SQUEEZED LEMON JUICE
- 1/4 CUP SOY SAUCE
- 1/4 CUP DRY VERMOUTH
- 2 CLOVES GARLIC, CRUSHED
- 1 1/2 TEASPOONS SALT
- 1/2 TEASPOON COARSELY GROUND BLACK PEPPER
- 2 TEASPOONS DRIED TARRAGON, DIVIDED
- *fresh tarragon, for garnish*

Wash and dry the hens. Combine the olive oil, lemon juice, soy sauce, vermouth, garlic, salt, pepper, and 1 teaspoon of the tarragon. Place the hens breast side down in a glass baking dish. Pour on marinade and sprinkle 1/2 teaspoon tarragon over the top. Cover and refrigerate overnight.

When ready to bake, turn the hens breast side up and sprinkle with the remaining tarragon. Bake in a preheated 400 degree oven for 50 to 60 minutes until tender, basting 3 or 4 times during cooking. Garnish with fresh tarragon.

Serve with French Rice Casserole (page 107). Delicious, elegant and easy to prepare, the hens make a perfect entrée when time is important.

8 SERVINGS

Abbazia di Rosazzo 1 9 8 9 Muller Thurgau (Friuli - Venezia)

BAKED ASPARAGUS

- 1 POUND FRESH ASPARAGUS, WASHED AND TRIMMED
- SALT, TO TASTE
- FRESHLY GROUND BLACK PEPPER, TO TASTE
- 2 TABLESPOONS CHOPPED FRESH PARSLEY OR OTHER FRESH HERB
- 2 TABLESPOONS OLIVE OIL

Place asparagus in a single layer in a shallow baking dish. Sprinkle with salt, pepper and parsley and drizzle with olive oil. Cover with foil and bake 15 minutes in a preheated 400 degree oven. Asparagus should be slightly crisp. Serve immediately.

This tastes better than steamed fresh asparagus, with less effort. Try it with Duck with Fresh Raspberry Sauce (page 141).

4 SERVINGS

BURGUNDY MUSHROOMS

Prepare at least 8 hours before serving.

- 4 BEEF BOUILLON CUBES
- 4 CHICKEN BOUILLON CUBES
- 2 CUPS BOILING WATER
- 1 POUND BUTTER
- 1 QUART BURGUNDY WINE
- 4 POUNDS FRESH WHOLE MUSHROOMS, CLEANED
- 1 TEASPOON GARLIC POWDER
- 2 TEASPOONS FRESHLY GROUND BLACK PEPPER
- 1 TEASPOON DILL SEED
- 2 TABLESPOONS WORCESTERSHIRE SAUCE

Dissolve beef and chicken bouillon cubes in boiling water. Melt butter in a large stockpot and stir in bouillon mixture and Burgundy. Add mushrooms and season with garlic powder, pepper, dill seed and Worcestershire sauce. Bring to a slow boil over medium heat. Reduce heat to simmer and cook, covered, 5 to 6 hours. Remove cover and cook another 3 to 5 hours until liquid barely covers mushrooms. Serve in a chafing dish.

The mushrooms can be cooled and frozen. They make an excellent accompaniment to standing prime rib roast or beef tenderloin.

The long cooking time actually enhances the flavor of this dish. The mushrooms remain firm but still absorb the rich flavor of the Burgundy sauce.

16 SERVINGS

Wild Horse Pinot Noir 1 9 8 9 (Santa Barbara)

BAKED POTATO SALAD

- 1 CUP HOT WATER
- 2 TEASPOONS INSTANT CHICKEN BOUILLON
- 2 TABLESPOONS INSTANT MINCED ONION
- 1 TEASPOON INSTANT MINCED GARLIC
- 1/4 CUP OLIVE OIL
- 2 TABLESPOONS WHITE VINEGAR
- 2 TEASPOONS DRIED TARRAGON LEAVES, CRUSHED
- 1/4 TEASPOON FRESHLY GROUND BLACK PEPPER
- 2 POUNDS SMALL RED POTATOES, QUARTERED

Preheat oven to 350 degrees. Combine water, bouillon, onion and garlic. Let stand 10 minutes, then add oil, vinegar, tarragon and pepper. Place potatoes in a shallow 3-quart casserole. Pour dressing over potatoes and toss to coat. Bake uncovered until potatoes are fork-tender, about 35 to 40 minutes, stirring occasionally. Serve at room temperature.

4 TO 6 SERVINGS

MAGIC POTATOES

4 TO 5   BAKING POTATOES, OF UNIFORM
          SIZE AND THICKNESS
    8   TABLESPOONS BUTTER
          SALT, TO TASTE
          FRESHLY GROUND BLACK PEPPER, TO
          TASTE
    2   TABLESPOONS MIXED, DRIED HERBS

Scrub potatoes thoroughly, peel and slice into 1/4-inch rounds. Arrange in staggered layers in a 3-quart glass baking dish. Melt butter and pour over potatoes, tipping dish if necessary to coat top layer. Sprinkle with salt, pepper and herbs and bake in a preheated 350 degree oven for 1 hour.

The "magic" of these potatoes is that they can be held for up to 45 minutes in the turned-off oven while other preparations are underway. Serve as an accompaniment to Salmon Cakes with Cilantro Butter Sauce (page 161).

8 TO 10 SERVINGS

COGNAC CARROTS

    2   POUNDS CARROTS, THINLY SLICED
  1/2   CUP MELTED BUTTER
    1   TABLESPOON SUGAR
    1   TEASPOON SALT
  1/3   CUP COGNAC

Place sliced carrots in a lightly buttered 2-quart casserole. Combine butter, sugar, salt and cognac and pour over carrots. Cover and bake in a preheated 300 degree oven for 1 1/2 hours.

This is a quick, easy way to dress up an ordinary vegetable. Serve as an accompaniment to Braised Quail with Hunter's Sauce (page 143).

8 TO 10 SERVINGS

ICED BERRIES AND CREAM

Prepare 4 hours before serving.

2 PINTS FRESH BERRIES (RASPBERRIES, STRAWBERRIES, BLUEBERRIES, BLACKBERRIES, OR A COMBINATION)
1 PINT HEAVY CREAM, WHIPPED
1/4 CUP BRANDY, RUM, KIRSCH, OR A SPLASH OF BALSAMIC VINEGAR
1 CUP BROWN SUGAR

Cover bottom of 2-quart soufflé dish or glass casserole with berries. Add liquor to moisten fruit well. Spread whipped cream over top and cover generously with a thick layer of brown sugar. Refrigerate 4 hours.

Before serving, place under preheated broiler to brown lightly and quickly (1 to 1 1/2 minutes). The brown sugar should caramelize and crack on top, leaving the berries chilled underneath.

Kirsch, Eau de Vie or Bonny Doon Raspberry Infusion

RED, WHITE AND BLUEBERRY

1 PINT STRAWBERRIES, RINSED AND HULLED
1 PINT RASPBERRIES, LIGHTLY RINSED
1/4 TO 1/2 CUP SUGAR, TO TASTE
2 TABLESPOONS FRESHLY SQUEEZED LEMON JUICE
1 TABLESPOON GRAND MARNIER LIQUEUR, IF DESIRED
1 POUND MASCARPONE CHEESE
1/2 PINT BLUEBERRIES, RINSED

In a mixing bowl, gently combine strawberries and raspberries with sugar, lemon juice and Grand Marnier. Press fruit lightly with back of spoon to release juices. To serve, place a spoonful of mascarpone on each dessert plate. Ladle a spoonful of berries over cheese and sprinkle with blueberries.

Reserve any remaining juice and mix with fresh berries for a fruit sauce that is a perfect addition to ice cream, sliced poundcake, or shortcake.

6 TO 8 SERVINGS

Bonny Doon Marionberry Infusion (California)

HOT SPICED BLUEBERRY SAUCE

1   PINT FRESH BLUEBERRIES, RINSED
1/4   CUP SUGAR
1/2 TO 1   TEASPOON CINNAMON
1/2   TEASPOON NUTMEG

Combine blueberries, sugar, cinnamon and nutmeg in a small saucepan. Bring to a boil and cook 5 minutes, uncovered, stirring occasionally. Serve warm with ice cream or cold, over lemon sherbet.

This almost-instant dessert sauce keeps well in the refrigerator and can be frozen. It can also be used to add flavor to a plain vanilla pound cake.

MAKES ABOUT 2 CUPS.

BALSAMIC STRAWBERRIES

1   PINT STRAWBERRIES, RINSED, HULLED AND SLICED
2   TABLESPOONS BALSAMIC VINEGAR
4   TABLESPOONS SUGAR, DIVIDED
4   TABLESPOONS PINE NUTS
    A PINCH OF GROUND CLOVES
vanilla ice cream, as an accompaniment

Combine strawberries, vinegar and 2 tablespoons sugar in a small bowl. In a small heavy skillet or saucepan, combine remaining 2 tablespoons sugar, pine nuts, and cloves. Stir over low heat until sugar melts and pine nuts are golden brown, about 4 minutes. Transfer to a bowl if not using immediately.

Spoon vanilla ice cream into bowls, top with strawberries and then with pine nuts. The strawberries may be prepared up to 1 hour ahead.

Almonds, walnuts or pecans may be substituted for pine nuts.

4 SERVINGS

ALMOND TORTE

BAKER'S PARCHMENT
2 TABLESPOONS UNSALTED BUTTER
7 OUNCES ALMOND PASTE,
CUT IN SMALL PIECES
3/4 CUP GRANULATED SUGAR
3 EGGS
1/2 TEASPOON ALMOND EXTRACT
1 TABLESPOON KIRSCH OR TRIPLE SEC
LIQUEUR
1/4 CUP ALL-PURPOSE FLOUR
1/3 TEASPOON BAKING POWDER
CONFECTIONERS' SUGAR

Line bottom of an 8-inch round cake pan with baker's parchment. In a mixing bowl or food processor, cream butter, almond paste and sugar. Beat in eggs one at a time. Stir in almond extract and liqueur, then add flour and baking powder and stir or pulse several times with metal disc. Do not overbeat. Pour into pan and bake in a preheated 350 degree oven for 35 minutes, or until a cake tester comes out clean.

Let cool, invert onto serving platter and dust well with confectioners' sugar. Serve plain or with fresh fruit.

This torte is simple, quick and easy to prepare, but elegant to serve.

8 TO 10 SERVINGS

Anselmi Recioto del Soave Capetelli 1 9 8 8 (Veneto)

RED HOT ORANGES

6 MEDIUM NAVEL ORANGES,
UNPEELED
2 1/2 CUPS SUGAR
2 CUPS WATER
1 CUP CANDY RED HOTS

Place whole oranges in a stockpot and cover with water. Bring to a boil, cover and simmer for 45 minutes. Drain and cool oranges. When cool, cut each orange crosswise into 8 slices. Arrange orange slices in a 9- by 13-inch baking dish.

Combine sugar, water and red hots in a small saucepan and cook over medium heat until sugar and candies are dissolved. Pour the syrup over the orange slices, cover loosely with foil, and bake in a preheated 350 degree oven for 1 1/2 hours. Refrigerate until ready to serve.

These sweet, spicy hot oranges make an unusual accompaniment for seafood salads, or grilled beef or chicken. A few drops of red food coloring may be added for a deeper color.

10 TO 12 SERVINGS

ORANGE PECANS

1 1/2 CUPS SUGAR
1/2 CUP ORANGE JUICE CONCENTRATE, THAWED
4 CUPS PECANS

Cook sugar and orange juice in a heavy saucepan until the temperature reaches the soft ball stage (235 degrees). Remove from heat and add pecans. Stir until syrup looks cloudy. Quickly drop by spoonfuls onto wax paper. Separate into individual pieces or clusters. When cool, store in a covered tin.

These keep well and can be stored in decorative containers for gift giving.

MAKES 4 CUPS.

Emilio Lustau Rare Cream Sherry nv (Spain)

RASPBERRY CORDIAL

Prepare 2 months before serving.
2 CUPS SUGAR
2 PINTS FRESH RASPBERRIES, RINSED
1 QUART VODKA

Pour sugar into a 3-quart glass jar with a tight-fitting top. Add raspberries and vodka and seal tightly. Stir once a week for 2 months. The cordial is then ready to use.

Make the Raspberry Cordial at summer's end, when fresh raspberries are plentiful, and keep until mid-winter. Use the cordial over ice cream and crêpes.

ACKNOWLEDGMENTS

THE COMMITTEE

CHAIRMAN:
Maureen V. Gamble

EDITOR:
Crennan M. Ray

RECIPE CHAIRMAN:
Candy Linn

COMPUTER CHAIRMAN:
Jo Ann Krekel

WINE CONSULTANT:
Doug Frost, Master Sommelier

PLANNING COMMITTEE:
Michael S. Churchman
Maureen V. Gamble
Ellen R. Goheen
Helen B. Windsor

RECIPE TESTING COMMITTEE CHAIRMEN

APPETIZERS:
Carolyn C. Williams

SOUPS & BREADS:
Courtney R. Earnest

PASTA & GRAINS:
Barbara Aiken

MEATS:
Heather W. Jordan

POULTRY & FISH:
Judith M. Cooke

VEGETABLES:
Barbara Aiken

SALADS:
Pam Gradinger

SAUCES & ACCOMPANIMENTS:
Diane A. Gibson

DESSERTS:
Janné Abreo

BEST KEPT SECRETS:
Candy Linn

MARKETING CHAIRMEN:
Cathy L. Hedlund
Jean Lerner

ACKNOWLEDGMENTS

André's Confiserie Suisse, Marcel
  Bollier
Answer with a Personal Touch,
  Marilyn McGovern
Asiatica
The Better Cheddar
Beyond Words, Ann McElhenny
Boyle Meat Company
The Classic Cup
Keith Coldsnow Artist's Materials
Consumer Consultants
Coopers & Lybrand, Edward F.
  Halpin
Gragg's Paint Co.
Hall's, Plaza
Harmon Smith Inc. Advertising,
  Austin Harmon
Constance Leiter Inc.
Longview Gardens
Matney Floral Design
Jan Michael
Mozzarella Company
National Pork Producers Council
Rozzelle Court Restaurant, The
  Nelson-Atkins Museum of Art
Rosehill Gardens, Inc.
Seasonal Sensations
Smith and Burstert Oriental Rugs
  and Decorative Arts
Rama Sola
Trapp and Company
Tutterri's Pasta
Williams-Sonoma Inc.
Vedros & Associates Photography
  Ron Berg
  Scott Hepler
  Mike McCorkle
  Jim Thomas
  Mike Lee
  Scott Murray
Bonnie Winston

RECIPE CONTRIBUTORS AND TESTERS, COMMITTEE MEMBERS, VOLUNTEERS AND FRIENDS WHO MADE CULINARY MASTERPIECES POSSIBLE:

Sam Abramson
Janné Abreo
Helen Ace
DeSaix W. Adams
Rebecca Adams
Barbara H. Aiken
John L. Aiken
Mary Alexander
Christi Allen
Gloria M. Allen
J.D. Allen
Nancy Allen
The American Restaurant
Doris J. Anderson
Kay Arnold
Laurie Arnold
Gloria Asner
Barbara Atlas
Jody Aussem
Cindy Avery
Ken Axetell
Mary Axetell
Diana Azar
Jean Azar

Joann B. Baldwin
Molly Banta
John E. Bargetto
Louise Barton
Ann W. Basore
Cecelia G. Baty
J.W. Baty
Logan Bay
Richard Bay
Cynthia A. Bell
Marian C. Bell
Heather Berger
Sharon Berges
Joan Berkley
Anita B. Berkowitz
Carol Berkowitz
Marjorie K. Bernard
Nan Berry
Lorena L. Bestor
Debe Biddle
Doris A. Biellier
Betty L. Bikson
Donna Birdsong
Lisa Birtciel
Katherine Black
Debbie Blair
Tom Blanck
Becky Bland
Sheryl Blasco
Shirley W. Blaul
Wheadon Bloch
Olive L. Bloom
Terry Bock
Louise Bodziony
Helen M. Boedeker-Eckels
Joe Boer
Vanessa Bonavia
Anne W. Boose
Pat Boppart
Betty K. D. Botts
Julia Boutross
Patricia T. Bowers
Maureen P. Bradley
Julie Brake
Julia L. Brettle
Stevi Brick
Lavinia S. Bright
Robert W. Brizendine
Karen Brookfield
Barbara Brown
Carolyn Brown
Rhonda Brown
Saurine Brown
Stephen S. Brown
Vivian Brownell
Polly P. Brunkhardt
Laurie Buckley
Gretchen Budig
Margaret Buie
Joan Buinger
Kent O. Bumgarner
Cynthia F. Burcham
Wendy H. Burcham
Pat Burke
Wilma J. Burnett
Bruce Burstert
Betty L. Burum
Jean Butler
Eileen Buttron
Café Allegro
Café Lulu
Therese Caillot

Susan Cain
John Callison
Kay Callison
Martha Calloway
Ann Canfield
Melinda Cannady
Barbara Capuzelo
Patricia H. Carlin
Benecia Carmack-Monaco
Janice H. Carmichael-James
The Carriage Club Staff
Jean Carson
Cindy Cart
Arlene C. Cartmeil
Karen Caskey
Dorothy H. Catlin
Pat Chapman
Marcia Charney
Anne Chasnoff
Pati Chasnoff
Della Chester
Chris Chitwood
Carolyn Christman
Judith K. Church
Jean W. Churchman
Michael Churchman
Barbara Cipolla
John L. Cipolla
Gail A. Clair
Carole W. Clark
Barbara ClaryRobinson
Jolene Clark
Judy Clouston
Lenore Coats
Stewart S. Cochrane
Gwen Cockrell
Robert J. Cody
Gloria Cohen
Joni Cohen
Sachiko Colom
Jane Conley
Marla Conley
Pauline E. Conley
Judith M. Cooke
Gigi Cooley
Frank Cooper
Jill Coppess
Mary Alice Corbett
Lisa Cornett
Barbara Cosgrove
Carole Coulter
Tammie Cox
Karen W. Craft
Caroline Crownover
Michael R. Crownover
Dorothy Curry
Alma W. Dallam
M. Pétra Danielson
John David
Mindy Davis
Ronald G. Davis
Danna Deeter
Peggy Derks
Betty J. Dewey
Cindy Dillard
Barbara Diment
Susan S. Dinges
Lori Dobbels
Tommye B. Dodd
Ann M. Dodson
Kenneth J. Doll
Katholeen A. Donnelly

248

Carole Douglas
Tillie Dowd
Lindsay Downing
Lynne Drennen
Nancy Duboc
Jane Dubois
E. Martin Duncan
Ann T. Dunn
Cynthia Dunn
Hilary Dunnaway
Sue Dunphy
John Dyblie
Courtney R. Earnest
Joshua Earnest
Sue Edwards
Aileene K. Embrey
John K. Enenbach
Ann E. Erbacher
Geri Erftmier
Missy Eubank
Gary Evans
Judy Evans
Susie Evans
Dee Everist
Eva L. Fabian
Susan Fagan
Barbara Lee Fay
Carol A. Fay
Helen Feingold
Alan Feingold
Mary Francis Fencl
Gertrude Ferguson
Marnell Fey
M. Karen Finch
JoLee Fishback
Helen Fisher
Kay Fisher
Mildred Fisher-Dentler
Tom Fletcher
Patsy R. Flynn
V. Margie Folz
Irene Forch
Lucille A. Forsythe
Julie Foster
Fred D. Fowler
Jeanne B. Fox
Beverly A. Frank
Eva Frank
Marie K. Frazier
Joseph Fulgenzi
Larry R. Gamble
Maureen V. Gamble
Joyce Games
Linda Gail Gardner
Carolyn Garfinkel
Janice Gartrell
Janet Gass
Joan Gastinger
Edward O. Gaus
John M. Gazda
Judy Geer
Mary Ann Geha
Julienne Gehrer
David Gerson
Diane A. Gibson
John R. Gibson
Julie Gilchrist
Mercer Gilmore
Linda Ging
Dorothy Glanville
Rena P. Glazebrook
Kate Goetz

Ellen R. Goheen
Julia Goheen
Jacqueline Gough
Meredith Gordon
Janet Goss
Lynn Gover
Pam Gradinger
Patricia Graham
Teresa Green
Babs Grinter
Sally Groves
Arvind R. Habbu
Betty Hachinsky
Pat Hagemeier
Louise Haines-Sherman
Jayne Hall
Julie Haller
Sharon Hide Hamil
Betty J. Hancock
Lois P. Hancock
Sarah Hancock
Kay Hanes
Jennifer Hardy
Marga L. Harris
Mary Harrison
Mary F. Hart
Barbara J. Hataway
Marsa D. Hatfield
Peter Hathaway
Libby Hayes
Beverly Hechler
Cathy L. Hedlund
Jean Marie Heisberger
Alison Heisler
Jalia Henderson
Joan Henges
Joan Henige
Pat Hennessey
John F. Herbst
Jean Herrick
Joy Hesler
Paget G. Higgins
Susan Hildebrand
David Hiler
Geraldine J. Hill
Susan F. Hill
Nanci Hirschorn
Sue Hoevelman
Jane S. Hogan
Ethel M. Hoke
Ethel Hopkins
Nancy Hornaday
Karen Houston-Howell
Paige Howard
Helen R. Howig
Carol Hudson
Dee Hughes
Jo Hughes
Jean Hullsick
Rosalee T. Hume
William J. Hundelt
Mary R. Hunkeler
Annemarie Hunter
Martin Hunter
Terrie Huntington
Hyatt Regency Crown Center
Carol C. Inge
Sarah Ingram-Eiser
Margaret W. Jackson
Bryce Jacobson
Stephanie H. Jacobson
Alison Jager

Carole James
Sarah Jantzen
Joan Jaska
Adele W. Jay
Tikie Jenkins
Jeanne Jennings
John Jennings
Rebecca Jessee
Denise L. Jobe
Glenda Jobe
Charlotte B. Johnson
Nellie Johnson
William A. Johnson
Linda Johntz
Barbara Jolley
William C. Jolley
Carol Jones
Christopher J. Jones
Janell Jones
Joy Jones
M. Frank Jones
Madeline P. Jones
Nancy Jones
Susan Jones
Heather W. Jordan
Paula W. Jordan
Kathleen F. Joyce
Nancy Kain
Donna Karney
Helen Louise Kassebaum
K.C. Rib Doctors
Kathy Keener
Margaret S. Kelly
Sean Kelly
Margaret A. Keough
Evelyn Kessler
Kathy Killip
Andie Kipke
Dorothy Kleinbeck
Diana Kline
Barbara Kluetfel
Alice Mae Knight
Sarah Knight
Susan Knight
Anne Knopke
Sarah H. Koenig
Carol Kornitzer
Jo Ann Krekel
Carolyn Kroh
Mary Lou Kroh
Susan Krozinger
Martha M. Lally
Janet LaMarche
Joyce E. Lambert
Paula Lambert
Nora B. Lamkin
Ginny LaPointe
Carol Larson
Raymond Larson
Erlene R. Lasley
Elizabeth Latimer
Sally A. Lauer
Laura Laughlin
Sherri Laughlin
F. Jay Lawrence
Iris Lawrence
Robert Lawrence
Leawood Women's Club
Susan Lee
Carolee Leek
Shirley A. Legg
Violet Lehman

Ann M. Leiter
Boots Matthews Leiter
Carol P. Leiter
Jay Leiter
Suzanne H. Leiter
Lisa Leonard
Jean Lerner
Vicki Levine
Missy Levy
Beverly Lewis
Kathy A. Liebst-Hudon
Alfred H. Lighton
Grace M. Lilgendahl
Larry Lillis
Pat Lillis
Betty Linn
Candy Linn
Donald Linn
Kari Lipscomb
Laura K. Lloyd
Ann Lombardi
Nancy D. Long
Virginia M. Long
Matthew Love
Stacy Luallen
Betty Lucas
Nano N. Lueders
Ruth Luhnow
Julia Lundberg
Jeen Lysaught
Wendy MacLaughlin
Lori Maguire
Jeannette Mallin
Maggie Mandel
Frances B. Manson
Aaron G. March
Kathy Marcos
Gary W. Marsh
Martha Ann Marshall
Mary E. Marshall
Barbara Martin
June Martin
Patricia L. Martin
Matthew Mascotte
Dorothy Mask
Jamie Mason
Bobbie Mathes
Catherine G. Mathews
Alfred Matthes
Lara Maughn
Tanya Maurin
Norma Jean May
Maura McCarthy
Carolyn McCaul
Megan McClarney
Michael G. McCoy
Marcia McCullen
Susie McElvain
Sacha S. McGibbon
Marjorie McHenry
Julia McKanna
Adena McKemey
Jan McKenna
Elizabeth B. McLaughlin
Mary McPherson
Pat McRobert
Dolly McTavish
Jim McWilliams
Sharon Mellor
Patricia Merlie
Lois Metheny
Nadine Miller

Rita Miller
Lori A. Milton
Sue Mindlin
Richard Mindlin
Deanne E. Mitas
Linda Mitchem
Kay Moffat
Irene A. Moore
Kathleen M. Moore
Alice Morgan
Richard Morgan
Sharon Morgan
Carla Morley
Mary Louise Morris
Linda Morsman
Alexandra Moschell
Ruth Moss
Charlotte Mueller
Rozan P. Mueller
Daisy Muff
Colleen Murbach
Betty Murfey
Scott Murray
Denise Nelson
Eleanor Nelson
Mary Alice Nelson
Peter Newcomer
Kris Newcomer
Wendy Newcomer
Marty Nichols
Angela M. Nielsen
Frankie Nisbett
Martha B. Noland
Pat Norris
Vicki Nulton
Nancy Nussbaum
Harolyn O'Brien
Rita O'Connor
Gina O'Neal
Orlando's Restaurant
Barbara R. Ostby
Frederick P. Ostby
Rhonda Owen
Page A. Palmer
Sally Papreck
Ruby Park
Dianne Patejdl
Laura Patterson
Ritchie Patterson
Marie Pawsat
Deanne Pearson
Cindy Peine
Libby Pence
Graham Pendreigh
Mindy S. Pendreigh
Lee Pentecost
Joan Peschka
Andre Phillips
Mary Ann Pinkerton
Joseph Pinkerton
Brenda Pittenger
Maurice P. Poindexter
Lori Poskin
Tom Pott
Cheryl Powell
Nancy L. Powell
Mary June Pranger
Harriet Prevan
Carol Price
Kathleen Pugh
Kate Quimby
Sharon Quimby

John Ralston
Alison Randall
Julie T. Randall
Walt Randall
Virginia L. Rau
Crennan M. Ray
Ethyl K. Ray
Christine B. Raya
Judy Rayl
Johine Reck
Jack Rees
Fajen Reinhart
Julia Reitzes
Kay Reusser
Jan H. Riedel
Gus Riedi
Nancy Rieger
Anne Ritchie
Arlene Ritche
The Ritz Carlton Hotel
Barbara M. Roberts
Cindy H. Robertson
Linda Robertson
Janet Rogers
Lisa Rolf
Stephanie C. Roselle
Jean Ross
Linda Rostenberg
Gary Roush
Anne Rowe
Sandra Kay Rozen
Rozzelle Court Restaurant
Marie Rueschhoff
Billie V. H. Runnels
Bob Russell
Elaine H. Russell
Joanne L. Ruzek
Ann P. Ryan
Stephen M. Ryan
Nancy Ryger
Shirley J. Sabal
Kathleen H. Sadilek
Jim Sajovic
Robert T. Salsman
Jean Paul Sams
Margaret J. Sams
Donna Claire Sanders
William F. Sanders
Edith Sanderson
Charles Satkewich
Marion G. Sauer
Cammie Savage
Lisa Schlagle
Jeannine M. Schmedding
Patty Lee Schrader
Helen M. Schumacher
Burch Schuman
Audrey Schwegler
David Scott
Lee Scranton
Ann Scrogham
Richard V. Seaboldt
Penny Selle
Don Shanks
Susann Shinkle
Kathy Shoemaker
Francis Shoup
Diane S. Shumacher
Aletha Simon
Gary L. Simpson
Mary Beth Simpson
Susan E. Sims

Marianne Skorupsky
Jo Sledd
Shirlie J. Sly
Robbie Small
Carole L. Smith
Cathy Smith
Chris Smith
Dana Smith
D. H. Smith
Karen Smith
Kathy Smith
Kit Smith
Patricia Smith
Patricia O. Smith
Phyllis W. Smith
Rebecca Smith
Terri H. Smith
Carol S. Spachman
Melinda Speak
Mardi Speer
Betty Stafford
Nancy Stanley
Robin P. Stanley
Irma Starr
Michael Staudte
Clara M. Stegmaier
Joy Steincross
Gladys C. Stern
Liz Stetson
David Stickelber
Lois Stratford
Eugene Strauss
Gerre Strauss
Pam Straussbaugh
Mary T. Stringer
Jo Ann H. Sullivan
Greg Suss
Gloria D. Swain
Jackie Sweet
Sarah Taxman
Dawn Taylor
Lannie H. Taylor
Alarie Tennille
Chick Thompson
Courtney Thompson
Diane G. Thompson
Bill Thomson
Christine B. Thomson
Raymond G. Thornton
Jeanne Tinberg
M. Jane Todd
Mary Bell Toevs
Lynn Towse
Jackie Tramposh
Robert Trapp
Beverly B. Tregoning
Kathryn A. Trigg
David R. Tripp
Prudence F. True
Billie E. Tsakonas
Ann Tucker
Dianne K. Tudor
The University Club
Alice van der Pas
Marian Van Der Veen
LLouise Van Osdol
Zoe Vantzos
Gaile M. Varnum
Patty Vedros
Jeanne Ventola
Venue
Nancy Verseman

Kevin Vivers
Joyce B. Vogel
Michael Vogel
Sally Von Werlhof-Uhlmann
Elizabeth Vrabac
Halli Vrooman
Paula Walker
Judy K. Walsh
Steven L. Walter
Lenise R. Ward
Mildred Ward
Paul Ward
Roger B. Ward
Martha Warren
Courtney Watkins
Nellie R. Bregg Weatherman
Carolyn Weaver
Judy Welch
Elizabeth W. Welker
Charlene Welling
Rita Wells
Linda Welty
Cynthia E. Wendlandt
Sally West
Fifi White
Cynthia Whitlock
Virginia Whitman
Virginia Whitmore
Evelyn A. Whittaker
Muriel B. Wildman
Bernice W. Williams
Carolyn C. Williams
Valerie J. Williams
Alice Wilson
Elizabeth Wilson
Whitney Wilson
Helen B. Windsor
John H. Windsor
Bonnie Winston
Irena Winston
Kristie Wolferman
Marilyn S. Wollard
Cathy Wood
Della Wooddell
Mary Edith Woodward
Elizabeth H. Woolcolt
Brian N. Woolley
Bill Wren
Alertha Wright
Theo Wright
Robert Wyatt
Nancy Yedlin
Danny Zeih
Joyce Zeldin
Joline R. Zwart

INDEX

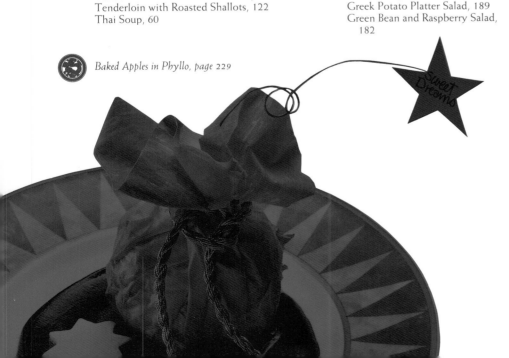

Baked Apples in Phyllo, page 229

CREDITS

CONCEPT, DESIGN & ART DIRECTION
Mary Lou Kroh

PHOTO STYLING
Annemarie Hunter

PHOTOGRAPHY
Nick Vedros